KEEPER OF THE GATE

Selwa "Lucky" Roosevelt

SIMON AND SCHUSTER
NEW YORK · LONDON · TORONTO
SYDNEY · TOKYO · SINGAPORE

SIMON AND SCHUSTER
Simon & Schuster Building
Rockefeller Center
1230 Avenue of the Americas
New York, New York   10020

10   9   8   7   6   5   4   3   2   1

Library of Congress Cataloging-in-Publication Data

Roosevelt, Selwa.
    Keeper of the gate / Selwa "Lucky" Roosevelt.
        p.   cm.
    Includes index.
    1. United States—Foreign relations—
1981–1989. 2. Rosevelt, Selwa.
3. United States. Dept. of State. Office of Protocol—
Officials and employees—Biography. I. Title.
E876.R673   1990
327.73'009'048—dc20   90-38479
                                                           CIP

ISBN 0-671-69207-0

The author is grateful to A. P. Watt, Ltd., and
James Sherwood for permission to quote from "Hassan," a play in five acts by James Elroy Flecker
(1922).

To My Beloved Archie
For forty wonderful years

Contents

Acknowledgments

S OME WAG once said that the two dumbest people in the world are your predecessor and your successor—but in my case, that just isn't so. To Lee Annenberg, who turned her job over to me with such grace, and to Joseph Verner Reed Jr., who followed me with such a generous spirit—thank you both. And a special thanks to the nine other previous chiefs of protocol who supported me through it all.

My heartfelt gratitude to the people who are the Office of Protocol and who for seven years gave me their support and friendship and made my job both effective and enjoyable. My story is their story—and if I don't mention each one in the text, please know that I value all of you. I can cite only a few—my three deputies, Tom Nassif, Tim Towell and particularly Bunny Murdock, who is a legend in her time; my extraordinary secretary Dee Lilly and that wonderful driver so many chiefs have come to love, Eugene Lewis.

To my former State Department colleagues George Shultz, Al Haig, Walter Stoessel, Dick Walters, John Whitehead, Mike Armacost, Ron Spiers, Evan Galbraith, Nick Veliotes, Dick Murphy, Ray Seitz, Tom Enders, Roz Ridgway, Chet Crocker, Gaston Sigur, and Elliott Abrams—thank you for all that you taught me.

I also appreciate the friendship and support of many other

Reagan-Bush officials—Bill Clark, Cap Weinberger, the late and much loved Mac Baldrige, William French Smith, Howard Baker, Don Gregg, Peter McCoy, Chuck Tyson, Jim Rosebush, Muffie Brandon, Elaine Crispin, Susan Porter Rose, Laurie Firestone, Ken Duberstein and Charles and Mary Jane Wick.

These were years in which I abandoned my friends. I forgot birthdays, missed weddings, and in times of sorrow I could not be with you. Thank you for forgiving me. I cannot name you all, but a special thanks to *les girls*—Mary Weinmann, Jean Lindsey, Maribel Pedroso, Ruthie Pratt, Elaine Atkins, and Joan Tobin.

Thank you, dear friends—Antony and Jenny Acland, Susan and Jim Baker, Arnaud and Alexandra de Borchgrave, Myrna Bustani, Carole and Bill Butcher, Oatsie Charles, the Forbes clan, Joan and Nicholas Gage, Kiki and Jerzy Kosinski, Carol and Paul Laxalt, Arianna Huffington, Marc Leland, John Hilson, Edmund and Sylvia Morris, Mandy and Betty Lou Ourisman, Aleko Papamarkou, David and Peggy Rockefeller, Karla and Liener Temerlin, and Ghassan Tueni.

To the memory of my dearest friend, Joan Humpstone Hanes, with whom I wish I could have shared the headier moments, and the late beloved Carol Hanes, the daughter I never had, who started me off with the sampler which hung in my office all seven years: "I know I'm gonna make it, cause God don't sponsor no flops." And to all the other Haneses especially Gordon, Johnnie, Philip, and David and their wives—thanks for so many happy memories.

To those who rallied when tragedy struck I owe a special debt—Bunny Murdock, Julie Andrews, Shelby Scarbrough, Becki Bernier, Carolyn Deaver, Pam Gardner, Carter Cunningham, Randy Bumgardner, Louise Bennett, Pat Bye, José Fuster, Buddy Carter, and Lynn Keith.

No words can adequately express my gratitude to my remarkable Mother, Najla Showker, a saint who has watched over me all my life, and always, always is there when I need her. I am also grateful to my understanding family, especially my sister Kay Showker, my stepson Tweed Roosevelt, and my niece Margot Hornblower.

For better or for worse, I wrote every word of this book myself, but along the way I had the encouragement and counsel of my agent Georges Borchardt, my publisher, Simon and Schuster, and my generous, talented and beautiful editor Marie Arana-Ward.

Most important of all, however, was the loving support of my husband Archie—my mentor, confidant, and booster—who, even while recovering from a devastating illness, gave me the strength to see this project through.

Author's Note

*L*ET ME WARN YOU before you begin. I'm not really mad at anyone; I've got no big ax to grind; this book is not written to get even. But wait—don't go away!

What I want to do is give you a picture of what it is like to be in a catbird seat—to move in the whirl of American diplomacy, to see and know all the people that occupy the front pages of the newspapers you read—and to give a few informed glimpses of presidents and princes, prime ministers and potentates.

For seven years I had one of the best jobs—albeit a tough one—in the U.S. government. As Chief of Protocol, I was privileged to be a small part of the foreign policy apparatus of the Reagan administration. I dealt with form, as opposed to substance, but as President Reagan once told me, form and substance are opposite sides of the same coin.

I would not presume to try to write an authoritative review of American foreign policy between 1982 and 1989. That will be for President Reagan and Secretary of State George Shultz to do— after all, they defined and articulated it. But I hope you will come away with a view of what we tried to accomplish—our successes and failures—as seen from my special perspective.

I witnessed with my eyes, ears, and heart—and I have tried to share with you what I saw, heard, and felt. With only one or two exceptions, I have limited myself to those with whom I was professionally involved.

I made a deliberate decision not to write in any detail about President and Mrs. Bush. It is too early to write about his presidency. But for the record, George and Barbara Bush were a joy to work with. I have the greatest respect and a special affection for them and I am deeply grateful to this marvelous couple for their friendship, loyalty, and support.

This book also tells briefly the story of my life—another version of the American dream—the odyssey of a Lebanese-American girl born and raised in East Tennessee who ends up in the Reagan White House.

Looking back, I realize that whatever happiness and success I have had is due to a brave decision by a sixteen-year-old lad—my late father—who at the turn of the century had the courage to leave his native land, stow away on a boat, and seek his fortune in America. He didn't make a fortune in the monetary sense, but he left me a glorious inheritance—he made it possible for me to be born a citizen of this wonderful country.

My mother, my idol and teacher, has endowed me with another great gift—a rich intellectual heritage.

The third gift came when I found the companion of my life, my husband Archie, who throughout our marriage showed me love, tenderness, and understanding and brought so much humor and adventure to our lives. What fun we had!

And finally, eight years ago, I received a very special gift—a chance to serve my country and give back a little of the bounty that has come my way. For this honor, I am indebted to President Ronald Reagan. I am especially proud to have served this President, for I share his vision of America.

I also share Ronald Reagan's optimistic philosophy of life. Like him, I tend to see the cup half full rather than half empty. When faced with sadness and suffering I try not to ask "Why me?" but instead "Why not me?" I believe that how we deal with adversity defines us. It also gives us the capacity to appreciate the joyous and the good. I am convinced that the mysterious zig-zags on the road of life, which at times seem incomprehensible, will ultimately have meaning, and one's destiny will be revealed.

One last word. This book is not true confessions time. No woman's life is complete without detailing the tragedies, the disappointments, the affairs of the heart. But I share W. H. Auden's view that graceful behavior—as well as graceful writing—demands a certain restraint.

PART ONE

Keeper of the Gate

ONE

The Lucky Locket

*L*UCK, FATE, and a benevolent God—I believe in all of them—but on a balmy February day in Brazil I almost became a convert to the cult of *candomblé*.

Those Afro-Brazilian gods worked their magic on me in Salvador, the capital of Bahia, where I had been sent to write a magazine piece on the province, and particularly about Jorge Amado, Brazil's most famous writer.

I spent several glorious days savoring this strange and wondrous world with Amado and his wife Zelia, and discovering the gods of *candomblé*, ancient deities brought by black slaves to Brazil from Africa. Together we celebrated the Festival of Iamenja, the Goddess of the Sea, as we threw flowers and gifts to her from gaily decorated boats.

"If the goddess is pleased with her gifts," Amado explained, "they will sink quickly to her lair at the bottom of the sea. This foretells a good year ahead. If Iamenja is not pleased, the gifts will float on the waters—a signal that she has rejected them." Happily, the goddess accepted our gifts; they sank with alacrity.

The next day we visited "Mother Menininha," the most famous *candomblé* priestess of Brazil, then almost ninety. (She died in 1986.) This once formidable black woman, now wizened and confined to her bed, was venerated throughout Brazil, and a private audience with her was considered an unusual honor.

19

As we entered her primitive and sparsely furnished house, strange odors of animal sacrifice and other *candomblé* rites overwhelmed us. I could imagine Robert Phillips, the photographer who accompanied me, wondering how this was going to play in *Town & Country*, the magazine that had sent us on this assignment.

Mother Menininha motioned me to her bedside and her wrinkled, bony hands enfolded mine. She paused, considering her words carefully. Then, with a stern expression on her face, she warned, "Be careful, for you are very strong. You will be famous—and soon." At the time, I took this about as seriously as I would a Chinese fortune cookie.

Finally, on my last day in Bahia, I decided to go shopping and found myself in a musty antique-jewelry shop. Not much appealed to me, but as I was leaving my eye fell on a charming gold locket with a turquoise in the center surrounded by seed pearls. Turquoise has always been my favorite stone, and everyone of Mediterranean ancestry knows that wearing turquoise wards off the evil eye.

I took the locket in my hand and, with a strange sense of the inevitable, turned it over. There, on the other side, was a large "L" in diamonds. I had no doubt that the locket was for me—"Lucky" had been my nickname since school days. I bought it without haggling over the price.

The next day I headed back to the snows of Washington. My mother, who had been house-sitting for me, handed me a clutch of messages, among them one saying, "Mr. Deaver called from the White House."

I knew that Michael Deaver, deputy chief of staff to the President, did not make phone calls just to chat.

"Mother, did Mr. Deaver give you any idea what he wanted?"

"He didn't say. I told him you were in Brazil."

"But why didn't you give him my telephone number?"

"Because I knew you were about to leave," she explained. "And anyway, I didn't think it was important."

I couldn't be exasperated with my mother. After all, she had done me the favor of coming to look after the house while I went to Brazil and my husband Archie toured Africa on a project for the Chase Manhattan Bank.

But I couldn't help finding it significant that the date Mike Deaver called was the day I found my Lucky locket.

When I finally made contact with Deaver, he said in that dry, expressionless voice I came to know well, "Lucky, I've been trying to reach you on behalf of the President to ask if you would be interested in becoming the next Chief of Protocol."

The position had just been vacated by Leonore Annenberg, an intimate friend of the Reagans. Although a Republican all my life, I had not been active politically. I scarcely knew the Reagans and had no reason to expect a presidential appointment.

I accepted at once. And, as I thought about it over the days that followed, I realized I had been preparing for this job all my life. All my experiences would finally fit together to form a coherent whole.

Still, you might ask, how did a woman whose ancestors undoubtedly rode camels in the Arabian Desert come to be appointed America's hostess to the kings and queens, presidents and prime ministers who come to this country on official visits?

How did this first-generation American find herself the nation's number one ceremonial officer and arbiter of what is correct and appropriate in American official matters?

And how did someone reared in the mountains of East Tennessee become the chatelaine of Blair House, the 110-room presidential guest house, overseeing its six-year restoration?

Therein hangs my tale.

TWO

The Reagans Arrive in Washington

WHEN THE REAGANS arrived in Washington, I did not know them well. In fact, I had supported George Bush in the primaries, partly because I thought I identified philosophically with him, but mostly because I knew him and Barbara and liked them enormously. Archie's parents and Bush's parents were next-door neighbors in Hobe Sound, Florida.

I first met the Reagans during the 1968 convention in Miami. I was one of the team covering it for the *Washington Post* and, being the most junior reporter, I was assigned to the "least important" candidate. At the time I felt cheated and condemned to obscurity— but, of course, a wiser hand was plotting my fate.

So the Reagans were my assignment, and one very hot July afternoon I found myself with Charlotte Curtis, one of my Vassar roommates and then an editor at the *New York Times*, waiting side by side for a press conference about to be given by Mrs. Ronald Reagan.

Impeccably dressed as always, Nancy Reagan made a hesitant entrance and immediately struck me as being very shy. I was surprised that a former actress and politician's wife could be so ill at ease and inarticulate, and my sympathy went out to her. One sensed she hated being there and felt a great antagonism toward her inquisitors. And I also felt the press's dislike for her. It puzzled me and made me determined in my own perverse way to try to elicit something from Nancy Reagan that the others could not. Was there any way of reaching her—of making real contact with this reserved and guarded woman?

I had taken the precaution of arranging with some conservative friends to have a private interview with Mrs. Reagan following the press conference. One on one, she was more forthcoming, and although it was not a great interview, I certainly had more of a story than my colleagues.

The next morning the *Post* carried an interview with my byline, but as I read the lead I realized it was not my story at all. They had taken the first paragraphs from the wire services—all rather negative—and then added some of my story.

I was stunned. Having just recovered from major surgery six weeks earlier, I felt fragile and in no mood to be trifled with. I stormed into the makeshift offices at the *Post*'s convention center looking for Howard Simons—a terrific editor and one I greatly respected. But that day I was breathing fire.

"How could you put my name on something I didn't write?" I asked. "Not only that, what you did publish was inaccurate and showed no perception or understanding of Nancy Reagan. No wonder people don't believe what they read in newspapers."

Pretty cheeky stuff from a fledgling reporter, but to my amazement Howard looked into the matter and told me, "Lucky, you were right. This was inexcusable."

After the convention was over and we had all returned to our respective cities, I wrote Mrs. Reagan a letter enclosing the carbon of my original story to show her what I actually wrote. I don't know if she ever saw it, but I received a nice thank-you note from an aide.

My first experience with Ronald Reagan came some years later when he spoke to the Women's Press Club in Washington, D.C. I remember some of the older regulars—cynics all—wondering why the club had invited a "lightweight" like Ronald Reagan who "had no political future" to address them. I, who rarely attended these gatherings, was curious to assess this attractive and simpatico politician in the flesh. He revealed himself to be generous-spirited, self-deprecating, and smarter than I thought.

After that evening I never made the mistake of underestimating him. And I noticed that my fellow journalists gave him a standing ovation.

These were my only encounters with the Reagans until they came to Washington as the President-elect and his wife, shortly after the 1980 election. However, the Reagans brought with them some fellow Californians, among them Peter McCoy, Mrs. Reagan's chief of staff, whose wife Kacey is the daughter of the Patrick Dohenys—close friends of ours. We had known Kacey since her childhood and of course we wanted to introduce her to our Washington friends. In turn, we met many of the Reagan inner circle at the very beginning of the administration, including Mike Deaver, Peter's boss.

Charlotte Curtis wrote me, "The Reagans are delightful people even if they are Republicans, and I think you'll enjoy them if not necessarily the people around them. Furthermore, they are great hosts, which will be a very nice change from Nixon, Ford and Carter. But don't count on them culturally. It's the same old conventional stuff."

During that first year, we went to parties attended by Mrs. Reagan and she came to lunch at our Georgetown house. Even a small luncheon for the First Lady, I soon learned, results in six good friends and a thousand enemies, so I decided to ask only writers—and out-of-town writers, at that—hoping none of my Washington friends would get angry with me. Fat chance. One close friend, who earlier had invited me to lunch with Mrs. Reagan, was furious. It took her months to forgive me.

The lunch was a culinary disaster. My party cook, who had never let me down, simply fell apart at the thought of Nancy Reagan eating her food. The salmon was overdone, the mayonnaise had curdled, the dessert didn't jell. However, the guest list was a big success.

I had invited Edmund Morris, author of *The Rise of Theodore Roosevelt*, the Pulitzer Prize–winning biography of Archie's grandfather, and his wife Sylvia Jukes Morris, author of an equally fine biography of Archie's grandmother, Edith Kermit Roosevelt. I had sent both books to the Reagans, and they loved them.

In the course of the luncheon, Sylvia told Mrs. Reagan that Edith Roosevelt had burned all of her husband's love letters to her and what a calamity this was for historians.

"I have all Ronnie's letters to me," Mrs. Reagan said. "Do you suppose I should burn them?"

"Oh, no," we all shouted in a chorus, but I could see she had not considered the possibility that one day these might be public property.

Arianna Stassinopoulos, author of a biography of Maria Callas, was also a guest, and my husband Archie, another aspiring writer. This was in July 1981, some months after the assassination attempt on the President. I could see that Mrs. Reagan would never get over the shock of it, but she had handled herself with great dignity. However, she was bewildered by the negative attitude of the press toward her, which seemed to get worse by the day.

The very style and elegance she had brought to the White House were about to become her undoing. Stories began appearing about her redecoration of the White House family quarters and about her acceptance of a gift of china for the White House paid for by a patriotic citizen (whose name no one even remembers now, despite the furor). At the time, the press never got around to mentioning the fact that all Mrs. Reagan did was receive this gift on behalf of a grateful nation. As the months went by, the criticism became more shrill. It was open season on Nancy Reagan, and it seemed unfair to me.

In a fit of outrage, I called Charlotte Curtis, by then editor of the *New York Times* op-ed page. "Aren't you shocked by these intemperate attacks on Nancy Reagan?" I asked.

"Well, Lucky," she said, "if it bothers you so much, why don't you write a piece for the op-ed page and I will print it."

I wrote the article, but for some reason did not send it to Charlotte. The draft sat on my desk for days, and I don't know why I hesitated.

Then one morning in November I picked up my *Washington Post* and read a column about Nancy Reagan by Judy Mann, which concluded with these words: "The fundamental problem with Nancy Reagan's image is Nancy Reagan."

That did it. I took the draft I had written for the *New York Times*, revised it, and showed it to Jeremiah O'Leary, a former colleague of mine at the *Washington Star*. I wanted to be sure I hadn't lost my own objectivity. Jerry didn't suggest any changes, so I called my neighbor Meg Greenfield, editor of the editorial page of the *Washington Post* and one of the journalists I most admire.

"Meg, I think the press has gone too far in their attacks on Nancy Reagan. I've written an answer to Judy Mann's latest. Will you consider it for publication?"

Meg was interested. A few days later the *Post* published the following article, which I quote in part:

> Fun's fun, but the pummeling of Nancy Reagan has gone on long enough . . . . [Judy Mann's] article prompts me to blow the referee's whistle. When is the press going to give the first lady a break? When are you going to stop expecting her to conform to certain criteria to please the fourth estate—criteria, I might add, that change as frequently as the hemline and seem just as capricious?
>
> How fickle you are and how short your memories. Only yesterday you were making fun of Bess Truman's avoirdupois and Mamie Eisenhower's bangs. You laughed at their dowdy clothes and pedestrian friends.
>
> Along came Jackie Kennedy and you extolled in her the very things you now deplore in Nancy Reagan. . . . And although Mrs. Johnson was one of the richest first ladies in history, no one ever asked what she paid for her clothes or what she gave to charity.
>
> You maligned poor Pat Nixon for being so determinedly middle-class . . . candid Betty Ford you liked for her gutsy battle with cancer and because she was an outspoken defender of the ERA and other pet projects of yours. . . . And finally, hark back to Rosalynn Carter. . . . You couldn't wait to pounce the minute she overstepped her "wifely" role. . . .
>
> Let's face it. Most first ladies can't win, whatever they do. But in the interests of fair play . . . I would like to venture some observations about this first lady especially vis-à-vis the press.
>
> Mrs. Reagan is shy, sensitive and vulnerable. . . . She

cannot dissemble. . . . She feels apprehensive and defensive with the press. She is hurt and bewildered by their hostility. . . . She is a real lady and loyal friend. . . . She has no doubt about her priorities. Her life is dedicated to Ronald Reagan. . . .

Mrs. Reagan has been first lady less than a year. In this time she has suffered the shock of an assassination attempt on the President; she has renovated the White House in record time without spending a cent of public funds. . . . She has been more accessible than almost any first lady in recent memory.

One need not agree with her viewpoints on everything . . . but one has at least to grant her the right—indeed the duty—to be true to herself and to chart her course as first lady in keeping with her personality, her upbringing and her own interests.

The response to this article was overwhelmingly favorable. The *Post* editors were surprised by the vehement feelings reflected in the letters they received, and they published an unprecedented number. Through the *Post*'s wire service, the article appeared all over the country; it was reprinted in many publications, and was even entered in the *Congressional Record*. I was invited to appear on NBC's *Today* show and other programs.

Knowing that I had struck a responsive chord and spoken for many Americans who were too shy or too disgusted to speak out was gratifying. Mike Deaver and many others in the administration called to compliment me. Nancy Reagan was surprised and grateful. She followed her call to me with a note beginning "Thank you, thank you, thank you!"

Later, when I was named Chief of Protocol, many of the stories about the appointment mentioned this article and said that it alone was the reason for my nomination. Certainly, it brought me to the administration's attention; however, I resented the implication that this was the only reason for my being named—as if my qualifications were of no significance.

I must add one postscript. I have never met Judy Mann, the writer who triggered my article, but I tip my hat to her for a generous gesture. In January 1989, as the Reagans were about to depart, Mann wrote another column about Nancy Reagan—this one entitled "Some Kind Words for a Class Act":

> Nancy Reagan . . . managed one of the more remarkable turnabouts of the Reagan presidency. Severely criticized at the beginning of her husband's first term . . . she has emerged in the end as one of the most popular and highly regarded first ladies in history. She's worked hard.
> . . . History ought to judge her kindly not only for the crucial role she played in ousting [Donald] Regan, but also for her war on drugs. She was given an opportunity to do something extraordinarily valuable for her country. And she did.

THREE

Any Skeletons in Your Closet?

$\mathbf{M}$IKE DEAVER cautioned me that my appointment as Chief of Protocol could be in jeopardy should the news leak prematurely. "I have to touch a few bases first," he warned, "and I want you to call on Secretary of State Haig to be sure he is on board."

But when Archie telephoned me from Africa, he seemed far enough away that I could risk it, so with a certain amount of double talk I told him the good news, swearing him to secrecy.

"Can't I tell David?" he asked. He was traveling with David Rockefeller, chairman of the International Advisory Committee of the Chase Manhattan Bank.

"No," I warned, sure that Cinderella would turn back into a scullery maid if she broke her word.

But nothing in Washington stays a secret, and the beans were spilled by none other than William Clark, the President's National Security Adviser, who casually mentioned my appointment at a dinner party. Donnie Radcliffe, of the *Washington Post*, immediately picked it up, and on March 2, 1982, broke the story, forcing the White House to announce the next day the President's "intention" to nominate me.

The State Department is even more of a sieve than the White House, and by the time Archie got to the next stop on his African itinerary the local ambassador greeted him with a hearty "Congratulations, Archie! We are all so pleased about your wife's new job."

Mike was right to warn me. I still had to go through a security clearance, a financial check, and a political clearance. And, of course, confirmation by the Senate for the rank of ambassador. I never had a moment's worry about any of this until Mike summoned me to his office that first week.

"Tell me," he said. "Do you have any skeletons in your closet? Is there anything in your life we ought to know about that could embarrass the administration?"

I thought long and hard because I realized, having lived in Washington all my adult life, how important it was not to give the President any surprises.

"Mike, you should know that I am an active member of NARAL, the National Abortion Rights Action League, and my pro-choice sentiments are diametrically opposed to the President's position on abortion."

His face fell.

"Mike, I feel so strongly about this issue that I would not compromise on it—if I am asked, I will have to tell the truth. Of course, if right-wing ideological purity is expected of me, then I'm not the person for this job."

Mike wisely noted that my attitude on abortion and being a good Chief of Protocol were totally unrelated, and he felt that this would not be a problem. "Please, just don't make any speeches," he added.

I felt I could live with that, but I told him, "If I'm asked in press interviews about feminist issues, I have to be honest and say I am pro-choice."

He nodded, and the subject was closed. (I would never hear another word from the White House about my abortion views during the years I served as Chief of Protocol, even though I did state my position frequently in interviews.)

"There is one other thing," I continued, "that might be a problem. I am of Lebanese origin, and Tom Nassif, the deputy chief of protocol [chosen by Lee Annenberg], also happens to be of Arab background. He is doing an excellent job and I certainly would want to keep him. The Israelis, or even some American Jews, might not like having two Lebanese-Americans heading the Office of Protocol."

Mike assured me that the President did not think in such terms and that ability and suitability were more important than ethnic origins.

(I was right to mention it, though, because shortly thereafter someone—they did not tell me who—called the Republican National Committee to denounce my appointment because I was of Arab origin. Mike, and the RNC as well, dismissed that with the contempt it deserved.)

Mike sent me over to meet Secretary of State Alexander Haig, who was outwardly hearty and cordial, but who struck me as coiled and tense on the inside. He praised Lee Annenberg for the talent and commitment she had brought to the office. And he gave me his blessing, saying the Chief of Protocol's job was "far more important than most people realize. To tell you the truth, I never realized how important it was until I took this job."

I had known every Chief of Protocol since John Farr Simmons in the first Eisenhower administration. The demands of the job were not news to me. It is often cited as one of the toughest jobs in Washington, and I knew the pitfalls were deadly—the "goof factor" the frequent subject of front-page news. (George Shultz would later say, "If protocol goes well, no one notices; if you make a mistake, it's all over the front page.")

In many countries there are two offices of protocol—one serving the chief of state, and the other serving the foreign ministry. In our system, I covered both, but my offices were in the State Department. Officially, my title was "Chief of Protocol of the United States of America." The job description stated that I reported directly to the President with "oversight" by the Secretary of State.

In preparation for my congressional hearing, I was given the following list of duties I would be expected to perform:

1. Plan and execute detailed programs for visiting world leaders and accompany them during their official travel in the United States.

2. Make all arrangements for delegations named by the President to represent him at inaugurals, funerals, weddings, independence day celebrations, and similar ceremonies abroad.

3. Coordinate arrangements for foreign press accompanying visiting dignitaries.

4. Organize the presentation of credentials of foreign ambassadors to the President.

5. Arrange all official entertainment by the Secretary of State, and any by the Vice President when host to foreign dignitaries outside his residence.

6. Plan and support the Secretary of State's official events at the United Nations General Assembly.

7. Suggest official gifts to be given by the President, Vice President, and Secretary of State and their spouses; select, purchase, wrap, deliver, and maintain records of same.

8. Accompany the President on official trips abroad, and coordinate planning with the White House advance office and First Lady's staff.

9. Assist at certain public events such as inaugurals, state funerals, joint sessions of Congress, Democratic and Republican conventions, and ceremonies where the diplomatic corps is involved.

10. Manage Blair House, the President's guest house.

11. Maintain a New York office to support visits and ceremonial functions.

12. Accredit all diplomatic officials assigned to Washington, to the United Nations, and to the Organization of American States. Register all other employees of these embassies and international organizations.

13. Publish the diplomatic list, the list of diplomatic missions, and the list of foreign consular offices in the United States.

14. Determine the eligibility of diplomatic and consular officials for rights and immunities; issue credentials; advise state and local governments on same.

15. Resolve disputes between the diplomatic corps and local law enforcement officials, especially those involving crimes or unpaid financial obligations.

16. Help negotiate consular conventions and other treaties involving rights and immunities of foreign diplomats.

17. Arrange customs courtesies for foreign VIPs.

18. Help new diplomatic missions set up their embassies.

19. Promote development of the Washington International Center as a place to build new embassies, thus avoiding zoning battles.

20. Maintain and update the precedence list.

I couldn't wait to begin. But first came a brief session before the Senate Foreign Relations Committee—an experience most appointees dread. But I was indeed lucky. The chairman, Senator Charles Percy, was my Georgetown neighbor; the ranking minority member, Senator Claiborne Pell, had been a neighbor; and my sponsor, Senator John Warner, was a friend of many years.

Said Senator Percy: "The Chief of Protocol occupies a unique position within the federal government. . . . Given the significant and substantial responsibilities, [she] . . . must be well versed in U.S. foreign policy concerns and at the same time be comfortable working with the wide assortment of people and interests that make up the Washington diplomatic community. . . . She is an outstanding choice for this very demanding post."

Senator Pell thought Mrs. Roosevelt would bring "grace, sensitivity and common sense" to the job, and added, "I only hope that when she is all through with this, she will write somewhat expurgated memoirs of her tour of duty . . . which can serve as a guidebook to those who follow her."

A hint of exasperation came from Senator Larry Pressler, who said he was tired of protocol chiefs coming before the committee for confirmation and noted that since 1968 "we have only managed to keep people on this job for an average of 1.2 years."

Senator Pressler's complaint was well taken, I thought, and I assured him that I would stay as long as the President wished.*

And when Supreme Court Justice Potter Stewart swore me in as the nation's twentieth Chief of Protocol little did I dream that I would serve almost seven years, longer than anyone in the history of the office.

*After my retirement in January 1989, Senator Pressler was so pleased at my staying the course that he gave a luncheon in my honor in the Senate Dining Room!

FOUR

Protocol—Keeper of the Gate

THE ROLE of the chief of protocol is an ancient and honorable one. As early as the fourteenth century, the Spanish-Arab historian Ibn Khaldoun mentions the "Holder of the Ink Well," or Dewadar, in the court of the Mamelukes, as "the official who introduces ambassadors and others in audiences with the Sultan, and who supervises the rules of etiquette in presenting oneself to the sovereign and saluting him. He has as subordinate officers the Secretary of State and the Masters of the Post."

Though not quite so exalted today, a chief of protocol still exists in every government in the world—be they monarchies, dictatorships, or democratic republics such as our own.

Basically, protocol is concerned with form—how things are done, how events are facilitated, the rules which govern the conduct, as opposed to the content, of our international relations. Hence the chief of protocol is the orchestrator, the chief ceremonial officer of any government.

He is also the principal interlocutor between the chief of state and the diplomatic corps, and represents his government on all matters to do with accrediting diplomats and granting diplomatic immunity. In the case of Washington, with almost 150 embassies and some 30,000 diplomats and dependents, it is like being the mayor of a small town with a very demanding constituency.

All state visits and official visits of high-level foreign dignitaries are planned under the supervision of the Chief of Protocol. In the process, the protocol office is in touch with the offices of the President and First Lady, the Vice President and spouse, the Secretary of State, the National Security Council, Andrews Air Force Base, the foreign embassy involved, Blair House, the Senate and House of Representatives, the Military District of Washington, the Secret Service, the press, interpreters, hotels, limousine companies, caterers, and florists.

During an official visit, the Chief of Protocol is also the personal representative of the President. I was surprised, my first week on the job, to learn how literally this is interpreted in other countries.

Queen Beatrix of the Netherlands was my first state visitor, and we had planned almost ten days of activities across the United States beginning on April 17, 1982. Months before my appointment, however, I had agreed to co-chair an important benefit in Washington for the Folger Shakespeare Library.

At one of the planning sessions with the Dutch Embassy, I explained that on April 23 I would have to leave the Queen in New York, fly back to Washington to preside at this benefit, and then rejoin Her Majesty the next morning in New York.

The Dutch diplomat frowned. "But, Ambassador Roosevelt, I do not think this would be acceptable to my government."

"Good heavens," I answered, a little put out. "Nothing official is planned for that night, and I'm sure the Queen would understand. Furthermore, my deputy will cover for me."

"But we would perceive this as a discourtesy to the monarch. You are President Reagan's personal representative. Your presence confirms his hospitality and our Queen's status as his guest. If you leave her, that would be a serious breach of protocol in our eyes."

I had visions of causing a protocol flap with my first sally into this arcane world—and decided that the Folger Library would have to do without me.

It was my good fortune to work for a Secretary of State who understood protocol and used it as a weapon in his diplomatic arsenal. When George Shultz took over the department in July 1982, one of his first acts was to send for me. "Tell me about protocol," he said.

This was my initial meeting with him and I was somewhat intimidated by the inscrutable blue eyes. Long pauses did not embarrass him, nor did he feel compelled to fill silences with innocuous conversation. He gave new meaning to the phrase "a man of few words."

"Mr. Secretary, protocol is a universal language which is designed to make diplomatic relations easier." And I added, "I could give you a long list of dos and don'ts, but basically, protocol is good manners and making the other person feel comfortable. Most of the time your own instincts will guide you to do the right thing."

I gave him an overview of my department—a staff of sixty, two of whom were posted to New York. My alter ego was Deputy Chief Tom Nassif, later replaced by Timothy Towell, our current ambassador to Paraguay. We kept three secretaries and a driver busy from dawn to midnight. Associate Chief Richard Gookin was our liaison with the diplomatic corps; and three assistant chiefs—for visits, for ceremonials, and for administration—completed the hierarchy. (Later, the manager of Blair House would also be accorded the rank of assistant chief.)

Shultz asked what the different types of visits signified. I explained that the state visits, for chiefs of state, such as Queen Elizabeth of Great Britain or President Mitterrand of France, usually lasted a week, splitting the time between Washington and any other cities of their choosing. The President gave a state dinner for the visitor.

An official visit, for heads of government, such as Prime Minister Margaret Thatcher or Chancellor Helmut Kohl, was exactly the same with one exception. Reigning monarchs and presidents got a twenty-one-gun salute and prime ministers got only nineteen guns at the ceremonial arrival at the White House. There were about ten state/official visits a year.

An official *working* visit—long on substance and short on ceremony—consisted of a two- or three-day stay. No state dinner, but lunches or dinners given by the Secretary of State and/or the Vice President. Definitions varied with each administration, but these were the rules in place when I took over.

Shultz balked when I told him he would have to go to the airport to greet on state visits. (For a working visit, the VIP was brought from the airport to the Washington Monument grounds by helicopter, and the Secretary greeted him there.)

"Mr. Secretary, not too long ago the President of the United States himself greeted a chief of state at the airport—only security considerations prevent it now. Furthermore, when President Reagan goes abroad, he will almost always be met at the airport by the ruler of that country."

Indeed, in many cultures, notably in the Middle East and the Far East, the formal welcome is more important than the substantive discussions. During the Eisenhower administration, the state visit of King Ibn Saud of Saudi Arabia almost got canceled because the King refused to come unless he was met at the airport by President Eisenhower.* Cables flew hot and heavy while the chiefs of protocol thrashed it out. Finally, Ike caved in and went to the airport. For Ibn Saud, it was a matter of honor and ancient tradition. In the old days, as a great tribal leader, he might ride out three days in advance to escort—and thus protect—a visiting chieftain to his oasis.

I stressed to the Secretary the importance of being consistent—no matter what format he adopted. That way, no visitor could feel shortchanged or compare his reception invidiously with another.

It didn't take long before Shultz learned what I meant. Shortly after Shultz took office, King Hassan of Morocco was to head an Arab League delegation to Washington in response to an important American initiative on the Middle East. The King sent word he would not come unless Shultz met him at the airport. Since this

---

*Understandably, Ike did not want to set a precedent, although in 1957 he met Queen Elizabeth at the airport. Ike also sent Chief of Protocol John F. Simmons all the way to London to accompany India's Prime Minister Nehru to America. And Lyndon Johnson ordered his protocol chief to London to escort the Queen to Washington.

was not a state visit, it was a problem for Shultz; every royal who came to Washington would expect the same treatment.

But protocol is also charged with finding inventive ways to rewrite the rules when necessary. "Why don't you simply announce that since the King is representing the entire Arab world, and to underscore the importance of this mission, the Secretary of State will accord him the signal honor of meeting him at the airport," I suggested. And it worked.

Shultz would come to appreciate the importance of his personal attendance. He always escorted the VIP to his hotel or to Blair House and had a friendly cup of tea with him and his advisers. Shultz was a master at making the visitor feel welcome, and this set the tone for future meetings with the President. The Secretary also found this unstructured preliminary get-together an effective way to sound out any problems or apprehensions on the part of our foreign guest.

During the six years Blair House was closed for repairs, we allowed our guests to choose their hotel. We paid all rooms and expenses for the principals and an entourage of twelve. Anything over that came at the expense of the visitors. A wise cut-off point, because many visitors felt the size of their retinue was an indication of their importance and they often arrived with 747s full of retainers. (Lucky's law: The smaller the country, the larger the entourage.)

For each visit we offered a similar package: Secret Service protection if requested, helicopters between Andrews Air Force Base and Washington, D.C., and Air Force transportation within the United States. We only paid for five limousines, no matter how large the entourage.

All these matters we negotiated with the chief of protocol or the ambassador of the visiting country. One of my first such encounters was with Moulay Hafid el-Alaoui, Morocco's protocol chief, and a relative of King Hassan.

An elderly, pugnacious man, who often wore a white burnoose, Moulay Hafid fixed his steely eyes on me as we sat down on opposite sides of the conference table. He decided he could make mincemeat of a woman, and began chiding me in French, translated by Alec Toumayan, the State Department's star French interpreter.

"Ambassador Roosevelt, don't you think it is disgraceful that this great rich country of America is so ungenerous and counts pennies with the King of Morocco, when my king is so hospitable to all American officials who visit the kingdom. Take, for example, the matter of autos. His Majesty provides any number you ask for in Morocco, but here, you humiliate us with only five cars." Moulay Hafid continued in this vein, citing other examples of our failings as hosts.

My deputy, Tom Nassif, was getting hot under the collar and started to interrupt this tirade, but I put a restraining hand on his arm. "Let me deal with this," I whispered. And I summoned up whatever insights I had into Arab psychology.

"Oh, Moulay Hafid! My face is blackened! Everything you say is true. Your king is indeed a man of legendary generosity; no one can match his hospitality, his munificence. But you must understand that my president, Ronald Reagan, is also a true prince, a man of great heart who wants to receive your king in a manner worthy of him. However, under our constitution the power of the purse rests with Congress—and unlike your king, who is accountable to no one, my president, alas, is accountable to the legislature on financial matters."

I waved my hand in a gesture of dismissal. "Please, Moulay Hafid, let us hear no more about this awkward matter. You are a gentleman and you will not wish to embarrass me further."

His manner changed completely, and as we left the room he said to Tom, "You listen to her. That woman knows what she's doing."

Much to my chagrin, I soon discovered that most people thought the Chief of Protocol's main duty was to determine where people should sit. Certainly, of all my areas of responsibility, none was more contentious than the question of rank and seating. People who are otherwise delightful and in fine mental health can behave like lunatics if they think they have been slighted or seated incorrectly.

Indeed, historical precedent is not on the side of sanity. In the seventeenth century, France and Spain almost went to war over a matter of ambassadorial precedence. About a century later, at a court ball in London, the French and Russian ambassadors got into a violent quarrel over their respective places, settled by a duel in which the Russian envoy was wounded. Even the Pope once tried to establish an order of precedence, but to no avail. Not until the Congress of Vienna in 1814 was the matter of diplomatic precedence codified, and the rules established then are still operative today.

In brief, an ambassador's ranking is determined by the date he presents his credentials to the host country's chief of state. The ambassador who has been *en poste* the longest becomes dean of the diplomatic corps.* Chiefs of state outrank heads of government, and within categories, rank is determined by the length of time in office, or in the case of monarchs, from the time they ascend the throne. A simple solution adhered to by every nation in the world.

Even today departures from protocol can cause dramas. When I first took over, the state visit of Italy's President Alessandro Pertini had just concluded—a great success, with only one sour note: the Italian foreign minister had not been properly seated at the state dinner.

"It was all I could do to persuade him not to leave the White House in a rage," I was told by the Italian ambassador, who had to bear the brunt of the ministerial ire.

At another state dinner, John Cardinal Krol of Philadelphia was given a place of honor at the head table and Archbishop Pio Laghi, the Pope's ambassador to Washington, was seated "in Siberia," an understandable decision since cardinals normally outrank archbishops. However, Archbishop Laghi was the Apostolic Delegate to the United States, thus the ranking ecclesiastic in the U.S., taking precedence even over cardinals. Both men were embarrassed by this breach of protocol.

*The only exception occurs in some Catholic countries where the Vatican's ambassador—the Papal Nuncio—is automatically accorded that honor.

I remember, an innocent young aide at the USIA who decided that seating an international luncheon meeting was a breeze, and proudly presented her seating chart for my inspection. She could have started several wars—she had Greeks and Turks at the same table; Argentinians and British together at another; and Arabs and Israelis at still another.

While errors or omissions can cause international incidents, creative seating can also be very effective in achieving foreign policy objectives. My favorite examples are the seatings we devised for the seven different events hosted by President Reagan in honor of the participants in the Williamsburg economic summit.

The players were the same at all the meals—the President of France, the Prime Ministers of Canada, Great Britain, Japan, and Italy, the Chancellor of Germany, and the head of the European Community. We looked for ingenious ways to seat them—still according to protocol, but giving President Reagan a chance to have different people beside him at each meal.

My final task was to call each chief of protocol of the countries involved and explain our plan to them. All were delighted save perhaps the French, who grudgingly accepted with the caveat, "We agree, but President Mitterrand must be to the right of President Reagan for the first event."

At the time, I thought the French protocol chief was being tiresome, but I realized later he was a step ahead of me—he was thinking of the photo op, and if Mitterrand was not next to the President at the first event, the French press would immediately assume a rift.

That's exactly what happened in a photo of the seven at a more recent summit. Japan's Prime Minister Noboru Takeshita appeared at the end of the lineup—out of protocol order. This was interpreted in Japan as a sign of strained relations with the United States.

Every new administration toys with the list of precedence of American officials, making subtle changes that often tell a lot about the players. I got many letters from government officials who thought their position too low on the totem pole. (Obviously, no one ever complained about being too high!) They made amusing reading: the petitioner always asserted that he would never write me if it were a matter of his own prestige—indeed, he simply wanted recognition given to his agency, representing umpteen thousand employees, so they could deal more effectively with foreign powers, Congress, etc.

I could make recommendations, but the final arbiter was the President himself or the Chief of Staff, acting in his name.

Despite their importance to the individuals involved, precedence and seating occupied only a minuscule portion of my time. At least one-third of my staff dealt exclusively with matters relating to the diplomatic corps, especially the accreditation process which confers privileges and immunities on diplomats assigned to Washington.

The principle of diplomatic immunity— the personal inviolability of the diplomat as well as the sanctity of the embassy—is recognized by every nation in the world, and is essential for the conduct of foreign relations. The rules and regulations governing diplomatic immunity are set forth in the Vienna Convention on Diplomatic Relations, and almost all countries adhere to this agreement.

Protocol is the office of record for those granted diplomatic immunity, and when I took over in 1982 these files were still in the quill-pen stage, each diplomat's name and status laboriously entered by hand onto card files. I fought for funds to computerize our data, so important to other areas of the government as well as to my office. The process took years and cost more than $500,000.

Ambassadors came to see me on a variety of problems— crimes by diplomats and their dependents being among the gravest. (The acronym for chief of protocol is appropriately enough COP.) When I assumed office, I felt that the State Department was too lenient with diplomatic offenders, especially the juveniles protected by their parents' immunity. I even sent home a few diplomats whose children committed the more egregious crimes, such as dealing in drugs or assault. Word got around that this Chief of Protocol was no pushover!

At first, some of my colleagues at State thought I was too

tough, but actually my stand helped deflect a really serious threat to diplomatic immunity launched by Senator Jesse Helms of North Carolina. The senator's favorite pastime was micro-managing the State Department and he finally got into my bailiwick.

Resentment had been building up in Washington and New York against "diplomatic crime," and a book came out in 1987 making sensationalist charges that we were condoning a crime wave among the diplomatic corps. (The statistics: out of some 79,000 crimes committed in the Washington area from June 1986 to May 1987, only 147 were by persons with diplomatic immunity, and of those, the largest portion were incidents of shoplifting.)

Senator Helms called a hearing, and with lots of publicity accused the State Department of being "soft on diplomatic crime." He introduced bills to curb diplomatic immunity so severely that other countries would have retaliated, and our own diplomats abroad, especially in unfriendly countries, would have been in serious danger.

The department finally got alarmed, and sent me to the Hill to do battle with Helms. At the beginning of the hearing, Helms said to me, "Young lady, before you begin, I just want to say that I am upset with the State Department for sending a pretty girl to testify instead of some ugly old bureaucrat that I can beat up on."

By the time I finished reading my twenty-page prepared statement, I think Senator Helms was less than enchanted with the "pretty girl." At one point, I departed from my script and looked up at him and said, "Senator, you and I come from the same part of the country, and where we come from a gentleman's word is his bond. We, as a nation, have put our signature to an international treaty, promising to uphold the principle of diplomatic immunity. We cannot unilaterally repudiate our commitment."

And then I added, "Senator, we are not an Iran. We are an honorable nation. We do not break our word; we do not violate diplomatic immunity."

Afterward, Helms paid me the ultimate compliment: "Young lady, I don't ever want you to testify before my committee again!"

Although Senator Helms continued to oppose us, it was on a

more rational basis and, in the end, we did tighten up many of our procedures.

For years I had remonstrated with certain embassies about their overdue bills. Diplomatic immunity protected them from bill collectors, and nothing annoyed me more than to see our local merchants, hospitals, banks, etc., unable to dun these deadbeats. We did everything in our power to collect the bills—but in some cases, particularly the poorer nations, they were too broke to pay.

Among the worst offenders was the Zairian Embassy, and yet a free-spending President Mobutu—with billions reputedly stashed away in Swiss bank accounts—constantly courted Congress for aid to his country. When I let it be known that we were considering reporting to Congress and the press every embassy indebtedness of more than six months' duration, Zaire's bills finally got paid.

Upholding the principle of diplomatic immunity was one of my most delicate missions, but the conferring of immunity—i.e., taking ambassadors to present their credentials to the President—was one of my favorite tasks.

The ceremony begins when a senior protocol officer goes to the embassy to collect the new ambassador and his family in a limousine. A flourish of trumpets greets them as they arrive at the diplomatic entrance of the White House, met there by a smartly saluting military aide. Ambassadors often wear national dress and are encouraged to bring their wives and children.

The most dramatic, I thought, were the Africans, in their magnificent robes and headdresses, either white trimmed with gold, or striking blues, purples, and yellows. A close second were the Asian ambassadors and their wives, in bright orange and pink silks from Thailand, Burma, the Philippines, Malaysia, Brunei. Sometimes the Arabs of the Gulf states wore their handsome desert garb—black abas and white kaffiyehs trimmed with gold.

Following the exchange of letters (no longer read out loud), President Reagan posed for photographs, first with the ambassador and then with the entire family. They were then ushered out of the Oval Office to the waiting limousine, a little dazed because it had gone so fast. I always felt it was too hurried, although President Reagan made up for the brevity with his charm.

(Almost every diplomat assigned to Washington returns home to play a leadership role in his native country. I did not feel that our government paid sufficient attention to them, and in my parting recommendations to the Bushes I stressed the importance of these envoys, who often later become foreign ministers and heads of state. Now President Bush is giving more weight to the credentials ceremony, and I note with pleasure that Barbara Bush is also participating and greeting the wives.)

Anytime the diplomatic corps was invited as a group to an event—the President's State of the Union message, addresses by visiting heads of state to joint sessions of Congress, the Republican and Democratic conventions, the presidential inaugural—my office was in charge of them.

They had been in the habit of arriving for these events each in his own chauffeured limousine, causing a 150-car traffic jam. It seemed to me we could do better. I conferred with the dean of the diplomatic corps, then Ambassador Dobrynin of the Soviet Union, and suggested that the diplomats come to the State Department in their limousines, and from there we would transport them to the Hill or to Arlington National Cemetery, or wherever, in specially chartered buses—a secured motorcade complete with police escort.

Change does not come easily, and Dobrynin was quite skeptical—afraid that riding in buses would offend ambassadorial dignity! But after the first try, the envoys loved it. No more traffic jams and no more waiting—sometimes as much as an hour—for their cars.

The ambassadors also appreciated the trips we organized to acquaint them with the United States—to the Spoleto Festival in Charleston, the Winterthur museum and botanical gardens in Wilmington, the 100th Anniversary of the Statue of Liberty, and the 200th Anniversary of the Constitution in Philadelphia.

Even on such innocuous expeditions we could have problems. In Philadelphia, a group of black activists were determined to turn the celebration into a protest against apartheid by embarrassing the South African ambassador. While I sympathized with their cause, I also had a duty to prevent harassment of an envoy in my care. So I persuaded the leader of the activists to publicly hand *me* a letter condemning South Africa, which I promised to pass on to the ambassador.

We normally took the ambassadors to both the Republican and Democratic conventions, but in 1988 the Democrats rejected our assistance because they did not want the South African envoy to attend, and they knew that we could not eliminate any country with which the United States had diplomatic relations.

The protocol office also had to organize American delegations sent by the White House to foreign funerals, inaugurals, weddings, and independence day celebrations. The delegates—usually political payoffs—could sometimes be difficult and demanding. This was their brief moment in the diplomatic spotlight, causing an epidemic of preening and posturing. My staff were always a bit nervous about delegations, aware that the White House would blame them if anything went wrong.

Maureen Reagan, the President's peripatetic daughter, went on a number of our delegations to Africa—and instead of being a pain in the neck, as everyone expected, she turned out to be a wonderful sport and a great ambassador. At one stop, Maureen was provided with only a quart bottle of water for bathing; at another, she sat in a sweltering stadium for six hours watching countless tribes, as well as pigs, chickens, and other native fauna, pass in review.

An Air Force officer detailed to my office wrote in his report, "This eleven-day whirlwind trip to Africa proved to be stressful, exciting and exhausting. But to the delegation and to the countless thousands of Africans that she came in contact with, Ms. Reagan proved to be a person of substance and stamina."

People often asked me, "How do you prepare for being Chief of Protocol?" Strangely enough, there were no written guidelines and very little briefing. I was grateful to have behind me my years as a journalist covering the diplomatic beat, and the three tours of duty abroad with Archie as an embassy wife.

But there's no question that Protocol stretches one's administrative capacities to the utmost. In addition to the representational aspects of the job, I had to run an office and be in touch with myriad departments of the government. I couldn't have done it without a car and driver and a cellular phone.

It was my policy to return all phone calls—the same day if possible. If not, my secretary Dee Lilly called and, in her most solicitous voice, explained why I couldn't telephone. I noticed that in government, the more important the person the more courteous he or she was about returning calls—and that included the President and First Lady. (Secretary of Defense Caspar Weinberger stands out in my mind as being particularly polite in this respect—as in all others.)

My only quiet periods came while waiting in the President's outer office for a VIP to finish his meeting; then I would always take work with me. I had to finish my reading and sign all letters and documents by the end of the day, even if it meant working very late. I am a clean-desk person, and cannot bear to have unfinished business cluttering my "in" basket.

Archie and I considered ourselves lucky if we had a free weekend together. Dignitaries generally arrived on a Saturday or Sunday so they could start the week fresh and well rested. That meant no real day off for me or the visits officers.

In such personal matters as decorum and appearance, I held my staff to high standards. It was not enough to be bright and enthusiastic—the protocol office should also set the example. Chewing gum and wearing jeans didn't seem the right image, and some of the younger staffers had deplorable manners. I was made sadly aware of this the day I took Mrs. Bush on a tour of the office and several employees did not have the courtesy to stand up when introduced to her. Barbara Bush, great lady that she is, pretended not to notice. (I also forgot my manners at times. Once while seated on the dais at a luncheon in honor of the President of Mexico I pulled out a compact to repair my lipstick while the visitor was speaking. I received two letters zinging me for my lapse.)

It took about two years to pull together a superb group of men and women. And in the State Department I heard nothing but compliments about the high quality, attractive demeanor, and professionalism of the protocol staff.

To work in protocol one had to be a coper. Life was a series of on-the-spot decisions, and no one was better at making them than Catherine "Bunny" Murdock, assistant chief of protocol for visits, later my deputy. Like the weekend the King of Spain, returning from a skiing vacation in the Western United States, stopped to refuel in Washington. The mechanics found a serious problem and the plane could not take off until the next day. Bunny and her staff were alerted, the owners of the Grand Hotel themselves were pressed into service, and the King and his party of seventy never knew the effort involved in getting rooms and meals ready on a Sunday night when most of the maids and the chef were off.

The protocol team's favorite example of "mission impossible" was the First Ladies Drug Conference, when seventeen wives of heads of state convened in Washington at the invitation of Nancy Reagan. "How on earth are we going to get seventeen First Ladies up at the crack of dawn, coiffed and dressed and ready to depart in one motorcade?" Bunny wailed. But she pulled it off.

And there are certain vignettes I will never forget: explaining the complexities of American football to the King and Queen of Nepal when I escorted them to Texas to see the Dallas Cowboys play the Washington Redskins; Bunny pressing the Portuguese president's trousers after learning there was no weekend valet service at the Waldorf-Astoria Hotel; a frantic call from a hotel asking what to do with a trunkload of elephant meat left behind by an African visitor; Gahl Hodges, as the visits chief negotiating with the Secret Service so that the Omani delegation could wear their ceremonial daggers in the White House.

The protocol officers were a gutsy crew. Tiny Becki Bernier broke two ribs when she fell while escorting the President of the

Dominican Republic around Abraham Lincoln's birthplace in Springfield, Illinois. She insisted on continuing with the visit, even though she was in agonizing pain.

Julie Andrews, a tall, stunningly beautiful blond officer, was literally thrown off a helicopter by Zairian thugs accompanying President Mobutu. She told me about it only months later, and Mobutu himself apologized for their behavior on his next trip. However, Julie did not tell me that two of the Mobutu entourage were overheard complaining that our protocol officers had small breasts! The Zairians also chastised Bunny Murdock for not providing call girls for them; they said they had been much better treated in France.

No matter what we did in protocol, however, we were always haunted by one little demon—the goof factor.

FIVE

The Goof Factor

WE ALL HAVE a touch of *Schadenfreude*—joy in misfortune—in us. And whenever I get into a discussion about the life of a Chief of Protocol, everyone—and I do mean everyone—wants to hear about the disasters.

Of course, calamities are inevitable. And although one has to be a big-picture person, one must also pay fanatic attention to detail. That's where the goof factor lurks, waiting to pounce.

I had a mental picture of the "goof factor"—a little devil, agile and mischievous, constantly throwing hurdles in our path. But we also took great pleasure in outwitting him. The goof factor could strike, but we tried to repair the damage before anyone found out about it.

We were pretty smooth. No one ever knew that when the Japanese Crown Prince arrived at Arlington National Cemetery to lay a wreath, there was no wreath for him to lay. The Japanese Embassy had forgotten to order one! Our advance protocol officer simply stole flowers from various wreaths around the cemetery, paper-clipping them onto a frame of greenery, and the ceremony went off with no one the wiser.

Our visitors came and went fast on each other's heels and sometimes ceremonial flags became a problem. Mary Masserini, Protocol's press officer for the past thirty years, spotted the Portuguese flags still flying from every flagpole in the White House area when the Irish prime minister was on his way for his traditional St. Patrick's Day call on the President. Somehow they got the Irish flags up just as the motorcade sirens were heard approaching. (That day Sam Donaldson shouted at me, in front of the entire White House press corps, "Hey, Lucky, how come you have on a purple dress on St. Patrick's Day?" The truth was I didn't own a green dress.)

Goofs multiplied like bacteria when it came to flags and national anthems. More than once we played the wrong anthem or flew the wrong flag because countries modify their flags or change their anthems and forget to let the rest of the world know.

We were expected to advise people on how and when to wear decorations. We sent appropriate National Day greetings from the President to various statesmen around the world. And we had daily inquiries, and occasional carping, from Congress. One of my favorites was a curmudgeonly letter from Senator Patrick Moynihan of New York to Secretary Shultz criticizing a motorcade for President Samora Machel of Mozambique, which he described as "six screeching outriders followed by eleven cars . . . enough automatic weapons to equip a company of marines."

As a result, Senator Moynihan introduced this resolution: "It is the sense of the Senate that the Department of State, in arranging visits of foreign dignitaries to the Capitol, shall have in mind that ours is a republican institution which . . . conducts its affairs with a minimum of display. . . . The recurrent spectacle of screeching, self-important, heavily armed caravans of limousines . . . bearing foreign visitors is discordant, disruptive and scarcely a service to the visitors themselves. The Department of State is urged to consider that two unadorned automobiles and no motorcycles would ensure foreign visitors a warm welcome and make clear to them that they are visiting the representative body of a democratic state, and not some besieged citadel of a fearful tyranny."

Jolly good stuff—except, as Shultz pointed out in reply, the Secret Service, not the State Department, is responsible for protecting visiting heads of state and determines the level of security required.

•   •   •

As Chief of Protocol, I planned my wardrobe carefully, but even so, there were unexpected problems. Just before the Queen Beatrix visit, I was told that wearing red and black combined would be a faux pas—too reminiscent of the Nazi colors. Of course, the very dress I had bought to wear to the first gala was a red-and-black organza.

Several years later, we were expecting a state visit from the Grand Duke and Duchess of Luxembourg and, feeling very smug about my foresight, I warned everyone not to wear red and black together—the Luxembourgers also had suffered under the Nazis. I called Gahl Hodges, then social secretary at the White House, and told her to alert Mrs. Reagan. I sent word to the Shultzes and the Bushes.

As I was leaving the State Department the evening before the visit, the special exhibit of photos and products in honor of Luxembourg was just going up—and the background colors were a dramatic red and black. But it was too late to change the exhibit. We would just have to tough it out.

I worried all night. The next morning, with heavier bags than usual under my eyes, I stood beside the President and Mrs. Reagan waiting for the royal car to pull up to the White House. "Hail to the Chief" had just concluded, and now sounded the fanfare for the arrival of a chief of state.

The Duke exited first, followed by the slim, elegant Duchess—wearing a black dress with bright red draping her torso!

Sometimes, however, being a worrywart paid off. When any important foreign official died, it was my duty to go to his country's embassy, sign the book of condolence, and leave calling cards on behalf of the Secretary and other top State Department officials.

During the transition between the Reagan and Bush administrations, the Emperor of Japan died. All the top officials of our government were expected to go to the Japanese Embassy and sign the condolence book. I was one of the first to go and, unthinking, wore a light-colored fur coat over a burgundy dress. When I got to the embassy, the ambassador and his wife were in unrelieved black, as were all the embassy officials lined up to receive my condolences. And the TV cameras were rolling for transmission back to Japan. I died many deaths as I signed the book, clutching my coat around me. I decided the fur would be more acceptable to Japanese viewers than the dark red dress. As soon as I returned to the office I telephoned the Bushes, Shultzes, Quayles, and Bakers, warning them to wear subdued clothing.

Chiefs of protocol spend a surprising amount of time on official gifts, for that is part of the pageantry of a state visit. Kings bearing gifts is a tradition that goes all the way back to the Bible. And throughout history there are frequent references to gift exchanges between potentates. In the eighth century Haroun al-Rashid, Caliph of Baghdad, sent the Emperor Charlemagne "aromatics, fabrics, a water clock and an elephant"—especially exotic at the time, for elephants had not been seen in Europe for centuries.

From that day to this, elephants have not gone out of fashion as state gifts. Prime Minister Indira Gandhi on her state visit presented an elephant to the Honolulu zoo. But a baby female elephant from President Jayewardene of Sri Lanka to President Reagan caused us more logistical headaches than the entire state visit. The elephant, named "Jayathu" (literally "May you be victorious"), was presented on the eve of the 1984 election. And since the elephant was the symbol of both Reagan's and Jayewardene's political parties, this seemed an auspicious gift.

But Tim Towell, my deputy, warned me, "We've got problems. Instead of a chubby, cuddly creature we have a thin, somewhat ill baby elephant whose ribs are showing. How are we going to organize a presentation ceremony and photo op when the poor thing looks like she's about to expire?"

Jayathu was being boarded at the National Zoo, her ultimate destination. But for that hot June day we smothered her in ceremonial robes and she looked adorable in the photos. Alas, she died a few weeks later. We wrote letters of condolence to the Sri Lankan ambassador and plunged into mourning, and I vowed that would be the last animal we would ever accept. But I did not reckon with the determination of certain heads of state.

Eagles were next. American presidents often give porcelain or glass eagles, since it is our national bird. The Germans also have the eagle for their country's symbol. Aha, said the German president—or was it his chief of protocol?—why not give President Reagan a pair of bald eagles. Live. There were no repeat performances of that presentation ceremony.

My worst experience, however, was having to persuade Indonesia's President Soeharto *not* to give the Reagans a Komodo dragon. We were on an official visit, staying on the island of Bali, when American environmentalists heard that the President was being given an endangered species—a six- to eight-foot lizard which comes from the island of Komodo. The advance men warned me that I would have to prevent this—no matter what. We finally compromised, with the Soehartos presenting the Reagans a wooden carving of the dragon.

We had a full-time gift officer, Christine Hathaway, who did nothing but shop, purchase, record, and prepare official gifts to be given by the President, the Vice President, the Secretary of State and their wives—mostly when they went abroad.

It sounds like fun—all that shopping—but it was not easy to be creative on a limited budget and to tailor each gift to the tastes of both the giver and the recipient. Furthermore, the gifts had to be made in America. We tended to be traditional—Tiffany silver, Lenox china, Steuben glass. Williamsburg craftsmen also designed gifts for our exclusive use, and we purchased handicrafts, such as quilts from Appalachia. Occasionally we commissioned sculptures by outstanding American artists such as Wheatley Allen of California or Walter Matia of Virginia. I had a particular affection for well-chosen sets of books and old prints of the city of Washington, which I encouraged the Reagans to give. We did not take coals to Newcastle. No glass to Sweden, no porcelain to Germany, no leather goods to Italy or Morocco.

We tried to deal with purveyors who were discreet, who would not discuss the gifts before they were given or their cost.

Shultz had a special round-the-world clock in his office and wanted to give a similar one to Soviet Foreign Minister Eduard Shevard- nadze. When we finally tracked one down, the manufacturer promptly told the press, thus spoiling Shultz's surprise gift. Shultz was so annoyed he canceled the order.

In earlier administrations, President Johnson traveled with a planeload of silver gifts and an engraver who could personalize them on the spot, and in 1973 President Nixon lavished on Rus- sia's Leonid Brezhnev a Lincoln Continental with black velour upholstery, donated by the manufacturer.

Even in today's more modest times, on my first big trip with the President—to Paris, the Versailles summit, London, Bonn, the Vatican, and Rome—we took seven steamer trunks full of gifts. We found that foreigners appreciated most of all a signed photo of the Reagans or a gift commemorating the occasion, engraved with the President's or First Lady's signature or the Presidential Seal.

Some gifts, far from pleasing the recipients, can actually of- fend them. No clocks to the Chinese or Thais, as clocks symbolize the ticking away of one's mortality; owls are a bad omen to Arabs; no calfskin picture frames or briefcases for Hindus, no pigskin items for Moslems. Nearly everywhere a knife or letter opener is considered unlucky.

In most countries, gifts are put on display at the state dinner, so that everyone can see them. But that is not our custom. In the beginning President Reagan exchanged gifts with his guest in the Oval Office, but when he saw how much time was taken in unwrapping and politesse, he decided it cut too much into the substantive discussions. Henceforth, the exchange was done by the chiefs of protocol and the gifts were opened in private. Of course, in all this was an element of charade. Government offi- cials, including the President, cannot accept gifts of more than nominal value (at present $180). All others must be turned in or, as in the case of the Reagans, sent to the Presidential Library.

Pamela Gardner, the assistant chief for ceremonials, was in charge of all our entertaining—guest lists, food, flowers and dec- orations, music, platforms and audio equipment for toasts. She even had a calligrapher on her staff, who prepared the thousands of place cards and other embellishments for formal occasions.

Planning menus was one of the trickiest jobs in the ceremonials office, and an error was not easy to correct once the meal was under way. For each visit we sent a list of dietary restrictions and suggestions to the White House and the Vice President's staff, and carefully vetted the meals being served to our visitors at other sites such as the Pentagon or the Hill.

We planned every menu for the Secretary of State's events, and I insisted that the menu cards be written in English (most fancy ones are done in French). I had two unbreakable rules: never serve exotic ethnic food, and never serve the visitor his own cuisine. "They can always prepare their national dishes better than we can, and furthermore they have come to America to learn about us—they want to try our food," I told my staff.

Consequently I had the bright idea of serving a traditional American Thanksgiving meal to the President of Germany. It was such a disaster that Bernard Gwertzman, the affable *New York Times*' State Department correspondent, actually complained in print about it. That's when we learned how difficult it is to serve turkey and stuffing to two hundred people and keep it elegant and hot. But I did have one triumph—pumpkin ice cream!

We tried to take note of certain foreign customs where appropriate. For example, in Brazil it is inhospitable to offer only one dessert, so for Brazilians we gussied up the dessert course considerably.

Sometimes we were misinformed. Having heard that the Chinese do not like cheese, we counseled everyone to scratch the cheese course. So what did Premier Zhao have for breakfast every morning? A plate of cheese washed down with beer!

Californians and Texans think they know all about Mexican food, and time and again I had to talk people out of serving Tex-Mex cooking to our Mexican visitors; they consider Tex-Mex an embarrassing corruption of their own cuisine.

Likewise, everyone tried to serve Middle Eastern visitors lamb and rice—as if they weren't sick to death of it! Instead, we served them chicken or game and occasionally veal or beef, but they did not like beef rare. Africans also had an aversion to rare meat, and almost all foreigners preferred their game well done.

Most people know that neither Moslems nor observant Jews eat pork, but often they forget what that excludes. It means no spinach salad with bits of bacon scattered over the top (this happened more than once when we were on the road); it means no avocado mousse with a circle of Canadian bacon underneath it, such as happened at the Vice President's house—the caterer added the bacon without clearing it with Mrs. Bush's staff.

If Jewish guests let us know ahead of time that they kept kosher, we tried to accommodate them. At one of Secretary Shultz's luncheons Cynthia Ozick, the writer, asked for a kosher meal and then didn't show up. But we forgot to tell the waiter at her table, and somehow Roger Mudd, the television commentator, ended up in her seat and was presented with her kosher meal. When he asked, "How come I don't have roast beef like everyone else?" the waiter insisted, "This you order. This you eat. Special meal for you."

When Indonesia's President Soeharto and his wife visited, I reminded everyone that Indonesia was the largest Moslem nation in the world. We cautioned the stewards on the Air Force plane that would be taking us around the United States. But when assorted cold cuts were passed to our guests, the Indonesians took one look and refused, visibly upset. I rushed to the back of the plane to confer with the stewards.

"Ambassador Roosevelt, these are kosher cuts. There's not an ounce of pork in them," the steward insisted. But to our guests the sliced meats looked like pork, and they simply did not believe us. After that, new orders: no cold cuts, kosher or otherwise, for Moslems.

Liquor was also a troublesome question. We usually served wine and champagne, but for strict Moslems we offered a sparkling apple juice. Still, we had trouble convincing them it was not alcoholic. Moslem visitors asked that after-dinner remarks be called speeches rather than toasts, in case the folks back home were watching.

In our decorations we took care to avoid certain color

schemes. No blue and white—the colors of the Israeli flag—for an Arab visit. No green, the color of the Prophet, for an Israeli delegation.

When the Sri Lankan president came, his ambassador objected to the standard blue-and-white program with a blue tassel we used for the White House arrival ceremony. We had to substitute black ink and white tassels because blue and white were the colors of the opposition.

And so it went. Details, details, decisions, decisions. I was asked hundreds of questions per day. All requiring instant answers, with little time to look up references or historical precedents.

SIX

The Care and Feeding
of Royals

*I*F I SEE another king, I think I shall bite him," said Theodore Roosevelt. I never felt that way, even though I dealt with dozens of royals. In fact, I generally found them the easiest to handle of all my VIPs.

Emperors and empresses, kings and queens, princes and princesses—they understand about protocol. Their lives are governed by it. The care and feeding of royals was once the most important function of a chief of protocol, and monarchs found protocol an effective tool to reinforce the mystique of royalty as well as a way to keep the hoi polloi at a respectful distance.

Of course, the royal families of Europe are by far the most democratic, since they are constitutional monarchs whose roles are largely ceremonial. The most awesome, I found, were the Far Eastern rulers, who are still bound by rigid court protocol. And somewhere in between, a curious blend of autocracy and democracy, are the Middle Eastern potentates.

I wish I could tell you that once you get to know them, today's royals are just like you and me, but it ain't so. Not only are royals different—their lives focused on the duties and privileges they were born to inherit—but most ordinary mortals react differently to them. I have seen suave, articulate men rendered speechless on being presented to the Queen of England and the

60

most dignified women become fawning and meeching in the royal presence.

As a journalist during the Eisenhower administration, I covered many royal visits, the most important being the 1957 state visit of Queen Elizabeth. I alerted my mother: "Watch for me on TV when the Queen arrives—you will find me hovering in the background with eight hundred other reporters." I wrote reams about the visit, including an interview with Chief of Protocol Wiley Buchanan—never dreaming that one day I would be in his shoes. (Imagine my mother's pleasure almost thirty years later watching her daughter officially greet the British monarch as she arrived for another visit.)

I also learned that some Americans do *not* like the fuss we make over royalty, viz. this letter from an annoyed reader:

"Selwa Roosevelt really has outdone herself . . . writing about the imminent visit of the fabulous British Queen . . . and how Mrs. Ike, like the rest of us, is all agog . . . she said that Mamie even loaned some of her own 'bibelots' for the Queen's chambers. Hoity, toity, how gracious indeed. . . . But I want to know, when does a mere curio become a bibelot. Or aren't we trying to be what we ain't by such grandiose language?"

As I have mentioned, my first state visitor on assuming office was Queen Beatrix of the Netherlands and her husband, Prince Claus. I started with a bang—a reigning monarch, an appealing and forceful personality, and a woman who knows her own mind. She was delighted that the first person to greet her bore the name of America's most famous Dutch immigrant. The original Roosevelt, Nicholas by name, came to New York in the sixteenth century from the Dutch village of Oud Vossemeer, in the province of Zeeland.

"I understand we're your first visitors," Queen Beatrix greeted me in perfect English, as I boarded her aircraft and prepared to rattle off my little speech of welcome. She gave me a bright, dimpled smile, and I forgot everything I was going to say. However, I did remember *not* to curtsey. My predecessor had been excoriated mercilessly by the press for bending the knee to England's Prince Charles when he came to the States.

Normally, I rode with the visitors in their limousine as they went through their paces. We always checked ahead of time, and if they wished to ride alone, I would follow in the protocol car. The Dutch preferred to have me with them so they could be briefed from one move to the next. Naturally, I sat on the jump seat so they could be more comfortable.

"Oh, no," Queen Beatrix insisted. "You must sit with us. Look, there's plenty of room for three."

"But, Your Majesty," I demurred, "as we get in the car, I must let you both pass first and I will end up by a window. The crowds want to see you and Prince Claus. I will block their view."

"Then you will get in first and sit in the middle," she said, and I learned anew what the word "imperious" meant. You do not argue with queens, even when they are screwing up protocol.

Privately, the Queen and Prince Claus were cozy and fun, but in her public appearances she was every inch a queen. Generations of breeding and training leave their mark. I reflected on that as I watched her address a joint meeting of Congress, as had her mother, Juliana, in 1952 and her grandmother, Wilhelmina, in 1942. (Addressing a joint session is something almost every visitor wants to do, but few are accorded this privilege jealously guarded by the Congress. Queen Beatrix was the first to be so honored after a five-year hiatus.)

I admired particularly her discipline and punctuality. Indeed, the queens I escorted—Beatrix, Elizabeth II, Sofia of Spain, and Noor of Jordan—never kept anyone waiting. (Kings are another matter, and give the lie to the phrase that promptness is the courtesy of kings.) Of course, royals arrive last and leave first from any function. I remember a time when Princess Margaret was guest of honor at a party at the American Embassy in London and was having such a good time she wanted to stay late. But she left and drove around the block, giving the early-to-bed types a chance to depart, and then she returned.

Queens have certain characteristics in common, starting with stamina. They never seem to get tired. They never ask for the ladies' room, and I never saw them repair makeup or fuss with their clothes. Queens usually wear hats, so they do not have to worry about hairdos, come wind or rain. They wear sensible shoes. They need an endless supply of white cotton gloves, which get worn and dirty after a round of handshakes. Because it is difficult to sit gracefully in a narrow skirt, which also tends to show creases, queens usually wear easy skirts at modest lengths.

Unless they are in mourning, queens never wear black for public events. And indeed one rarely wears black in the presence of royalty. In the daytime queens tend to underdress, preferring conservative good taste to flamboyance and high fashion, but all restraints are off in the evening, and they are not afraid to wear magnificent jewels, since our royal visitors are protected every moment of their stay.

But now it can be told. During Queen Elizabeth's California visit, the plane took off leaving the Queen's jewels, and the footman responsible for them, forgotten on the tarmac! We had him follow, carrying the jewels, on a later plane.

Loyal subjects, when being *protocolaire*, never refer to "the Queen" but to "Her Majesty." As a journalist, I used to be amused by the friendly American crowds yelling "Hi, Queen," but as Chief of Protocol I winced when photographers shouted "Hey, Queen, look this way!"

The worst, however, were importunate fans who tried to get royal autographs. This is a no-no. Even when giving a photograph—a much coveted gift—royals do not write anything except their signature. However, I was pleased that Queen Beatrix made an exception on mine and wrote: "To Mrs. Roosevelt, with our warmest thanks and very best wishes—in remembrance of your first state visit!" It was my first photograph of a head of state, and would soon become a part of a collection of hundreds.

No one could be more regal than Queen Elizabeth of Great Britain—five foot two, eyes of blue notwithstanding. And during her ten-day official visit to the Western United States, her aplomb was put to the test.

Arriving in late February 1983 on the royal yacht *Britannia*, the Queen and Prince Philip were to bask in the California sun-shine as they sailed from San Diego to San Francisco. Instead, the royal couple were greeted with a freak tornado, torrential rains, mud slides, floods, high winds, and eighteen-foot waves.

At one point, water flooded the pier where the sleek 412-foot yacht had anchored and the only way we could get the royal visitors off the *Britannia* was by commandeering some school buses from the nearby naval base. Imagine my amusement at seeing the Queen and Prince Philip sitting in the front seats of the bus laughing like schoolchildren. (I was told this was probably the first time she had ever been on a bus!)

A few days later, instead of helicoptering to President Rea-gan's ranch, as the original scenario provided, rain and fog grounded us, so several four-wheel-drive vehicles were organized to take the royal party up the treacherous mountain road.

The intrepid Queen seemed totally unconcerned. I climbed into the jeep directly behind hers, the one carrying most of her Secret Service contingent. Bob Alberri, the head of the detail, a handsome man with a roguish charm, couldn't resist teasing me as I averted my eyes from the sheer drops on either side of the road. "Madam Ambassador," he said, "we're talking three-thousand-foot drops!"

The weather played havoc with the Queen's wardrobe. When she came down the gangplank the first day in a blue-and-white costume and rakish Dutch-boy cap, that was the last the general public saw of her new ensembles. Instead, the Queen had to cover herself with an olive-drab raincoat and huddle under an umbrella. She even resorted to a plastic rain hat tied under her chin as she rode around Walter Annenberg's Palm Springs estate in a golf cart. Finally Princess Margaret, observing the royal visit on tele-vision in London, telephoned her sister and protested, "Don't you have anything else to wear besides that horrible old mackintosh?"

The royal party ended up flying instead of sailing to San Francisco, but the social events went on as scheduled and I dined four nights on the royal yacht. We arrived in San Francisco early, and despite meticulous advance planning, no one had foreseen a free day. Mike Deaver decided to organize a dinner at Trader

Vic's, and the Queen loved it—the first time in sixteen years that the British monarch had dropped in at a restaurant anywhere.

Months earlier, when we were beginning our preparations for the Queen's visit, I had been hurt and upset because Mike Deaver wanted to take over my duties on this visit. "The President would like me to be the Queen's official escort," he informed me. I was surprised because I knew the President never bothered himself with these details.

"Certainly, Mike—whatever the President wants. I'm sure the Queen will be honored by the President's decision." I'm afraid Mike missed the irony in my voice. He seemed relieved that I did not make a fuss.

I assumed, of course, that this was Mrs. Reagan's wish, but I decided to bide my time. They would soon find out how much they needed my protocol team, and in the end Gahl Hodges, the head of our visits section, would do much of the work. Actually my guardian angel was looking after me. Having Mike Deaver and the White House advance team out front on this visit meant that we had easier access to the U.S. Navy and Air Force. My staff and I could never have coped with the fantastic logistics problems we encountered because of the weather. And every day I said a little word of thanks to the Good Lord who had protected me from falling flat on my face.

In the end, it all worked out for the best. Mike and I shared escorting honors, and when the Queen and Prince Philip had separate itineraries I went with the Prince. Not a bad assignment. There are few men in the world more attractive than Prince Philip, with his aquiline features and military bearing. He kept me laughing, to the point that once I felt the Queen was giving us a disapproving glance. I could imagine her saying, "We are not amused."

The Queen is far lovelier than her photos, and her manner is not nearly so austere as her public moments would indicate. Her glowing skin is a triumph of nature—even as she approached her sixtieth birthday, she had scarcely a line in her face. And when she smiled, she looked like a mischievous little girl.

But Prince Philip had a short temper, and nothing annoyed

him more than the security cordon around them. One afternoon I accompanied him on a series of activities, during which he kept up a lively running commentary. It was dark when we returned to the yacht, and as we drove along the streets Philip noticed that crowds had gathered to greet him. He turned on the light inside the car, so people could see him.

"I'm sorry, sir," the Secret Service agent riding in front said. "I must ask you to turn off that light. It makes you too easy a target."

The Prince was livid. "I'm damned if I will! Why do you think these people are out here? They want to see me, and I want to wave to them."

It took all my courage to say, "Sir, these men are only doing their job. If anything happens to you, it would be due to their negligence. Please do not take it out on them. They have their orders."

When we arrived at the yacht, the Prince, still fuming, tore out of the car and slammed the heavy, armored door in my face, just as I was following him. He could have done me serious injury. Suddenly, he reversed his stride and came back. He grabbed my hand, thanked me, and apologized for losing his temper.

I was scheduled to dine on the *Britannia* that evening, and was afraid the Prince would be out of sorts. Not at all. That night I recognized a kindred soul. I too have a short fuse, but like him I never stay angry. I sat on his right and had a wonderful time. No one would have guessed that just two hours before he had almost killed the Chief of Protocol.

Two years later, the Prince and Princess of Wales came to Washington on a "private" visit—and succeeded in causing even more excitement than the Queen. I was caught in the middle of the juggling for invitations and the social angst that seemed to afflict *le tout* Washington.

Frankly, I was bewildered by the hysteria, which also gripped the press. With the exception of Mikhail Gorbachev's visit, I never had so many media inquiries and requests for interviews. Charles and Diana are a delightful and attractive couple, but I was surprised at the massive crowds lining the route everywhere they went—larger even than for Gorbachev. Young girls jumped up and down and screamed with excitement when the motorcade passed by. If they managed to shake the Princess's hand, they almost fainted from joy.

While attention was focused on the Princess of Wales, with her youth and beauty, I found Prince Charles the more interesting of the two—he was well read, spoke beautifully, had his father's charm and a great sense of humor.

When a visit is "private" it means that the U.S. government is not the host, is not paying the bills, and does not have responsibility for the visit. In these cases, my office worked closely with the embassy involved, but the arrangements were largely theirs. However, no one believes that. So my office was besieged with people wanting to participate in some way in the activities surrounding the royal visit.

The most coveted invitations were to dinners at the White House and the British Embassy. Mrs. Reagan regarded the dinner for Charles and Diana as a private party—even though that was the only part of the visit the State Department was paying for. When it was private, she had total control of the guest list, and took few suggestions from government agencies. (The State Department, the White House congressional liaison, the Chief of Staff to the President, and others did suggest guest lists for official dinners, but again she was the final arbiter.)

Mrs. Reagan's list probably made a much more amusing party than one full of boring officials, but it also made a lot of people angry and earned for me the undying enmity of one congressional wife who thought she had been excluded from the dinner by me.

The royal couple for whom I developed a great personal affection were Crown Prince Akihito and Crown Princess Michiko, now the Emperor and Empress of Japan. Before they arrived, I had read extensively about them and decided theirs was such a rarefied atmosphere that our relationship would perforce be stiff and distant.

Japanese protocol is the most precise and exacting in the world, particularly anything to do with the imperial family. I had seen the way every Japanese referred to them in hushed and reverential tones.

(Japanese protocol is equally solicitous of foreign guests. For example, in planning the visit of Sweden's King and Queen to Japan, they asked the Swedish ambassador what the King preferred for breakfast. A regular continental breakfast, the ambassador answered. What size cup? Medium, the ambassador replied. *Exactly* what size cup? Somewhat exasperated, the ambassador grabbed a piece of paper and drew a cup. The Japanese whisked that piece of paper away and had a cup made exactly the size drawn, plus an extra dozen in case of breakage!)

Archie and I were to accompany the Crown Prince and his wife, both in their early fifties, from their arrival in Boston, to Lexington, Concord, Fairhaven, and Plymouth Rock, through their program in Washington. I had visions of my husband causing an international incident, with his laid-back manner and wicked wit, as we escorted the heir to the Chrysanthemum Throne.

We friendly Americans find it difficult not to touch people. When Queen Elizabeth was in San Diego, the acting mayor placed his hand on the Queen's back as he squired her around a museum and the British press gleefully reported his gaucherie. A friend who watched the Reagans' visit to Japan on TV told me that the Japanese had been shocked when Mrs. Reagan was shown crossing her legs and laughing in the presence of the Emperor. He warned me never to touch a member of the imperial family.

These strictures were enough to make anyone a nervous Nellie. But the minute we met the royal couple I knew we would hit it off.

Crown Princess Michiko was exquisite. She moved with an economy of motion that would make most Americans look like hyperactive children. Her hands formed poetic gestures, and her eyelids fluttered modestly as she looked down, waiting for her husband to precede her at all times. The movements of the couple were like a well-choreographed ballet—so smooth one scarcely noticed that they were highly formalized.

Akihito, now Emperor, is the 125th monarch in a line dating back to 660 B.C. and he carries the weight of tradition and veneration well. At first he seemed shy, but as soon as we started on our rounds he was animated and interested in everything we did.

With their charming, gentle manners, they communicated joyousness and remarkable thoughtfulness. They walked slowly through various receptions, having genuine conversations rather than a perfunctory greeting for each person they met. They asked questions and actually listened to the answers; they seemed not to notice crowds pressing in on them.

At the Washington Home and Hospice I was touched by the tenderness the Crown Princess showed to each senior citizen. In fact, it was the only time I ever wept while on duty, and I had to drop back and compose myself before I could go on.

Another emotional moment came at the Museum of American History when we inspected an exhibit of photographs and memorabilia from the internment camps where we had herded so many Japanese-Americans following Pearl Harbor. We were not particularly anxious to take the Japanese visitors there, fearing to reopen old wounds; however, the Japanese themselves insisted on seeing it.

Afterward Crown Prince Akihito said to me, "It says so much about your democracy that you would hold such an exhibition, and in a government institution."

Akihito loved to play tennis, so we arranged a doubles match with Vice President Bush, Secretary of State Shultz, and Pam Shriver, the tennis star. We also took the royal couple to the Whittier Woods School, where American students conducted the entire program in Japanese. I don't know about our guests, but I was impressed.

Their visit, which had been scheduled to last three weeks, had to be cut short because Emperor Hirohito was thought to be near death. When we said goodbye to the royal couple, I knew that if I ever saw them again, it would be as Emperor and Empress.

Normally, royal visitors do not write their own thank-you

letters—that is left to ladies-in-waiting or equerries—so imagine my delight when I received a handwritten personal letter of gratitude from the Crown Princess upon her return to Japan.

A postscript. Hirohito rallied, and did not die until a year after the visit. Shortly after the presidential election of 1988, we in Protocol began to monitor Hirohito's health closely. We knew that after his death there would be a formal mourning period of forty days. Only then could the state funeral be held. Our question was, would it be a Reagan or Bush funeral delegation—or would it come at the very moment of our inauguration? As it happened, Emperor Hirohito died on January 6, 1989, and President and Mrs. Bush represented the United States at the funeral on February 24.

SEVEN

The Exotic Royals

THE MOST EXOTIC combination of traditional and modern I encountered was the King and Queen of Thailand, whom Archie and I met in the spring of 1988. We were on vacation—on one of our fantastic adventures with Malcolm Forbes. We had flown to Singapore, and then sailed on his yacht to Bangkok. Malcolm had been granted an audience with the King and Queen, and all his party were included: General Motors chairman Roger Smith and his wife, Apple Computer CEO John Scully and his wife, Malcolm's son Christopher, and Elizabeth Taylor, who arrived on the yacht with thirty-seven pieces of Vuitton luggage!

I had never met King Bhumibol, the longest-reigning monarch in Thai history. He had refused recent invitations to travel to America, even though he was born in Boston some sixty years ago, when his father was a student there. I had met Queen Sirikit once, when she came on a private visit. Their daughter, Princess Chulaborn, had dined on the yacht with us the night before and brought her two little girls, complete with small thrones and individual nannies.

The audience was like a scene from *Anna and the King of Siam*. We arrived twenty minutes early and were escorted upstairs past a series of Victorian drawing rooms with large portraits of former Thai kings. Precisely at the appointed hour we were ushered into the royal presence. The two monarchs were seated on thrones elevated on a platform. The Thai friends accompanying us immediately prostrated themselves—and I mean flat-out horizontal. No one had warned me, and I was mesmerized by the elegant wriggling on the carpet!

Each of us was presented in turn, and the Queen very kindly remembered my looking after her in Washington. When we sat down I had a devil of a time with my legs. "You must not point the toes of your shoes at the monarchs," we had been warned. "Do not cross legs. Sit with feet to the sides. You must wear stockings, and no black." The women were seated on one side of the room to converse with the Queen, and the men were gathered near the King.

Suddenly waiters scurried in on their knees, bearing tea and orange juice—individual trays for each guest. They must always be on their knees in the royal presence because their heads can never be higher than the monarchs'.

We were longing to taste the refreshments before us, but no one dared start until the King or Queen did. Throughout the hour-long audience the monarchs' trays remained untouched, so no one else took a single sip. I wondered why the King and Queen didn't invite us to begin—or take just a bit of tea to indicate it was all right for us to indulge.

At first the conversation was stilted. The Queen asked me, "How is Mrs. Reagan? I enjoyed so much my trip to Washington, especially the dinner Mrs. Reagan gave for me. It was so beautiful, not only the food tasted wonderful, but it looked so pretty. That is very difficult, is it not?"

I remarked how much Mrs. Reagan had enjoyed her recent visit to Thailand. And so it went. Meanwhile, the King, a bespectacled, scholarly-looking man, seemed very stiff until he discovered a soulmate in John Scully. The King was a computer freak; he had learned Sanskrit in order to devise an alphabet for his computer. The audience, which had been scheduled for a half hour, stretched to an hour as the King became engrossed in computer talk. Finally he got around to the main purpose of the audience— to confer a decoration on Malcolm Forbes.

As the audience ended, the servants reappeared on their knees, this time bearing books for each of us—wrapped in specially woven Thai silk. When we took our leave, the Queen, who had impressed us all with her beauty, said a curious thing to me: "I have fought the Communists all my life, but I cannot fight the menopause."

I took her to mean that she felt keenly her passing youth, but to my eyes she was still stunning.

For pure Arabian Nights fantasy, nothing can match my trip to Morocco as President Reagan's personal representative at the wedding of King Hassan's eldest daughter, Lalla Meriam.

Morocco was the first country to recognize the United States after we declared our independence. Now, after more than two hundred years of cordial relations, we were having one of the few really tense moments between our two countries.

The wedding was on September 15, 1984. Exactly one month earlier, the King—without telling anyone in advance—had proclaimed a "union" with Libya. The White House and the State Department were alarmed. King Hassan and Muamar Qaddafi, Libya's flaky leader, constituted an odd couple indeed. Nonetheless, at the urging of our ambassador, Joseph Verner Reed Jr., who later succeeded me as Chief of Protocol, the administration decided to send me to the wedding in Fez.

I had mixed feelings about returning to Morocco. Five years earlier, on an assignment for *Town & Country*, I had received a call in Marrakech telling me that Archie had suffered a heart attack and was in intensive care in a New York hospital. I can never forget the anguish of that flight home.

However, I am grateful to Joseph Reed for insisting on my presence, and for the memories that I took home.

The festivities lasted five days, beginning with the henna ceremony before the wedding, when they color the bride's hands and feet with a red dye. On the first night the approach to the palace looked like a set from *Ben Hur*. Thousands of Berber tribesmen paraded before us, bearing tributes from the provinces, and more thousands of dancers performed in colorful tribal costumes. Queen

Sofia of Spain and Imelda Marcos were among the VIPs seated in the reviewing stands. Observing the festivities with me were Ambassadors Vernon Walters, Angier Biddle Duke, and Robert Neumann.

Sharing this wedding day with the King's daughter were 250 betrothed couples from all over Morocco—each groom in a white djellaba and red fez and the brides in green and white, the colors of the Prophet. The King paid for their weddings as well.

After the parade, and the usual hour or two of milling around wondering what next (this is de rigueur in Morocco—everything is total improvisation and yet it all works out), we were admitted into a courtyard the size of two football fields. Water cascaded down the crenellated walls enclosing the courtyard, bougainvillea bloomed profusely against a background of arabesque forms, and the smell of jasmine was intoxicating.

We passed on, into a second courtyard, where each bride was carried around on a large tray by ululating tribeswomen. I met the Queen, who is never seen in public. Young and beautiful, she spoke English and had her feet propped up on a divan, taking it easy for a few minutes. She thought I was Moroccan and did not rise to greet me. Apparently this was later reported to the King (although I took no offense), who said to me, "I apologize that the mother of my children did not recognize you. She did not realize who you were." Later I also met the King's mother, a gracious and surprisingly modern lady.

Each day's activities were a mystery until some hidden tom-tom beat out the message. The next day we had no idea what to expect until an announcement in the hotel proclaimed that the King would receive the men at 6:00 P.M., black tie, and the women at 7:15, long dress.

Now picture this: Camels tethered at the palace gates laden with bridal gifts from the tribes. Another courtyard, even larger than the one the previous night, with two thousand guests helping themselves to mile-long buffets of sweets. All the royals and VIPs seated like a court around the bride, wearing white and her face painted white. The King joins Lalla Meriam for a while, giving his daughter an affectionate hug for the photographers. Then the King sends for me. Seated on a throne in the center of the courtyard, where everyone can see him but no one can approach close enough to hear us, he asks me to carry the following message back to President Reagan:

In sum, King Hassan believed that Americans were chagrined over his accord with Libya because it came at an "awkward" moment just before the presidential election. But, he added, "I am King of Morocco and I must judge my timing for what is best for my people."

He told me he considered Ronald Reagan his most important and closest international friend, "indeed more than a friend—a brother." He said he had not told the President or anyone else his intentions for fear of leaks to the press. "Tell the President to be patient. Ask him to wait and see. Trust me. Nothing has changed in my relationship with the United States."

He urged me to tell "my friend Weinberger" that the U.S. fleet must pay the planned call on Morocco and that the American navy would always be welcome in his ports. He expressed admiration for Secretary Shultz as a thoughtful man of great intelligence.

As we concluded the audience, the King offered me his private plane to take me directly from Fez to Paris. I declined, but as it turned out, on my last day in Morocco I got a terrible case of food poisoning at a private dinner and was so ill the King had me flown directly to the Concorde in Paris and from there I flew to Washington.

King Hassan's visits to Washington were among my biggest challenges. The King was capable of canceling a visit at the last minute if his astrologer decided the signs were not propitious, and he was notorious for being late. But not always. When he came to London on an official visit, he was punctual to the minute. But when Queen Elizabeth was his guest in Morocco, he kept her waiting for almost an hour.

A month after I became Chief of Protocol, the King paid his first visit to President Reagan. I warned Moulay Hafid, my protocol counterpart, that the Reagans were very punctual. King

Hassan had expressed a desire to call on Mrs. Reagan, and we set it up for noon. I came early to Blair House, to escort him to the White House. When twelve o'clock struck, I got worried and begged Moulay Hafid to alert the King that we were already late. The harassed protocol chief disappeared. When he returned, he announced that the King would be ready shortly. I telephoned and warned Mrs. Reagan's office of the delay. At twelve thirty, still no King. He would be another fifteen minutes. Again I telephoned the White House. Again, Mrs. Reagan was understanding. But when one o'clock struck, I took matters in my own hands.

"Moulay Hafid, please inform His Majesty that unfortunately Mrs. Reagan has another engagement now, and their meeting will have to be postponed to another time," I said. I wasn't sure if that was true but I thought it undignified for Mrs. Reagan to be kept waiting so long, without a word of explanation. The next day the King sent her a fortune in flowers by way of apology.

On the King's next visit, the following October, he went to have tea with Mrs. Reagan and arrived on the dot. He even sent his tea-makers ahead. They always traveled with him, carrying their silver teapots, Bunsen burners, and picnic hampers full of the makings of delicious Moroccan mint tea, which they served in the finest Bohemian glass. At the White House gates the uniformed Secret Service had to bodily restrain them, but they insisted that the King expected them to make tea for Mrs. Reagan.

Protocol rushed to the rescue. We sprang them from the guardhouse, explaining to the startled Secret Service that these funny-looking guys in pantaloons and striped vests, red fezzes and pointy bedroom slippers, were part of the King's retinue. The White House curator also had a few moments of panic as they plopped themselves on the red-carpeted floor of the main hall to make the tea, portable stoves ablaze!

The King had also brought a huge supply of pomegranates with him, and sent the aide in charge of pomegranate juice to the White House with a special squeezer to prepare this for his substantive meetings with the President and the cabinet.

An entourage of servants and aides accompanied the King

wherever he went—the coat-and-hat holder, the eyeglasses bearer, the cigarette server/lighter, the coffee/water server. Not surprisingly, his traveling party often numbered more than three hundred, and the Moroccans flew in planeloads of food and equipment to be used at the return dinner he planned. (Sometimes I was horrified by this, until I thought about the staff and equipment we brought with us on our trips abroad. President Reagan rarely traveled with fewer than six hundred tagging along, all presumably vital to our mission.)

King Hassan decided that since they both loved horses so much, he and President Reagan should go for a ride together. And actually, it gave the two principals several hours alone without the usual aides. Arranging that ride, however, proved to be a logistical nightmare.

Immediately after a White House lunch, the President and his guest would helicopter to the Quantico Marine base, where the ride would take place. At what point would His Majesty change into riding clothes? Did he prefer English or Western saddle? Did he want a spirited horse? Who would ride with them? In the end it was one-on-one, with only the military aide, security detail, and photographer at a discreet distance.

The Moroccans informed us that King Hassan wished to bring three horses with him as gifts, one for the President, one for Mrs. Reagan, and one the King would ride and then leave as a third gift.

There was no way the White House could accept them, and yet they did not want to offend the King. Word came from Mike Deaver's office: "Turn off the horses."

It was up to poor Bunny Murdock, who at that time was the gifts officer, to find a way to do this graciously. She telephoned the Moroccan Embassy and explained that American law prevented the President from accepting any gifts worth more than $120 (the limit then). This meant the horses would revert to the government and the American taxpayer would have to feed and board them.

"Are these horses worth more than a hundred and twenty dollars?" Bunny asked.

"But of course, they are the finest Arabians," said the Moroccan, shocked by such a question.

"Well," said Bunny, "I guess we'll just have to shoot 'em and stuff 'em and put 'em in the Presidential Library."

How that message was reinterpreted for the King's ears one can only wonder, but in any case, no more was said about bringing horses.

The protocol staff, while solicitous of all our visitors, had one clear favorite—King Hussein of Jordan, a ruler who could trace his lineage back a thousand years to the Prophet Mohammed himself. Over the thirty-some years of his reign, Hussein had come to Washington almost annually—the guest of eight successive American presidents. Blair House was like home to him—the cook produced his favorite hamburgers the minute he arrived—and he had the drill of state visits down to a science.

The King, thoughtful and courtly, had come to know many of our long-term employees and always greeted them by name. He was especially fond of James Payne, our logistics officer who handled the mountains of luggage and had never lost a piece in forty years. Sometimes, Hussein would appear in the staff office, just to chat with the secretaries and visits officers—something no other monarch ever did.

King Hussein spoke in a deep bass voice, and exuded wisdom and authority. He had the kindest eyes. And with his perfect English, he was extremely articulate and could make his points without resorting to the counterproductive rhetoric of some of his fellow Arabs.

Queen Noor, a vibrant young Arab-American beauty, usually accompanied the King. Almost every year she produced another adorable baby, who captivated the staff and turned them all into goo-gooing aunties. Luckily, Blair House is equipped with baby furniture for just such contingencies.

I must confess to a personal affection as well. My husband had known King Hussein since his early days on the throne, and in the 1960s we had warmly welcomed his brother, Crown Prince

Hassan, to our house in London anytime he wanted to get away from the rigors of Oxford University, where he was a student.

Jordan's Crown Prince also was a frequent visitor to Washington, and we always looked forward to seeing him, but a protocol miscalculation on my part almost ended a beautiful friendship. Because of my hectic schedule I greeted only heads of state or government at the airport, with the exception of the foreign ministers of China and Russia. Everyone else was met by a senior protocol officer. But because we were such old friends, the Crown Prince felt I should have met him at the airport, especially since the greeting is so important in Arab culture and I could not plead ignorance of their customs.

The rulers of the Persian Gulf states—Saudi Arabia, Kuwait, Bahrain, and Oman—all made state visits during the Reagan administration. They were our most colorful guests, with their flowing robes and tribal traditions.

While European monarchs were scheduled down to their last moment, a totally opposite approach was required for our Arab visitors. To them, timetables were a nuisance and even an affront. And yet it is impossible to conduct a state visit without adhering to a program.

And Arabs do things on a grand scale. When King Fahd of Saudi Arabia came in 1985, Blair House was still under reconstruction and so we offered our usual package of twelve hotel rooms, plus the master suite. The Saudis were much too polite to laugh, but they informed us they had rented the entire Hay-Adams Hotel for the officials accompanying the King. Fahd would stay at the residence of his nephew, Prince Bandar, the Saudi Arabian ambassador to Washington.

Bandar and his wife, Princess Haifa, daughter of the late King Faisal, with their five children, moved out and turned their mansion over to the King—a gesture totally in keeping with their sense of courtesy. The Arab code of honor is all tied up with their hospitality—the two are synonymous in their lexicon. And the king must be the most hospitable of all, hence the tradition that any petitioner can approach the king, partake of his food and coffee, and then get a resolution to his problem. (It would be rude to talk business before breaking bread.)

I found that something resembling a court, or *majlis*, gathered around each of these Arab leaders. They moved in a body with him wherever he went. For the Saudis, the motorcades carrying important ministers would form at the Hay-Adams Hotel, just across from the White House, then make their way under police escort to the Virginia estate of Prince Bandar. There, they would salute King Fahd and wait around, sometimes for an hour or two, until he signaled he was ready to depart for the White House. No one would dream of looking at his watch and saying, "Hey, boss, it's time to go!"

When we were planning the state visit, the first by a Saudi king since 1971, I asked Prince Bandar if the King would prefer my male deputy to escort him. I knew that women were strictly segregated in Saudi Arabia, and although I bemoaned that, my primary interest had to be the comfort of our guest. I did not feel it necessary to use that occasion to make a feminist statement. (I had had an earlier experience with the Sultan of Oman, who did not want to be televised in the company of a female. And the members of the Afghan resistance who called on the President asked me not to shake their hands, lest they be photographed touching a woman.)

To my surprise Prince Bandar replied, "On the contrary, Ambassador Roosevelt, His Majesty would be very offended if you did not accompany him. You are not only the ranking official, but you are a woman of Arab background. We are very proud of you."

The Amir of Bahrain, the ruler of a small sheikhdom that is the banking and trading center of the Gulf region, was one of the most genial and popular visitors we ever had.

For state visits I usually flew to the point of entry to greet the visitor, and in the Amir's case it was New York. I then accompanied him on his plane, a magnificently appointed 727 complete with a large salon outfitted like a throne room. There his entourage sat around in a circle, as in a *majlis* at home, and I was plied with caviar, smoked salmon, and other delicacies.

Everyone loved him, and at every opportunity he told me in his excellent English how much he appreciated all that the President and Mrs. Reagan had done for him, and how much he had enjoyed his stay. Yet, when it came time to say goodbye, he seemed very troubled.

"Ambassador Roosevelt," he began hesitantly, "I have been told about your laws that forbid you to accept gifts over a certain value. This upsets me very much. How can I express to you my gratitude for all that you have done for us, if I am not allowed to give you a gift worthy of you—or of me?"

"But, Your Highness"—this was the correct way to address him, unlike the other rulers who were Royal Highnesses or Majesties—"my reward is pleasing you. If you have enjoyed your visit, that is the best gift I could have."

"Well, I must think about this," he said. A while later he came back to the subject. "Ambassador Roosevelt, I have made a decision. I must give you these gifts, otherwise my own people will think that I did not show you the proper appreciation. I know you cannot accept them, but all the same, for my own honor, I must give them."

I opened the two packages. In one was a lovely gold watch, and in the other a string of Bahraini pearls. Alas, today, they languish somewhere on the bowels of the General Services Administration.

The visit of the Crown Prince of Kuwait, Shaikh Saad, illustrates another cultural difference. The Crown Prince was here when Congress was considering the sale of arms to Kuwait. Acting Secretary of State John Whitehead wanted senators opposed to the sale—primarily Inouye and Kasten—to meet with the Prince. But for protocol reasons Shaikh Saad refused to call on them. He was coming to Capitol Hill, however, to visit with the Senate Foreign Relations Committee.

I suggested that Vice President Bush offer the Crown Prince the hospitality of his office in the Capitol, as a place for him to rest and put his retinue. That way, the two senators could call on the Kuwaiti prince on *his* territory, so to speak, and thus protocol would be observed. The Kuwaitis liked that, and the senators were happy as well.

Of course, this attention to detail had a larger purpose. The Arab potentates were not mere ceremonial figures. They also represented authority. To offend them not only meant a protocol blunder, for which the Chief of Protocol would gladly take the blame, but it could result in retaliation on substantive matters for any presumed snub or slight.

In their culture, form and substance were the same.

EIGHT

Blair House—
Why Not Tear It Down?

A FEW YEARS after our marriage my husband and I bought a dilapidated house, circa 1842, in the Georgetown section of Washington. It took a year, and all the money we could scrape together, to restore it.

Afterward, I wrote an article about this adventure for the *Saturday Evening Post* in which I concluded, "If our marriage can survive redecorating a house, it can survive anything."

Well, our marriage certainly survived, but it threatened to come unglued once more when I undertook the restoration of Blair House, the President's guest house—a complex of four nineteenth-century townhouses patched together, comprising 110 rooms—located across the street from the White House.

Blair House falls under the jurisdiction of the Chief of Protocol because it is used primarily to lodge foreign leaders invited to Washington by the President. By providing a setting that reflects the best of our heritage and traditions, this national treasure has a subliminal message which helps us achieve our foreign policy objectives.

Little did I know that the restoration of Blair House would become the most difficult, the most consuming, the most exciting challenge I have ever faced.

The project took six years and over $15 million in government and private resources. It also took the combined efforts of thousands of Americans in both the private and public sectors. But before I go any further, I will let you in on a secret: some people on the Hill thought a better alternative was to tear it down!

One of the important landmarks in Washington since its construction in 1824, Blair House and its companion Blair-Lee House embody the history of Washington. An army of ghosts inhabit those rooms. Sometimes when working there late at night, I could sense their presence:

• President Andrew Jackson meeting informally with Francis Preston Blair, a distinguished editor, and other intimates in the kitchen of Blair House in order to keep warm in the cold Washington winter. From this came the term "kitchen cabinet."

• President Martin Van Buren continuing the tradition in his administration and consulting almost daily with Mr. Blair, whose descendants lived in the house for more than a hundred years.

• General Robert E. Lee, turning down Blair's offer, extended on behalf of President Abraham Lincoln, to take command of the Union Army. (Lee's portrait and Lincoln's both hang in the room where this historic encounter took place on April 18, 1861.)

• William Tecumseh Sherman being married there to the daughter of the first Secretary of the Interior, with President Zachary Taylor, Daniel Webster, and Henry Clay in attendance.

• Franklin Roosevelt, who decided in 1942 to purchase Blair House as the nation's guest house.

• Harry Truman, who spent four years of his presidency at Blair House while the White House was under repair. Truman barely escaped death in an assassination attempt foiled by guard Leslie Coffelt, who was killed in the melee on the front steps of Blair House.

As the Presidential Guest House, more lore has been added to this already legendary complex. Almost every important world leader has stayed there, and the staff has become so accustomed to their vagaries that nothing fazes them.

Many times, guests bring their own chefs and truckloads of food and equipment, including linens, cooking utensils, goat's milk, and chickens! Once, a visitor smuggled in meat full of maggots, which caused Department of Agriculture inspectors not only to remove the meat, but also to burn the suitcases used to transport it.

One monarch insisted on his own special vibrating bed, and had eighteen mattresses spread out on the floor for his guards. The startled manager also found five naked men asleep across the threshold of her room.

Often the Blair House staff has had to cope with six different functioning dining rooms when the visitors' caste systems did not allow them to eat in the same areas. For religious reasons guests have taken down paintings depicting the human form, and requested that parallel beds be changed to perpendicular. They have brought in chairs to act as thrones, and some even set up their own exercise equipment.

My most poignant Blair House memory comes from my days as a reporter, when the diminutive Emperor of Ethiopia, Haile Selassie, was observed walking his tiny dog in the garden twice a day.

When my predecessor, Lee Annenberg, briefed me about my future duties, she said, "Lucky, what I regret most about leaving is that I did not have a chance to do anything about Blair House."

But Lee had commissioned a study to analyze what needed to be done and what it would cost. The answers were grim. Every system—electrical, plumbing, heating, air conditioning, sprinkler, and security—needed an overhaul. The study also recommended adding a new wing, to provide a secure master suite and a large special room for entertaining.

The price tag: about $9 million—and that was before one cent was spent for decorating and refurbishing. As we were digesting this shock, the manager of Blair House, Juliette McLennan, telephoned.

"We've just had to send for the fire department. The boiler malfunctioned and the place is filled with smoke," she reported.

Prime Minister Mzali of Tunisia was staying in Blair House, and I could imagine the international brouhaha if anything happened to him. It turned out that a gas valve had leaked explosive natural gas. A few weeks later, the chandelier in the master bedroom came loose from its supports and was hanging sideways by a thread when it was discovered. Fortunately, no one was sleeping there at the time, but two warnings were enough. Our luck might run out with a third incident.

My deputy, Tom Nassif, and I conferred with Mike Deaver, and he told us to close the house to overnight visits. "You will have to put official visitors in hotels until we can renovate the house," he added.

We would never find the millions needed for the restoration in the regular State Department budget. President Reagan and Secretary Shultz sent letters requesting special congressional funding to the appropriate Senate and House committees. But after a summer and fall of much talk and little results, I began to wonder if we would have to scale down our ambitious plans.

Richard Haase, commissioner of the Public Building Service (under the General Services Administration), had shown great enthusiasm for the Blair House project, and convinced me that we had to go for the entire package—especially the addition of the new wing. Haase suggested a different approach. Move control of Blair House, if only temporarily, to the General Services Administration. In the GSA budget, such an expensive project would not seem out of line with other big government building costs.

A stroke of genius. The GSA was authorized to spend $2 million on a feasibility study, followed by an architects' survey and then detailed drawings from architects John I. Mesick and John G. Waite of Albany, New York. By the summer of 1984 we felt the project was going smoothly, with $7 million additional funding about to be approved by Congress.

Then I got a call from Carol Somerville, acting manager of Blair House. "Something strange has happened on the Hill," she reported. "The Blair House funding has been cut to three million. No one—neither the White House nor State Department liaison— was aware of it. The GSA knows nothing about this. I gather there's little chance of reversing it."

This meant the Blair House restoration was dead. The problem, I soon learned, was Senator James Abdnor of South Dakota, chairman of the Public Works subcommittee controlling the project. I asked Deaver to try to persuade the senator, a conservative Republican, to restore the money.

I also asked for an appointment with the senator myself. Senator Abdnor was a Lebanese-American, a crusty bachelor known to be tight with the taxpayers' money. The Hill was uncharted territory for me; my work as a journalist had rarely taken me there, and the State Department had a special bureau to handle congressional relations. Normally, solo performances were forbidden, but this was no time to go through channels.

First I talked with Abdnor's staff, and they seemed convinced that the project was a boondoggle: "Who ever heard of a house costing more than eight million dollars to restore?" Why not tear the house down and build a new one—it would cost less money!

I warned them I would mobilize the city of Washington, and preservationists nationwide, if they tried that—and I think they realized I meant business. (Also, the house was protected as a historic monument.)

Next I was informed that the Secret Service had told Abdnor that Blair House was not worth saving and presented insurmountable security problems. I didn't believe that. So I went to see John Simpson, head of the Secret Service, and a man I respect enormously.

"Do you support the restoration of Blair House?" I asked, not dancing around the subject.

He assured me he was for it, would endorse my efforts and would so inform Senator Abdnor.

"Is it true that the Secret Service has doubts about protecting Blair House?" I persisted. He seemed offended at the mere suggestion and assured me they could protect the complex.

Armed with this, I called on the senator.

"Well, Mrs. Roosevelt, you certainly have been stirring things up," he said. "I've been hearing from Deaver and Shultz, and now even the President. I didn't realize there would be so much fuss over this."

"Senator, why did you cut our funding so drastically?"

"Back in my constituency in South Dakota, eight or nine million dollars to do over a house is an outrage," he huffed.

"Yes, sir. I'm from Tennessee, and I know what you mean. But it's not just a house—it's four large houses which need to be properly joined together, and it's a hundred and ten rooms. But that's only the beginning. The legislation prohibits us from using any public funds for decorating—and after the Congress pays for the structural work and the new wing, I still have to raise at least four million dollars in private funds to take care of the curtains, rugs, upholstery, furniture, and any other embellishments not funded by the Congress."

We parried some more, and I reminded him of the heritage we shared. My parting words were: "Senator, I don't see why you want to give a nice Lebanese girl so much grief!"

He gave me an amused and quizzical look and then muttered that he would have to discuss it with his staff. I was sure I had failed. But the senator restored the cuts. I never asked why or how, and I never looked back.

The structural work, begun in 1985, was supervised entirely by the GSA, under the direction of its administrator, Terence Golden, a political appointee from Texas who had taste as well as enthusiasm, and kept a sensitive and concerned eye on the project.

Golden is the unsung hero of the Blair House restoration. He visited the site regularly, trailing an entourage of his top executives jotting down instructions as he moved through. Whenever I had a complaint, he immediately addressed the problem—no bureaucratic gobbledygook.

Even so, we had problems. The gardens, for example. Not a dime had been allocated by the government for landscaping. We persuaded top landscape architects Richard K. Webel and his son, also Richard, to take on the project long before we had any money to pay them. Finally, thanks to a $250,000 donation by Arthur and Janet Ross of New York, we were able to proceed—but by this time all access to the garden had been cut off by the new construction.

Plans called for planting nine full-grown trees more than two stories high—four willow oaks, four magnolias, and one enormous maple—weighing five tons each. How would we get them, plus a dozen hollies, into the garden?

"How about a helicopter dropping them down?" was one of the more serious suggestions.

That would have been easy compared to what we finally did. We got permission from Mayor Marion Barry to cordon off several lanes of Pennsylvania Avenue for one weekend, and with the Washington police keeping guard, a huge hundred-ton crane hoisted the trees over the roofs of Blair House, dropping them in their assigned places in the garden.

Every time the crane swung a tree over, I mentally pictured the horror of a giant tree dropping through the roof instead. But everything landed in its proper place and, presto, instead of empty holes we had an instant garden. Fabulous. Except there was no way to water the trees. No one had thought to install water faucets in the garden!

Government funding also provided a nice big laundry room, but no sinks; no light switches for turning on the garden lights from inside the house; no vanities in the bathrooms—just the bare plumbing, with no place to hide even an extra roll of toilet paper! (One private donor was so offended by the coarse government-issue toilet paper that she sent a check for $1,000 to be used for the purchase of soft tissue.)

In the master bathroom, all rose-colored marble, the shower stall had no door; the tub had a shower guard, but no shower. The first-floor lavatories looked like the men's room at Grand Central Station—cheap white tile from floor to ceiling and urinals; it cost $25,000 in private funds to rectify and redecorate. We also had to use private funds to finish off the pantries, the walk-in silver closets, and the cloakroom. The government's budget made no provision for mantels for three rooms in the new wing, nor for much needed moldings and chair rails in the main hall of Lee House.

Steep, wide stairs connected the new wing with the older structure, and I complained that they looked like the approach to an Aztec temple. Thanks to Terry Golden we got them modified so that the transition was more aesthetic.

Every time I went over to inspect the work, a man would run ahead of me—like a town crier—wielding a stick. One day I found out why. With so much construction and excavation, rats were turning up all over the house. They had even gnawed away at the fine paneling in the Lee House dining room. The advance man was making sure that a rat wasn't lurking ahead.

Halfway through the construction phase, the project had become so mammoth that I pleaded with the State Department to provide an on-site project manager. Soon the GSA would be finished and the private contractors, the painters and others, would begin. I could not coordinate that and fulfill my normal responsibilities. They chose Michael Coughlin, a career Foreign Service officer who specialized in administration, and he became another unsung hero of this endeavor.

It was Coughlin who cleared up the mystery of the original wrought-iron fence which had once surrounded the Jackson Place houses, adjacent to Blair House. We felt sure that no one would have dared throw away the handsome, 120-year-old decorative ironwork, which we knew existed from early photographs. Finally, after some splendid detective work, Mike Coughlin called me one day, triumphant.

"We've found the iron fence. Stored in a GSA warehouse near Washington. They were about to get rid of it for scrap. It's in terrible condition, but most of it can be saved. It will cost a packet to save it," Mike reported. Thanks to Alyne Massey of Nashville, Tennessee, another generous donor, we redid the front gardens and restored the fence, and it adorns the façade today.

Whenever I asked Deaver for permission to form a Blair House committee to raise funds for the redecoration, there was always a good reason not to. Mrs. Reagan wanted to see Blair House restored, but she had been badly burned by all the adverse publicity over her White House refurbishing—done, I might add, very well and economically.

"Nancy wants nothing to do with the Blair House restoration," Mike emphasized. "You are on your own. And you must keep this away from her, both the fund-raising and any criticisms that might arise over the decorating."

It would be a GSA–State Department project, and no one in the White House was to be involved. Donations would not be solicited in the name of the White House. Mike instructed me to wait until after the presidential elections in 1984. So, six months into Reagan's second term, I finally got the go-ahead. Don Regan, who was my contact after Deaver left, was very supportive of the project.

I asked Anne Armstrong, former ambassador to Britain, and someone I had admired since our Vassar days, to head up a national council of forty members, each of whom would either give or raise $100,000 in cash or in kind. We wanted a bipartisan council, so for vice chairman we chose Democrat Robin Chandler Duke, wife of former chief of protocol Angier Biddle Duke. Robin had been active in an earlier redecoration during the Kennedy era. Investment banker John W. Hanes Jr. agreed to be treasurer, handling all incoming and outgoing funds. No government employee would have access to the private funds. Final decisions about the use of that money would be made by the private Blair House Restoration Fund.

In my time I've been involved in much fund-raising, but I've never known such an effective committee as this one, from the Eastern establishment—the Douglas Dillons, David Rockefellers, Brooke Astor, Annette Reed—to the West Coast moguls—David Murdoch, Armand Hammer, Anne Getty, Jerry Weintraub. In the South, Texas was heavily represented by the Ross Perots, Mrs. Eugene McDermott, Robert Bass, the Joe Allbrittons, and Nancy Wellin, who gave the largest single donation.

One of the most meaningful donations was $100,000 from John Johnson of Chicago, owner of *Ebony* magazine, and America's most famous black entrepreneur. He underwrote the refurbishing of the Lincoln Room and the purchase of a portrait of Lincoln.

We began on September 16, 1985, and in one year we had

raised $2.5 million. A benefit in Washington organized by Mary Jane Wick and Marion "Oatsie" Charles in September 1986 put us over the $3 million mark. Further gifts, plus a second benefit organized in New Orleans by Mrs. Brooke Duncan, with Princess Margaret of Great Britain in attendance, put us over $4 million by 1987. We decided to go for an endowment, so that the house would never fall into such disrepair again. As of December 1988, patriotic Americans had contributed $5 million, plus gifts-in-kind worth more than $2 million.

The actual redecoration, brilliantly conceived and executed by Mark Hampton and Mario Buatta of New York, took about two years. My charge to them was simple. "Blair House is not a museum; it is a beautiful hotel—the best we can offer. However, we do not want our guests to be so overwhelmed by the furnishings and their value that they cannot enjoy themselves."

Blair House already had a fine collection of English antiques—with occasional American pieces—purchased from the Blair family. I felt we should not spend money on furniture, except where absolutely needed. Instead, we should concentrate on upgrading the rugs, pictures, curtains, and upholstery. I asked Oatsie Charles and Katherine de Braganca of Winston-Salem to join me and Clement Conger, the curator, in overseeing the work of the decorators.

The final bill came in at around $4 million. When it was broken down, we found we had spent about $1 million for painting and architectural embellishments; $500,000 for fabric and wallpaper; ditto for window treatment and upholstery; rugs and wall-to-wall carpeting throughout the miles of corridors were another half-million; the same for the front and back gardens. The remainder of the expenditures went to consultants and decorators (at rates far below their normal fees), additional furniture, paintings, mirrors, and the restoration of existing furnishings.

After all this, more than $1 million remained for an endowment fund. No capital was ever used for operating expenses. These were paid for out of earned income. In the first five years, interest income exceeded operating expenses by $76,000.

The donors did not interfere with the decorating, and thus the house, instead of being a hodge-podge of tastes as it had been in the past, became a seamless elegant monument to one of the great periods of American and English decorative arts—the early nineteenth century.

Not only was the national council remarkable in its achievements, but the members expected little recognition in return. In a few rooms we placed small donor plaques in discreet nooks. But we decided that some acknowledgment of the major donors should be permanently inscribed on two Tiffany-designed plaques, tucked away in a side hall of the new wing. This would not interfere with the historic fabric of the original houses, but would assure that those who had contributed so selflessly would not be forgotten.

Before the restoration, Blair House had been a mom-and-pop operation. That gave it a certain charm, but I knew that when we reopened the vastly enlarged house—with the square footage increased by one-third—we would need to expand the staff in the same ratio.

Also, it was time to put management of the house on a professional footing. The manager and assistant manager had been political appointments, but I persuaded the Reagan White House to give the Blair House positions career status, not subject to political whim, and this remains in effect today.

Thus we had fifteen new employees to train for the reopening of the President's guest house. Besides the new manager, Benedicte Valentiner, and the assistant manager, Samuel Castleman, we hired an administrative assistant, secretary, engineer, butler, chef, assistant chef, housekeeper, three housemen, and three maids.

Secretary Shultz was enormously interested in every step of the restoration, and visited the house from time to time, donning a hard hat during the construction phase. But he was very pessimistic. "This will never be finished during the Reagan administration," he said.

I was determined to prove him wrong and held everyone to a strict timetable. The GSA, with hundreds of employees involved, the State Department, the Secret Service, Diplomatic Security, the White House (notably curator Rex Scouten and chief usher Gary Walters), the architects, painters, carpenters, restorers, lighting experts, the Fine Arts Commission, the Mayor's office, muralist Robert Jackson, as well as the decorating committee—all worked enthusiastically to meet the deadline.

As a final check, Sam Castleman organized "Operation Flush" in which every toilet was flushed and every tub was filled simultaneously to see how the water pressure and hot water held up. A huge success. We inadvertently proved the efficiency of the sprinkler system when two deliverymen, carrying a huge carpet aloft, set off the sprinklers. I happened to walk into the house just as a Niagara of sulfur-smelling water poured out of the ceiling. Luckily, it fell on the basement floor, and little damage was done.

President and Mrs. Reagan officially opened the house on April 25, 1988, in the presence of the two hundred people who had done the most to make the six-year project a reality. The President and George Shultz, in their remarks, were very generous to me.

I have to admit, however, the compliment that amused me most came from one of the men who had worked on the house and had seen me knock a few heads together. "Mrs. Roosevelt, I have to say—you got more of 'em than most men."

Six weeks later, over one thousand donors were invited to an open house, and the next day we held a press preview for several hundred print and TV journalists. Normally, the house is not open to press or photographers, nor is it available for tours. But interest in the restoration was overwhelming. Magazines and newspapers from all over the country—beginning with a big spread in *Architectural Digest*—did features on the house. All the major TV shows wanted to film it. Their reports were glowing.

We decided to suspend the normal rules until the house was actually ready for use as a guest house. We had a series of open houses—paid for out of private funds—for all State Department and GSA employees who had worked on the project; another for the National Association of Interior Designers, who were holding their annual meeting in Washington; another press event when the refurbished beauty salon was finished (it has been a part of the house since the Nixon administration). And in October, when all three gardens were finished, we had a special dedication ceremony to thank those who had helped create them.

As I prepared a final report for the Secretary of State on what had been accomplished at Blair House, nothing gave me greater joy than to know that everyone—from the President on down—had joined in the chorus of praise. And what did we accomplish?

The four houses that made up the Blair House complex were now joined together on each of the five floors. The basement, once a hodge-podge, became a unified work space housing state-of-the-art kitchens and utility rooms for every need.

A new wing was added, which gave us a handsome master suite and increased the capacity for official entertaining. The new garden room can be used for dinners for eighty or receptions for two hundred or more.

Every room has had the tender, loving attention of decorators Mario Buatta and Mark Hampton. The master suite was completely furnished with several million dollars' worth of the finest English furniture, a gift of the Heathcote Art Foundation. The conference room—the largest room in the house—which previously had been almost empty, was decorated with $250,000 worth of furnishings donated by various American manufacturers, members of the Stately Homes collection.

All systems were new—heating, air conditioning, phones, fire alarms. Security was upgraded throughout, and the house was equipped with a sprinkler system for the first time. The bathrooms were totally renovated; in many areas new floors and new roofs were installed.

The gardens in back were designed and planted from scratch. The formal front garden incorporates space taken over from the city on the Pennsylvania Avenue side of the Jackson Place houses—the two houses built in the 1860s and purchased by the government in the 1960s.

For the first time the house was fully equipped, thanks to gifts of 150 place settings of Tiffany flat silver, Lenox official china embossed with the Great Seal and BH initials, and crystal, similarly embossed, as well as sheets, towels, and table linens.

A handsome new book about Blair House was commissioned and published by the Restoration Fund to commemorate the renovation. And another book was compiled in which every donor's name was inscribed by a calligrapher, regardless of amount donated, and it remains in the house as a permanent record.

The new house was inaugurated with a visit from François Mitterrand, and who could have been more appropriate? As we entered the house, I showed him the portrait of the Marquis de Lafayette and reminded him that Lafayette was the first official visitor to the fledgling American republic after it declared its independence from England.

"I like the feel of this house," he told me as we arrived in the master suite and he looked out over the garden. "One has a sense of history here."

The French president could not have made me happier. But when the visitors left we discovered something quite puzzling. The antique glass doorknobs on one of the bedroom doors were missing. We searched the entire house, but they never reappeared. We could only guess that for some reason French security might have removed them. Still, it is, as they say, a puzzlement.

The last visitor to use the house before my tour of duty ended was Margaret Thatcher, who during earlier visits had stayed at the British Embassy on Massachusetts Avenue, one of the great houses of Washington. In her toast to the President at the White House dinner, she thanked him for being allowed to stay in the "beautifully transformed Blair House" and added, "I hope Antony Acland [the British ambassador] will forgive me for saying that it surpasses even that modest little log cabin of his up on Massachusetts Avenue."

NINE

Be Careful What You Wish For

THE JOB of Chief of Protocol is sometimes perceived as frivolous because of the heavy social duties that go with the territory. It was not unusual for me to put on an evening dress four or five times a week, and as I dressed for yet another black-tie event I often remembered the warning, "Be careful what you wish for—it might come true."

I thought back to my agonies as an insecure high school student who yearned to be the belle of the ball. I was convinced that I would go through life a perpetual wallflower. However, Mother kept things in perspective. "Be patient," she counseled. "Concentrate on your studies. There'll be plenty of time for boys and for parties."

Even my clairvoyant mother could not have foreseen that one day, as Chief of Protocol, I would routinely accept some five hundred party invitations a year—and turn down even more. These blue-ribbon affairs were often given by the Reagans, the Bushes, or the Shultzes, or by a visiting chief of state. I also represented the government at events given by some 150 embassies in Washington.

While this was a headier atmosphere, it was not vastly different from the life I had been leading since I married Archie. For years I had attended official functions. And as a Washington journalist my beat was the State Department, the diplomatic corps, and White House state visits.

But there was a world of difference. As a housewife or reporter, no one read great significance into whether or not I attended a party, when I arrived, or how long I stayed. But as Chief of Protocol my judgment—or lack of it—could embarrass the President or the State Department.

For example, in the early years of my job, the decision as to whether or not I should attend a Soviet Embassy reception honoring the October Revolution was made at the highest levels of the government, and attendance was limited to officials of my level. But after *perestroika* took hold, Secretary Shultz himself attended the annual celebration—the best signal we could send, in Soviet eyes.

Many times, my presence at an embassy function was meant to convey a message of support; my nonattendance, a message of coolness or disfavor, depending on the state of our diplomatic relations with the particular country. Sometimes when I couldn't attend for other reasons—illness, press of other duties, out of town—I took pains to be sure someone represented me and offered my apologies

When the Vice President or Secretary Shultz was in attendance at an official party, I often had yet another duty. I kept a discreet eye on him to be sure he wasn't being overwhelmed by the press or monopolized by some bore he couldn't shake. Sometimes, so he could leave early without appearing ungracious, it was my assignment to interrupt and point not too discreetly at my watch—giving him a chance to say, "Oops, the Chief of Protocol says it's time for me to leave." (And in protocol-conscious Washington this was important, because no one else could leave until the ranking guest departed.)

Normally, I didn't mind playing the heavy. But at one embassy party, when I gave Vice President Bush the signal he said in a loud stage whisper, "Gee, Lucky, do I have to leave? I'm having such a good time." The ambassador glowered at me for taking away his star guest and breaking up the party, and Bush continued protesting all the way out the door about how he hated to leave. But he gave me a conspiratorial wink as he got into his car!

Being seen so frequently on the party circuit made people think I was a social butterfly. I had managed to stay out of the spotlight during the years Archie was in the CIA and we lived abroad. And because I was myself a member of the press, I was not of much interest to my colleagues. I found it very comfortable that way. But when I became Chief of Protocol, I was no longer permitted the luxury of keeping a low profile.

I'll never forget an article by Diana McLellan, a naughty and funny writer for *Washingtonian* magazine, entitled "Springtime for Sycophants" in which she described the attributes of a Washington toady. Then she listed the "ten most-toadied-to citizens" in descending order of grovelability: "Katharine Graham, Nancy Reagan, Marion Barry, Howard Baker, Jim Wright, Selwa 'Lucky' Roosevelt, Bobby Byrd, Teddy Kennedy, Cap Weinberger and Ben Bradlee."

When I read that, I knew I was in trouble! That sort of article makes insecure people fear you. They perceive you as the dispenser of social favors. They will blame any slights on you. For me to be the source of someone's insecurity was shattering. People often telephoned or wrote me asking to be included in various events. I always transmitted these requests to the White House or the Secretary of State's office. Sometimes it worked and sometimes it didn't, but I never withheld a request.

In the course of an official visit, my office also had to organize many private events. The purposes of these were often misunderstood by the public. There were three people whom almost every foreign VIP who came here insisted on seeing—Katharine Graham, David Rockefeller, and Malcolm Forbes. We were the intermediaries in arranging these events, and in some instances were asked to assist with guest lists.

As publisher of the influential *Washington Post*, Kay Graham was much sought after by every foreign visitor. Mrs. Graham generously responded as often as she could; not only did she entertain newsworthy VIPs such as Corazon Aquino, but she also made time for leaders of small African or South American nations who were not hot news items. This might take the form of a working breakfast or luncheon with her editors at the *Post*, or perhaps a dinner at her Georgetown house. Her assistance was invaluable in making these visits a success.

The same was true of David Rockefeller. During his many years as CEO of Chase Manhattan Bank, David had traveled extensively around the globe and formed personal bonds of friendship with almost every chief of state. After his retirement from the bank, he retained the status of world statesman, and many potentates, presidents, and prime ministers who came here felt their trip was not complete unless they saw David Rockefeller. Better still, they wanted to be invited to one of his houses.

Whether a luncheon for the King of Morocco, or a dinner for President Zia of Pakistan, whoever the visitor, being entertained at the Rockefellers' Pocantico Hills estate on the Hudson River north of New York City was an experience no guest could ever forget. Sometimes it was a cozy—yes, cozy—lunch for twenty-four in the dining room of the main house, the table laid with the most stunning porcelain and crystal and vermeil flatware. Larger gatherings might be held in the Playhouse—a somewhat whimsical name for a complex which included an indoor tennis court and swimming pool, squash courts, bowling alleys, billiard room, and gym. And I remember a particularly beautiful summer evening when tables were set up around the outdoor swimming pool for a dinner honoring Sekou Touré, President of Guinea.

David often took his visitors on a personal tour of the extraordinary sculpture and paintings collected by his brother, Nelson, the late Vice President. David's wife Peggy drove guests around the estate in her own horse and buggy, showing them the fine cattle she raised or the panorama of the Hudson. Everywhere, accoutrements of great wealth, including a nine-hole reversible golf course, were at the visitor's disposal.

Once, as we left Pocantico, someone remarked, "Well, this just shows what God could do if he had money." And although money made it possible, there was something more important that the visit demonstrated to the VIP. David, with a beguiling modesty and charm, had a way of dismissing the importance of material wealth and emphasizing the intangibles instead—family and hospitality.

Another great host was Malcolm Forbes—the colorful publisher of *Forbes* magazine, whose eclectic collections of Fabergé eggs, toy soldiers, presidential papers, and Victorian paintings were almost as well known as his motorcycles, his hot-air balloons, his estates in France, England, Scotland, Fiji, and Morocco, and his fabulous series of yachts, each one larger and more luxurious than the last.

Long before I came on the scene, Malcolm had been making his yacht available to the State Department whenever it was needed for a special visitor in New York. For security reasons, these excursions were low-key and the media were rarely aware of them. Malcolm's two chefs produced sumptuous meals; a steward doubled as a bagpiper and guests were piped aboard; the fourteen-man crew gave the guests guided tours of the yacht. And as they circled New York harbor, no visitor failed to be moved by the majesty of the Statue of Liberty dominating the horizon.

Most people thought of Malcolm Forbes as a consummate showman who loved the limelight, but actually he never appeared on the yacht when he turned it over to the Secretary of State unless we insisted! However, with no disrespect to our Secretaries of State, we found that many of the VIPs were genuinely disappointed if they did not meet Forbes and his family.

Malcolm was responsible for the most exciting invitation Archie and I ever had—to join him and his son Kip on a trip up the great Amazon River in Brazil in February 1986. We flew to Manaus, boarded the *Highlander*, and continued upriver to Iquitos, Peru, where his plane was waiting to bring us back to New York.

Twelve days on the Amazon, sailing in a luxurious yacht through a forbidding primeval rain forest! So immense was the river, we felt as if we were looking at two sides of the universe, and the panorama which unfolded was better than the most gripping adventure movie. Playful pink porpoises followed us up the river, and we knew that crocodiles and piranhas were also lurking in the waters.

If we got tired of our view from the deck, we boarded the

helicopter perched on top of the yacht and pilot Chuck Dixson would fly us over the treetops so we could see the rain forest from above. We also carried two small boats to explore the many tributaries, where we saw monkeys, bright yellow birds, and mammoth insects.

We called to the occasional hardy soul who lived on the river and visited an Indian village, but few signs of the modern world intruded on this mysterious lush beauty.

On such a trip one has many precious hours to think—a luxury not often permitted me, or in fact anyone in my frenetic, busy world. I thought a lot about my Lebanese parents and my early life in Tennessee. I thought about Vassar and my marriage and my career as a journalist. God had been good to me. And what sorrows I had suffered, God had given me the strength to bear. I have never speculated about death, but on that trip an uncharacteristic thought crossed my mind. If I were to die now, I would already have had more than my share of the goodness of life. *More Than I Dreamed* is the title of Malcolm Forbes's autobiography. It could just as easily be mine.

PART TWO

From the Tennessee Hills to the White House

TEN

The Village of My Ancestors

ARSOUN, THE ANCESTRAL VILLAGE of my parents in the mountains of the Lebanon, is now a ghost town, the beautiful family home from the Ottoman period in ruins.

After surviving some two thousand years, the village was destroyed on one horror-filled September day in 1977 when Phalangist renegades swooped down on the community where Druze and Christians had lived in harmony for centuries. My feisty eighty-six-year-old Druze grandmother refused to flee at the sound of the approaching tanks and artillery barrage. Though only five feet tall, she was a true matriarch, and she intended to defy them.

"They will never harm an old lady," she reassured her family and neighbors who tried to persuade her to leave. And when the invaders finally arrived at her two-story stone house, she stood guard at the front door. She dared them to kill her as they fired bullets all around her. Fortunately, she was rescued by the Christians of the village, who persuaded the raiders to let her go—but the house was pillaged and set to the torch, as were many other houses that day in Arsoun. Thus, cruel fanatics of the twentieth century destroyed what successive waves of Romans, Crusaders, Arabs, Turks, and French could not.

The village, located in the part of Lebanon known as the Metn, had an ancient and proud history—and my family, the

Choucairs, were the earliest recorded landowners. They were Druze—a religious sect which was an outgrowth of Islam and took hold in the Lebanese mountains in the eleventh century.

The Druze feudal lords were the aristocracy of Lebanon until the eighteenth century. They had a tradition of strong, independent-minded women (as my husband noted even before we were married!) and, unlike other Moslem sects, did not permit polygamy. They opened the country to Western ideas and also brought in Maronite Christians from Syria as farmers and servants. Over the next two centuries the Maronites became the dominant religious group of Lebanon and the Druze were reduced to a minority, albeit an important one. (The Phalangists were the right-wing extremist faction of the Maronites.)

Tiny Arsoun, its population never exceeding five hundred souls, remained primarily a Druze village, but Greek Orthodox and other Christians lived peacefully in their midst. Being eight hundred meters above sea level, Arsoun has a salubrious climate and an abundance of water.

I was born in America, but as a child I spent two years in Lebanon, including many happy days in Arsoun. Even now, whenever I smell the sweet aroma of fig trees, the resin of pine forests, or herbs such as thyme and lavender, waves of nostalgia sweep over me and my mind wanders back to those tender days.

For two summers, my sister, Khalida, and I were the spoiled darlings of the village. Everyone fussed over us because we had come from America, and they proudly impressed on us the luster of our heritage. So we hopped from house to house as if they were our own—and indeed most were inhabited by our huge extended family. My mother and father even had the same last name, although they were not closely related.

I heard tales of many of our ancestors—judges, doctors, lawyers, military officers. My favorite story was that of Mother's uncle Najib Bey Choucair, who married a Turkish beauty and became the right-hand man to Izzat Pasha, the Sultan's vizier. Najib Bey was a great Arab nationalist, and in World War I when the Arabs revolted against Turkey and joined the Allies, he left Turkey secretly and went to Syria to help organize the independence movement. He and many other Arab patriots were caught by the spies of Turkey's cruel Jamal Pasha (the Arabs called him "the Butcher") and ordered to be executed. Most were hanged, but Uncle Najib's Turkish wife turned heaven and earth and, one hour before his scheduled execution, got him smuggled out of prison to Egypt, where he remained and became a dynamo in the Arab Nationalist Party until his death in 1927.

Mother's father had gone off to Brazil at seventeen to make his fortune, returned to Arsoun for ten years to marry and produce my mother and her four siblings, then left for Brazil again in 1921, never to return. Thus, Mother's grandfather, Sheikh Mohammed Dweik, a formidable blue-eyed tyrant who terrified me, was the patriarch of the family at the time of our visit.

At age five I fell in love with the Greek Orthodox priest of the village. He wore his long reddish-blond hair in a pageboy like Prince Valiant, and in his flowing black robes seemed the incarnation of Jesus Christ. What's more, he let us watch, greedy-eyed, as he made molasses, stirring the delicious, aromatic sweet liquid in a huge metal tub. He allowed us to sample as much as we liked, to my grandmother's dismay.

Looking back, I am proud of my discerning eye, for this hero of mine later became Elias IV, the Greek Orthodox Patriarch of Lebanon and Syria. (Incidentally, Ralph Nader is descended from a Greek Orthodox family of Arsoun.)

Arsoun was an agricultural village, with nut-bearing pine trees. In the early days mulberry trees made possible a profitable silk industry. But by the twentieth century the Turks, with little thought for the local inhabitants, had cut down the trees and destroyed the food supply as well.

My father's family were farmers, and before World War I his brothers fled Turkish oppression and went to the United States, where they married American women and prospered in the Shenandoah Valley of Virginia. Daddy, whose first name was Saleem, was the youngest son, and therefore he was expected to stay in the mountains and look after their aging mother. But Daddy would have none of that. If his brothers wouldn't send him the money to come to America, he would make his own way.

He slipped off to Beirut, and stowed away on a ship. He was caught, but persuaded the captain to let him work for his passage. When he arrived at Ellis Island in January 1914, he was sure that once his brothers saw him they would relent.

On the contrary, they were furious. They agreed to let him go to school and learn English, but they refused to help him start a business. So Daddy began as a peddler, and after acquiring a bit of capital finally settled down in Kingsport, Tennessee, where he opened a small dry goods store which became known as S. L. Showker's (the anglicized version of his name).

Meanwhile, back in Lebanon my mother, Najla Choucair, was growing up in a traditional and privileged family. The Turks had left, and the French now had the mandate to rule over Lebanon. But it was not a happy time for the Druze, because the French saw themselves as the protectors of the Maronites.

Mother was a spirited and beautiful girl of sixteen when my father returned to Lebanon in 1927, having prospered in the New World. He thought it was time to find a bride, and was smitten at the sight of Najla. But he was not considered a suitable match—and in any case she was betrothed to a wealthy, much older man. To escape this arranged marriage, she ran away with my father, attracted to the idea of starting a new and exciting life in that far-off place known as America.

Great-grandfather Dweik was furious. The rest of the family never became reconciled to her marriage, and my father never saw Lebanon again. When Mother went back four years later, taking me and my baby sister, their hearts melted toward her, but they never really forgave my father.

We returned to America in 1935. World War II intervened, and we were destined not to see Arsoun again until 1949—the year I was taken back to Lebanon for my own betrothal!

ELEVEN

Memories of
an Ethnic Childhood

Mother brought us back to a vastly changed America. By 1935 the Depression had overwhelmed my father, and whatever prosperity he had managed to achieve in the previous two decades was wiped out.

Daddy was barely able to keep going during those terrible years. He wasn't a very good businessman—his dream in life had been to be a doctor, but his brothers would not help make that possible and now it was too late.

To save money, Daddy had given up our little house in a middle-class section of Kingsport and moved us into an apartment over his store in a seedy downtown area known as Five Points. The five corners that converged there were peopled with the characters of my childhood—Dr. Bill Westmoreland, the indulgent druggist who slipped me ice cream cones; "Ommie" (Uncle) Haney, a jolly three-hundred-pound Lebanese grocer who was a combination of Santa Claus and Humpty Dumpty; Mike Kabool, the Lebanese owner of the Liberty Café, who served a wholesome lunch for twenty-five cents. His daughter Betty was my best friend. We were not allowed to go into Russell's Poolroom, but the Rialto Theater, Ketron's service station, and the Phoenix Café were all part of our playground. Every Saturday night, Salvation Army stalwarts gathered at Five Points, complete with big drum and tin cup, to urge us sinners to repent.

I certainly preferred the exciting life on the street to bringing my little friends up those dreadful stairs past the puce-colored hall and walls dotted with fingerprints. Our parlor was furnished with an apple-green rug and maroon velour living room "suite" festooned with antimacassars—security blankets of the bourgeoisie. My sister and I shared a bedroom overlooking a busy corner illuminated by brazen neon signs. Neither the kitchen nor the dining room had outside windows or proper ventilation. All the apartments were served by a huge communal storeroom, and we entered there with terror in our hearts, afraid of the rats which scurried away when we turned on the light.

Every morning Daddy got up early to stoke the furnace and we all held our breath, hoping it would start. We took turns visiting the one bathroom shared by four or five families. That bathroom—the ultimate humiliation—was to haunt me the rest of my life. I remember the joyous moment, a few years later, when our finances improved enough for us to build a new bathroom—ours exclusively—carved out of the storeroom. No doubt that bathroom would seem modest to me now, but then it was paradise. Pale green wallpaper with white lilies and swans, and so clean—a modern tub with no legs, a wide sink, and an odorless toilet.

Yes, that was happiness and a sign that we were climbing out of the Depression. And we did. But my nightmares of the communal bathroom and the big rats that terrorized us never ended.

Despite the near-poverty and insecurity, my parents did everything in their power to give my sister and me a happy home and ensure us a bright future. Daddy eventually got on his feet again and we moved twice more, each time to a nicer and bigger house. (I recently learned that President Bush's parents lived in Kingsport briefly in a house near ours.)

The East Tennessee city where I spent most of my first seventeen years was a storybook place—a small town of 25,000 snuggled in a valley in the heart of the Appalachian Mountains. Geography helped form the character of these quintessential Americans we lived among—independent pioneer types, of Scots-

Irish descent, who fought the Indians and, like Daniel Boone, became American legends. They were conservative and Republican and thought "government" was bad.

Most of Kingsport's citizens were decent, hardworking, churchgoing people who actually practiced their religion. Neighborly caring was a way of life. When friends were ill, one looked after them, rushing to their homes with food and necessities. When someone died, the townsfolk formed a comforting cordon around the grieving family. When tragedy struck, there were many outstretched hands and hearts.

Nonetheless, to grow up in the Tennessee hills in a city almost entirely made up of blond, blue-eyed Anglo-Saxons was for me a searing experience. And to look as exotic and dark as I did in the South of the 1930s and '40s was to learn compassion and understanding for all who have ever suffered the indignities of racial and ethnic slurs.

It began with the name. Mine was not bad, as ethnic names go. But even though my father had changed his name from Choucair to Showker, it sounded strange. No one ever got it right, and Selwa was even worse. It means "consolation" in Arabic, and was frequently given to a firstborn girl to "console" her father for not being a boy! It also means "quail" or "honey," but for me Selwa meant agony—teachers stumbling over it the first day of school, children teasing me with distortions such as "Sula" and "Saliva," and always having to answer the well-meant query, "Now, just what kind of a name is *that?*"

It builds character for a child to learn how to answer that question. You have to prove you aren't a "wop" or a "wog" and that Arabs are also nice human beings. John Jones and Jane Smith don't mean to torment you—anything different is simply an object of curiosity and viewed with suspicion until understood.

Thus, early in life I developed a sensitivity that made me want to put the other person at ease. I wanted to explain quickly to my interrogators why my name was different and why I looked different, so they wouldn't inevitably utter a slur that would wound me even more.

I'm not sure that other ethnics react this way. But just as

blacks say they can never forget their "blackness," so I was always aware of being "different." I hated my masses of black hair, olive skin, and long nose. To console me, Mother would tell me that a long nose was a badge of aristocracy, but I found that hard to believe.

Indeed, my mother would not allow us to sink into the psychological ghetto that entraps so many ethnics. She wouldn't put up with self-pity. She told me I could do anything I set my mind to. She accepted no excuses and simply held me to the highest intellectual and ethical standards.

Mother was sixteen when she married and came to America and seventeen when I was born. Two years later came my sister, Khalida. Soon after her marriage, Mother realized she had made a mistake. My father was a fine man, but wrong for her. Intellectually and socially they were worlds apart, and she seriously considered returning permanently to Lebanon. But after two years in Lebanon she changed her mind.

"I had brought you girls into the world and you deserved to have both parents and the opportunity to grow up in America," she told me years later. Indeed, as children, we never dreamed of any unhappiness or lack of rapport between our parents. Like most ethnic families, ours was close and loving.

My father was an exceptionally good and kindly man. He had little education and neither spoke nor read English well, but being a man of integrity and pride, he was well regarded in Kingsport. His two brothers who lived in Virginia had produced seventeen children in all, so we had cousins galore.

Dotted around the surrounding hill country were a surprising number of Lebanese families like ourselves, who visited back and forth across treacherous mountain roads in an attempt to preserve some semblance of their former life. Once or twice a year Shukri Barbary, a diminutive, courtly traveling salesman with a huge bulbous nose, came from New York to sell us our special Lebanese groceries—now the rage in health food stores, but back then too rare to find in Kingsport.

My sister and I felt keenly the dichotomy between our parents' generation and our own. We resented these old-fashioned people inflicting their old-country ways on us. Daddy, in turn, could not accept our Americanization, even though it was inevitable. He did not permit smoking or drinking, and when I started to wear lipstick at age fifteen it provoked an enormous family drama.

"What will the *nas* say?" my father asked. *Nas* was the Arabic word for people—meaning all those eagle-eyed, ubiquitous folks out there watching our behavior, eager to criticize and more to be feared than the Methodist minister's Sunday-morning wrath.

The *nas* were also any of our extended Lebanese family who dropped in on us at any hour of the day or night, and stayed and stayed, uttering one banality after another. As a child, I was not a candidate for "Miss Politeness." I would hide in my room, reading, and Daddy would search me out, warning me that my nose would grow long like Pinocchio's if I kept it permanently in a book.

"For shame," he would say. "What will the *nas* think? You must come and greet them and help your mother prepare food and Turkish coffee." And I *would* learn to be hospitable, for that was an unbreakable tenet of Arab culture.

In all the inevitable conflicts—clothes, dating, permitting me to work, social clubs—my mother was the buffer. A generation younger than my father, better educated (she spoke English, French, and Arabic and later learned Spanish), and from a more cosmopolitan background, she was the idol of my young life, a totally selfless woman, beautiful both in form and spirit. She was becoming an important force in our community, and in her early thirties was elected president of the Tennessee League of Women Voters.

After my father died of cancer in 1958, my mother went to college. She was in her mid-forties and completed her bachelor's degree in two years, graduating second in a class of 750. Then she won a Woodrow Wilson Fellowship and took her master's at Georgetown University. While teaching at Mount Vernon Junior College in Washington, she continued at Georgetown, acquiring all her credits for a Ph.D. in linguistics. She returned to Tennessee and became a college professor, until her retirement in 1980.

Mother's values and priorities were such that money was

never important to her, even though it was pretty scarce. Somehow she always found the extra dollars—either by working in my father's business or by teaching French privately—to give us piano, dancing, and art lessons. She surrounded us with books—everything from the Bobbsey Twins to Shakespeare, with Flaubert, Dumas, and Tolstoy and many other masters at hand. Anything not on our shelves I could find in the town library, where I consumed books like popcorn.

Mother took us to the Barter Theater in nearby Abingdon, Virginia, where I saw my first performance of *The Women* by Clare Boothe Luce, who one day would become a friend of mine. I saw my first opera, *Carmen*, at age eleven, and have been an opera buff ever since. We attended every concert that came to Kingsport, and among my childhood mementos is an autographed program of the Trapp Family Singers, later immortalized in *The Sound of Music*.

At age ten, I read *Gone With the Wind*, and like all Southern girls, I wanted to be Scarlett O'Hara. I hated mealy-mouthed Melanie and that ass Ashley Wilkes, and dreamed of the day I would find my Rhett Butler.

Although determined to expand our horizons, Mother always managed to be a "momma" as well. She comforted us when we were sick and worried about us when we were away, even years after we left home.

Like all Lebanese women, Mother was a queen in her kitchen. She loved to cook, and before my sister and I were teenagers we were taught to assist her. Lebanese food was one aspect of our culture I was proud of.

My friends loved to eat at our house because the food was so abundant and tasty—we grew up on hummus, kibbee, tabouli, and other delights. When I went to my friends' houses, I was fascinated by their eating habits. With us meals were warm, informal affairs. We sat down with all the food on the table, helped ourselves, and passed the platters around. In the houses of my friends—who seemed very rich to me, but in retrospect were average American middle-class families—they sat at austere tables, with placemats, something we rarely used, and ate in the dining room, which we only did when we had company. One course followed another in stately progression, usually served by a black maid, but I always left those fancy tables feeling a bit hungry.

Kingsport was in a dry county, so we grew up without alcohol in our social life, not even beer. For an out-of-town visitor, however, my father could be persuaded to drive to nearby Gate City, Virginia, to buy liquor. (One day Mother and Daddy drove over to buy some Haig & Haig scotch for a guest from New York. Daddy entered the store alone—ladies did not go into liquor stores—and in a few minutes came back to the car. "Najla, I can't remember. Haig—and what was that other fella's name?")

From the time we were toddlers, Mother was determined that we would grow up as part of the community. We were in the heart of the Bible Belt and so she raised us as Protestants, taking us every Sunday to the Broad Street Methodist Church and Sunday school. I was not aware of Jews, but I heard Catholics referred to in hushed voices as if speaking of the devil.

The church was the center of our social life. We learned the hymns and took part in the pageants—I was Mary Magdalene, but never the Virgin Mary! My favorite vignette from Sunday school is my little sister with her childish lisp singing "Jethuth wanth me for a thunbeam."

The Druze religion that my parents sometimes talked about seemed very obscure to me. I knew that the Druze were a small religious sect in the Middle East—neither Christian nor Moslem but respecting both. They were monogamous and believed in one God and the transmigration of the soul.

Always a minority, the Druze took on the dominant religion of any place they found themselves—protective coloration as it were. Thus, in Syria they were just another Moslem sect, and in Lebanon, until the recent troubles, they were frequently allied with the Christians against the Moslems. In Israel, they are regarded benignly. In America, all the Druze immigrants we knew raised their children as Protestants. And yet it was unheard of for a Druze to marry outside the clan. I was the first of our family to do so.

As a little girl, I hated to hear my parents speaking Arabic—they often resorted to it when they didn't want others to understand. It infuriated me and I would turn on them. "Don't do that! Everyone is looking at us."

I was also embarrassed by the foreign accents (Arabs have trouble pronouncing the letter *p*) and broken English of some of their friends. I'll never forget my chagrin when I walked into Ommie Haney's store one day wearing a gold cross. All my friends wore crosses, so I had to have one too. He looked at the cross dolefully and said, "Boor Jesus, when I see cross, it make my feel bad."

Our own speech, with its strong Southern twang, was very non-U. We didn't go to the movies, we went to the show. The midday meal was dinner, not lunch. We carried groceries in pokes, not bags. And we cut the lights out rather than turning them off. No one ever died—they passed away, passed on, or simply passed.

When Mother brought me back from Lebanon at age six, I had completely forgotten English, but she insisted on entering me in the second grade, convincing the principal that she could tutor me at home. "She will pick up English immediately," Mother insisted.

Tears rolled down my cheeks as I sat in the classroom ashamed, staring at a book I could not decipher. To this day, my mother has no idea of the torture she put me through. But in the end, she was vindicated. In only a few weeks I was speaking and reading English.

From then on, my marks were straight A's except for conduct—I was too spirited and sassy—and physical education. I was a disaster on the playing field, always the last to be chosen when teams were forming up.

I used to think how wonderfully American it would be to have a nickname like "Happy"—the most popular girl in my class, who was tall, blond, and blue-eyed, with delicious dimples. Alas, only after I went to college did I acquire my own nickname, "Lucky."

It was just the opposite for my sister. Even as a baby she insisted on being called Kay, and was always a superb athlete. She had fair skin and light brown hair and never seemed foreign at all.

My girlfriends wore blue and pink, but with my olive skin and dark hair I looked better in vivid colors. Stubbornly I insisted on wearing pastels, despite Mother's valiant efforts to persuade me otherwise. I also developed physically much earlier than my classmates. The dresses that suited their boyish figures simply accented my new curves and caused men to look at me in a way that made me very uncomfortable.

I don't remember my father ever taking a real vacation. Like most Lebanese immigrants, he and his friends worked long hours running their stores, restaurants, laundries, and dry cleaners. Daddy treated his employees well. Sometimes his workers cheated him, but Daddy was a forgiving and tenderhearted man.

My young world was peopled with characters cutting across all social barriers. At one time, my father owned a dry-cleaning establishment on the edge of a Negro slum. We knew many of the blacks in the neighborhood and had a deep affection for them. When a drunken black man attacked Daddy with a knife and severely wounded him, Daddy refused to press charges.

I was particularly fond of a truck driver who worked for my father—and who fancied himself a modern-day Rhett Butler. He regaled us with stories of his female conquests and, with knowing winks, patted the girls on their behinds. My mildly puritanical father would mutter his disapproval and scold him for "messing around" during business hours. (In today's humorless atmosphere that man would be accused of sexually molesting young girls, but I innocently thought this a rite of passage and rather enjoyed the attention.)

It seemed natural to me to hang around my father's store, and I loved nothing more than being allowed to wait on customers. Not surprisingly, at age thirteen, I took myself to Mr. Sam Anderson, manager of the largest department store in town, got a job selling perfume during the Christmas season, and thus earned my first paycheck—for thirty-five hours at thirty-five cents per hour. I proudly took home the magnificent sum of $12.13, the twelve cents having been deducted for Social Security.

With this check I opened my first savings account. I also learned to keep books for my father. Every cash gift, every dollar I earned automatically went into that account, so when it came time to pay my first year's college tuition, much of it came from my own savings.

When I was fifteen I announced to my parents that I wanted to go to Vassar College and that I wanted to be a writer. Vassar attracted me because at the time it was the oldest and most distinguished women's college in America. A cousin of mine, Dr. Najla Izzeddin, had been the first woman from an Arab country to come there as a student. (Now in her eighties, Dr. Izzeddin lives in Lebanon and has written numerous scholarly works about the Druze and the Arab world.)

Instead of patting me on the back and saying "bravo," my teachers, my high school principal, and most of our friends thought going to Vassar a terrible idea. "The girls at Vassar come from such privileged backgrounds," they warned. "They are snobs, and you will feel insecure and left out. You can't afford to participate in the social life and may find yourself struggling to keep up scholastically as well."

My father, understandably, was far more worried about financing such a "fancy" education, but I had the full support of my intrepid mother.

I was valedictorian of my high school class, thanks to marvelously challenging and caring teachers. But equally important to my education was my summer job at the *Kingsport Times*, an excellent newspaper of some 25,000 circulation.

My father had tried to stop me from taking that job the summer after my junior year, protesting that I was only sixteen, but Mother cajoled him into giving his consent.

"Najla, you have no idea what it's like on a newspaper," he warned her. "Selwa is too young. The men who work there will not respect your daughter. They all swear and drink too much. It is not a place for a nice girl."

Actually, it was more unsuitable than Daddy ever could have

imagined! But I savored every minute as I plunged into the world I came to love most—journalism.

Like most rookies, I was assigned obituaries and weddings but finally talked my way into writing features. Still, I had to put in time at city hall, the courts, the police station, and acquire a new vocabulary. "He was charged with L and A" (lewdness and adultery). "Fornication" and "sodomy" were not words bandied around our house, and I could only imagine what Mother and Daddy would have thought when the managing editor threw down his phone one day shouting, "Hot damn—a double rape!"

One editor had an eye for nubile girls and loved to photograph them in various stages of undress. "How would you like to pose for some pin-up pictures?" he suggested. I was delighted that anyone thought me attractive enough to photograph. "Just bring your bathing suit," he said, then added: "And don't tell your mother."

Afterward, I couldn't resist showing Mother the series of provocative photos. She had a fit and threatened to tell my father if I ever did such a thing again. That ended my modeling career, and probably just as well. I failed to tell Mother that the editor had tried to talk me into removing the top of my bathing suit for even more explicit photos, but just the thought of my parents' reaction stopped me.

One editor in particular, Herman Giles, a fine writer, became my mentor and patiently tried to teach me his craft. However, most of the men I encountered were typical Southern "good ole boys," and they made passes at me. Daddy was absolutely right—this was no place for a young girl. But I learned fast and was able to handle the situation. Essentially, their macho attitude was "nothing ventured, nothing gained." If I said no, even to a stolen kiss in the darkroom, they were good-natured about it. They liked my parents and knew that I had been strictly brought up.

In truth, I loved the badinage and irreverence of the newsroom. The four summers I spent at the *Kingsport Times* would prove to be a perfect counterpoint to my life at Vassar College.

TWELVE

Vassar and the Sheikess

Vassar College was my fairy godmother. It took almost two years to transform this Cinderella from an insecure Southern bookworm with all sorts of ethnic hangups to a rather sophisticated young woman hobnobbing with United Nations ambassadors or singing torch songs perched on a grand piano at Princeton, where I was known as "the Sheikess."

I never doubted that Vassar was the place for me. In my junior year in high school I persuaded a relative to drive me to Poughkeepsie, New York, to see the college and be interviewed. I refused to apply to any other college.

A somewhat absentminded dean of admissions interviewed me. Looking up vaguely from her file she said, "Now, let's see. You have a daughter who wants to come to Vassar in the fall of 1946?"

"No, ma'am. I am the student." I had just turned sixteen and was wearing my most grown-up outfit—a brown suit with velvet collar, and a hat. I had my hair pulled back in a chignon.

"You certainly do seem mature for your age," she said, not altogether approvingly. "Why do you want to go to Vassar?"

I explained about my cousin who had been the first Arab student at Vassar, and then added, "Really, I just want to go to the best women's college in America. If my parents are going to make the financial sacrifice and if I have to work every summer, I don't want to settle for anything less."

Apparently, I said the right things. So in September 1946 my mother, herself only thirty-four years old, accompanied me to Vassar. I had behind me two summers of working as a newspaper reporter and thought I was the cat's pajamas until I realized that every one of my classmates had been the best and the brightest in her school.

I had approached Vassar with a lot of bravado, but I was frightened—of failure, of letting my parents down, of not being up to the challenge.

Recently a former professor of mine described the way I looked to him some forty years ago. "You appeared in my office a most tearful and waif-like young woman," he wrote, "a mere slip of a girl . . . I think you must have been up all night, for it was quite early in the day and you looked like the legendary Edith Piaf in her most appealing role."

It was at Vassar that I heard the expression "anti-Semitism" for the first time. Being myself a Semite (Arabs are also of Semitic origin), I had experienced it in mild forms all my life, but I couldn't put a name to it. I was very embarrassed when some of my Vassar classmates made thoughtless and unkind remarks about Jews, for I felt they were also talking about me.

And yet, I soon learned that my unique background—being of Lebanese origin—was my greatest asset at Vassar. (In that world an Arab was rare indeed. Years later, Marietta Tree, daughter of the famous rector of Groton, Endicott Peabody, and later a delegate to the United Nations, told me she had never even met an Arab until she was appointed to the U.N.) As for all those snooty debutantes the folks in Kingsport were worried about— they were there all right, but they became and still are my closest friends.

The Arab-American community in New York was a small one, and they all knew each other, so when I went to the big city I had a supportive network of family friends to call on if needed.

In December 1946 one of these friends took me to my first diplomatic reception. I wrote home:

"I arrived just in time to go to a banquet at the Waldorf-Astoria in honor of Prince Faisal [the Foreign Minister, later to be King of Saudi Arabia]. Golly, I nearly passed out from excitement. . . . Everyone acted like it was an honor to have me there—and there I was thinking what a great honor it was for me. . . . Dr. Khairallah introduced me to the Prince. . . . He stood up and talked to me—right in front of everybody. I could hear people whispering, 'Who is she? Golly, she must be important,' etc."

Shortly after that, Prince Faisal, through the good offices of Dr. Khairallah, indicated to my father that he wanted me as a bride for one of his sons. Though flattered, I was not interested. I had my eye on an education and career and I knew it would be impossible in Saudi Arabia.

All this simply added to my exotic appeal among my Vassar classmates. After a few months we had settled down to certain patterns of friendship, and my two closest friends—both from Columbus, Ohio—were Charlotte Curtis, a petite redhead who later became the op-ed page editor of the *New York Times*, and Harriette Moeller, a tall gorgeous blonde who is now the Vicomtesse de Rosière. We were quite a sight together, each of us with striking coloring, and me sandwiched between the blonde and the redhead.

Charlotte, nicknamed Rusty, came to Vassar a Taft conservative, and decided to take on my political education. I showed alarming signs of becoming a liberal. Ironically, by the time we graduated, I had become quite conservative and Charlotte had become a bleeding heart. Until Charlotte's death in 1987 she and I remained fast friends, but on opposite sides of the political fence.

Harriette, nicknamed Ronnie, became my social mentor. She improved my hairdo and makeup, and with her fantastic clothes sense, tried to help me with my wardrobe—but it wasn't easy. As I wrote Mother, my clothes were "just plain tacky." And I was very specific and demanding about what I wanted: "If anyone does buy me a lapel pin [for a present] please see that it is tasteful. I don't want a gaudy costume jewelry piece. I would rather have a simple, plain one—with a dash of chic to it.''

The beautiful Harriette also had great success with the boys, and it was thanks to her that I started dating Princeton men. Harriette dubbed me "the Sheikess," and at Princeton football weekends we would end up in one of the clubs with me singing "Stormy Weather" or some other blues song in a low, throaty voice. I loved the attention even though I really didn't have a good voice.

Luckily, my first-year roommate, Joanna Foster, was a serious student like myself, who later became a distinguished writer and editor of children's books. A dear friend, Ruth Baker Pratt, invited me to my first big debutante ball at her grandmother's estate on Long Island, where I felt like a character out of an F. Scott Fitzgerald novel.

My most famous college friend was Jacqueline Bouvier (Kennedy Onassis). I was dazzled by Jackie and thought her the most beautiful creature I had ever met. So much hogwash has been written about this extraordinary woman that one would need another book to set the record straight, but for what it's worth, herewith my own impressions of Jackie in our student days.

She was wonderful company, and had a delicious sense of humor; she was keenly perceptive and widely read. Jackie had great panache—she wrote with flair and was a talented artist. But she was modest about all her accomplishments. I remember when we got our mid-term grades, Jackie was very quiet and I wondered if she had done poorly in her exams. As we walked along together I asked, "How were your grades?" and in the softest voice she said, "I made the dean's list."

Even then she had a breathless voice and glamorous aura. She was the debutante of the year, and we followed her activities with a certain pride and pleasure in her celebrity. She never referred to the social side of her life, and even seemed embarrassed by all the fuss. At that young age she already showed the poise and maturity that would carry her with such dignity through unprecedented fame and unspeakable tragedy.

Jackie was incredibly kind to me, and I have only the most tender thoughts about her. I appealed to her intellectual curiosity—

she had never met anyone of my background before. I had a photograph of a dashing Arab with whom I corresponded but had never met. My family wanted me to marry him. Jackie was fascinated. The idea that an American girl she knew was about to be betrothed in an arranged marriage was intriguing, and she would often question me about my intended.

At the time I married Archie Roosevelt, Jackie was abroad. On her return she sent me a wedding present with this note: "What a wonderful surprise your wedding announcement was— Mummy handed it to me in a bunch of mail as I stepped off the gangplank and I nearly fell into the water. I never really could picture you in veils on the back of the Sheik's charger."

Besides the culture shock of going from the Tennessee hills to New York's glitter, I also had a complex intellectual metamorphosis. My freshman grades were disappointing—only B's—but after that it was almost straight A's—and I was graduated with honors in international relations.

My Vassar professors came in all varieties—conservative, liberal, and even an avowed Marxist. Every class was stimulating, but I reveled in the intellectual challenge presented by history professor Evalyn Clark, surely one of the great teachers of our time.

She taught the most exciting course at Vassar—modern European history—but she also taught us how to think, how to question our sources and look at the motivations and credentials of writers and historians, how to discern propaganda from truth. The class was limited to ten or fifteen students and it was a feast of learning. Throughout my life I have blessed Professor Clark for teaching me to distrust the "conventional wisdom" about any given situation.

I was a student during the emotional days of the Rosenbergs and Alger Hiss. Overseas the Russians were showing their true colors, but the American intelligentsia could not face the obvious. In the beginning I was influenced by my more liberal teachers. I joined the Vassar *Miscellany News*—at that time the voice of the campus Left. The pressure was strong to conform to a party line, but gradually I began to resist. So even before coming under Miss Clark's influence I was beginning to be disillusioned.

Professor Clark gave me the scholarly underpinnings for my revolt against the authoritarian Left. She sent us to the bowels of the Vassar library to trace the zigzags of Soviet propaganda in Comintern periodicals; she made us read accounts from both the Nationalist and Republican sides in the Spanish Civil War—no Ernest Hemingway romantic was she! We read about World War I from the viewpoint of every major participant. We traced the developments of both Czarist and Communist Russia and saw how they coincided in the Russian concepts of manifest destiny and empire.

I also took courses in American history, the French Revolution, and Victorian England, and discerned a certain consistency in the historical figures that appealed to me. I preferred Alexander Hamilton to Thomas Jefferson; adored Disraeli, hated Gladstone; was a great admirer of Theodore Roosevelt, long before I married his grandson; and detested the priggish and self-righteous Woodrow Wilson.

While I was learning my history from books, I was getting practical lessons in international diplomacy. During my sophomore year I took a course on the United Nations, and part of my work included field trips to New York and to Lake Success, where the General Assembly was meeting. (Although not what my professors had in mind, I got involved in some extracurricular activities with polished diplomats and Latin lovers—excellent training for a future Chief of Protocol!)

This coincided with the year of the partition of Palestine by the United Nations, resulting in the birth of the State of Israel. As I read over the newspaper accounts of the time, *plus ça change, plus c'est la même chose* was never more true.

Camille Chamoun, a Maronite Christian later to become President of Lebanon, headed the Lebanese delegation and spoke eloquently on behalf of the Arab states in opposition to partition. With his Charles Boyer looks, the forty-eight-year-old statesman cut a dapper figure and was an effective spokesman for the Arabs.

He predicted the tragedy that would result—endless strife between Arabs and Jews over the same land—but the momentum for a Jewish state was overwhelming.

These were heady times for an eighteen-year-old Vassar girl. My letter to Mother describing my first meeting with Chamoun tells it best:

"I don't think I have lived a more fabulous week than this one . . . Wednesday I arrived at the Waldorf about 7:15 and was met there by Dr. Khairallah. We went to a reception in the Jade room and who do you think was first in the receiving line? Prince Faisal, of course. He remembered me and teased me about not speaking Arabic.* During the evening I met His Excellency, Mr. Camille Chamoun—undoubtedly the most handsome man I have ever met. He seemed to find me attractive and as soon as his duties had been taken care of, he had the waiter place his chair beside mine for dinner and stayed at my side the rest of the evening.

". . . when Mr. Chamoun asked me if I would like to go dancing, I told him to ask Dr. K. The good doctor was so flattered at the attention being showered on his protégé, he told me I was free to go. 'It isn't often a young lady has such an honor.'

"The suave Mr. Chamoun took me to El Morocco and you should have seen the way waiters bowed. . . . He's a terrific dancer. Then he took me to my train and saw me off, asking me to be his guest at a reception Friday night."

As a precaution I added, "I don't know how much of this you ought to tell Daddy, but use your judgement . . . Tell Daddy I wore a minimum of makeup, but of course, you know I didn't."

Over the next weeks, I saw more of Camille Chamoun. We lunched or dined with various delegates, and I had my first meeting with Russia's Andrey Gromyko, taciturn and dour—as he was forty years later when I escorted him to Ronald Reagan at the White House.

Chamoun was enough to mesmerize any college girl. Know-

---

*Prince Faisal once asked me if I knew any Arabic and I answered no, except for one phrase, "Curse your religion," which I repeated in Arabic. There was a hush, and then the Prince laughed and everyone else did—nervously. I later learned that for saying that phrase, which is almost a term of endearment in Lebanon, you could be arrested in Saudi Arabia.

ing I was a virgin from a proper Druze family, he did not try to seduce me, but clearly I found him devastating and he was amused by my hero worship. He made the college boys I had been going out with seem like puppies. One evening, I came to New York to have dinner with him, and as I waited in the sitting room of his Ritz-Carlton suite the door opened and in walked a beautiful and soignée woman—Mrs. Chamoun, no less. I had no idea she was in the United States.

Just then Camille arrived, instantly sized up the situation, and said, "My dear, this lovely child is a Lebanese-American at Vassar, studying the U.N., and I promised to help her."

Mrs. Chamoun was charming to me and pretended to believe his interest was only in my scholarship. But I could see that this situation was not new to her; she was keenly aware of the romantic appeal of her husband.

Up to this point I had never thought seriously about the impropriety of going out with Camille. I had convinced myself that this was an innocent friendship, or at worst, an exciting flirtation. The enormity of what it could mean—to be involved, however innocently, with a married man—finally sank in and, collecting my coat and books, I made as graceful an exit as I could. (I did not see Chamoun again until long after I married, but I always had a soft spot in my heart for him. He was President of Lebanon from 1952 to 1958 and died in 1987 at the age of eighty-six.)

I seemed to have recovered quickly from this episode, because my next letters home were full of my adventures with a Venezuelan diplomat, tall, dark, and handsome—and unmarried. My United Nations phase finally ended, and during the last two years at Vassar I dated a variety of young men, mostly students at Princeton, and fell deeply in love with one—a WASP from Philadelphia's Main Line. Alas, the differences in our cultures and background frightened him, and this rejection put me in the proper psychological frame of mind to retreat to my roots, to the Lebanese suitor that my parents wanted me to marry.

And so at the end of my junior year, my mother took me back to Lebanon, her first trip there in fourteen years, where the competition between my two worlds would finally be resolved.

THIRTEEN

The Sheik

WHEN MOTHER LEFT Lebanon and the fiancé her family had selected, I am sure she never expected to return to Beirut some twenty years later with a marriageable daughter of her own—all set to betroth me to the Druze suitor my relatives had chosen.

Of course, my reenactment of this ancient Middle Eastern drama had some modern twists. I was not dragged kicking and screaming to Beirut that summer of 1949. I was looking forward to the trip. A matchmaking aunt of mine had arranged for me to correspond with a fascinating Lebanese, the eldest son of a good family, who had been educated abroad and spoke fluent English, French, and Arabic—a fun-loving and debonair ladies' man in his thirties who felt it was time to settle down with the woman of his dreams. For three years he waited for me—writing me eloquent letters, sending me perfume, records of love songs, candies and cables on every important occasion.

"The Sheik," as my Vassar friends called him, added much to my intriguing persona at Vassar, and the girls flocked to my room to admire his photo. They speculated endlessly about our first meeting, our first kiss, our wedding night.

Even though he died some years ago, in deference to his widow and children I will not use his real name but stick to his Vassar nickname. Our romance began with a series of informative and amusing letters to acquaint me with the world of the Druze.

"Supposing a man wants to marry," he wrote. "The demand is great, the supply is limited. With us Druzes, one cannot often meet the girl and talk to her. So he asks his sisters or cousins to inquire about her. Say he spots his ideal girl, Phatatita. The first thing he does is tell his mother and father, then they in turn send someone to 'feel the pulse'—whether Phatatita's parents are agreeable. Let's, for continuity's sake, say they are; then the mother and father inform the family heads about it, get their consent and then choose a delegation to go and ask for Phatatita's hand formally. When that is done the groom buys the engagement rings, a gold one and a platinum one, and then he starts frequenting his fiancée's house more often and in the meantime the groom's family will be preparing the rest of the jewelry, the trousseau and the house furniture."

The Sheik's family were the leading landowners in a lovely village near Beirut, and as the eldest male (his father was dead), the villagers turned to him when in trouble. He ended up holding a *majlis* almost every evening.

"A week ago," he wrote me, "as I arrived back from Beirut, I saw a light in the sitting room at about 8:30 and was quite astonished to find seven sheikhs from the village, all with their long white beards . . . I saluted them, spoke to them about the latest world news, asked them about their farms and crops. A few moments later, the eldest of them asked Mother's permission to say a few personal words to me about a subject which they came especially for, namely, MARRIAGE.

" 'It's high time,' he said, 'that you get your better half and produce the son who is to carry your father's name. Your mother must be compensated for the loss of her man by a grandchild. Moreover, it's ages since we in this village have attended a proper marriage lasting the usual three days of ceremonies and festivals. We would like you to give us a favourable answer, so we may rest assured that you're still an ardent Druze and Arab.'

"I thanked them for their kind feelings and promised them something before my next birthday." And he added, "Don't let me down this summer; it's a nice trip, I assure you."

Indeed, the summer was a joyous one; my intended was an exciting man, both mentally and physically. But we were never permitted to be alone together. The one time we managed to escape our chaperons and sneak away for a quiet lunch in a seaside restaurant, my three uncles were livid, and threatened to kill him for bringing dishonor to the family.

(Matters of honor were not treated lightly among the Druze. A young cousin of mine was sitting in the movies, when a man behind him put his feet up on my cousin's seat. After the man refused to remove them, my cousin drew a gun and shot the offending foot. At the trial, he was found guilty, but because this was an offense to his honor his punishment was mild—banishment to Saudi Arabia until the dust settled.)

Despite my uncles' protectiveness, during our three months in Beirut I was surrounded with love—from both the Sheik's extended family and mine.

Beirut beckoned at its most beautiful—it was affluent and modern on the one hand, but enough of the old survived to find scenes evocative of an Orientalist painting: mustachioed men wearing baggy trousers and fezzes, elderly Druze women with their white head coverings, vendors insistently touting their wares. Donkeys and camels vied for space with the ubiquitous Cadillacs, and the smells of lamb roasting on spits and bread baking in ovens tantalized the senses. Jasmine necklaces were sold on every street corner, their perfume overwhelming.

Every meal was a banquet. My relatives, no matter how humble, outdid themselves to give the visitors from America a lavish welcome. Richer cousins put their cars and drivers at our disposal, and took us on delightful excursions to Tyre and Sidon and the Roman ruins at Baalbek, and to Zahle, a picturesque village on the road to Damascus. There we ate at a world-renowned restaurant beside a waterfall and sampled fifty different hors d'oeuvres, called *mezza* in Arabic. We often carried picnic lunches to the beach, and in the evening the Sheik and others took us to some of the glamorous night spots of Beirut.

Most evocative of all, however, was our return to Arsoun, after fourteen years' absence. The entire village came to call, especially the old crones looking me over as bride material. "*Haram*," they would say to each other, forgetting that I could understand much of what they said. "For shame. The poor girl is so dark and so thin, she will not easily catch a husband." Even in Lebanon, fair meant beautiful, and plumpness equaled desirability—at least among the less sophisticated villagers.

Arsoun had a special magic at night, for the village did not yet have electricity. With sundown came a heightened awareness of the heady smells of fig and pine trees and the thyme, mint, and parsley used in every Lebanese kitchen. Cicadas provided a whispering chorus as we munched on green olives from our own groves and white cheese topped with my grandmother's apricot jam.

We played cards by the light of kerosene lanterns; poker was my favorite game and we used watermelon seeds for chips. Sometimes the villagers would form a circle around a fire and recite poetry created extemporaneously in our honor. (Years later I was struck by the similarity of an evening in Seville, when the peasants on a large hacienda entertained us throughout the night with fandangos composed on the spot.)

Toward the end of the summer I received a letter from the Sheik—a proposal that would win any woman with an ounce of romance in her. "My very dear creature," he began, telling me he had fallen in love with me, and quoting some romantic lines from Wordsworth. He concluded, "My mind is made up, my heart set, my life's aim found. Need I make, rather frame, my proposal in the usual and common words of 'Will you marry me?' "

My heart was smitten, but my mind urged caution. Not only had I seen the beauty and tranquillity of life in Lebanon, but even then, I saw much under the surface which disturbed me.

Writing to Professor Clark, I said: "In a nutshell, I find that Lebanon itself is living on a completely false economy, and the time for a crisis must be near at hand. They manufacture almost nothing and import everything . . . the country's money instead of going for essentials, goes for flashy cars, fines wines and other luxury items. Politically, the country's leaders are very corrupt, fattening their pockets at the expense of their people. . . . They make fun of things American, yet it is a mark of distinction to claim that something they possess was made in America. . . . America caused the defeat of the Arabs (they never stop and question their own ineffectuality and lack of cooperation over the Palestine question)."

Yet, for all my criticisms, I concluded by saying, "Frankly, I'm in love with this country!" But my love was an ambivalent one, as was my feeling for the Sheik. I refused to give a definite answer to his proposal. I felt I had to get back to my familiar surroundings, finish at Vassar, and think about where and how I wanted to spend the rest of my life.

After I returned for my senior year at Vassar, we continued to write, and I realized how far apart our worlds were, especially on the subject of my having a career.

"May I tell you why I object to your getting a job here, once we're married," he wrote. "First, knowing you as I do, you would either do something well, or not at all; hence, if you took a job you would devote all your time and attention to it. You can do this only at the expense of your matrimonial life. Early to work and early to bed, no time for me, no evenings out, no social life. No more morning, lunch and evening smile that I crave coming back from my work. A household without its lady is like a ship without a skipper.

"Second, it's not in keeping with our social standing for you to be a working woman. Ladies do not, as a rule, work for a living. . . . In fact, it reflects badly on the husband . . . I couldn't bear the idea of having my wife obey someone else, or having her time and effort exploited other than for herself or for me. This is neither selfish nor egoism; it is self-respect and dignity. A woman is a man's recreation, a man's consolation, a man's protégée, a man's ambition and a man's counselor. How do you expect an employed woman to be any of those?"

Obviously, our visions of the future were wildly incompatible, and I reluctantly faced up to the realization that a marriage between us was impossible. Thus, when the moment of truth came, I knew that I could never leave home. And home for me was America.

As graduation approached, only one sadness marred this otherwise bright and happy ending to my first twenty-one years. The four years at Vassar had taken me far, far away from Kingsport, and especially from my father, whom I loved, but never had looked to for inspiration or guidance. His was a noble and generous heart—and he never begrudged me my close rapport with my mother, from which he was excluded.

He and Mother drove up for graduation and I, with the typical thoughtlessness and selfishness of youth, paid little attention to him. He did not fit in with my new friends.

That night, sitting in the hotel room in New York, Daddy appeared to be looking out the window, but I saw him brush the tears from his cheeks. I put my arm on his shoulder and he shrugged and turned away, saying with heartbreaking sadness, "What was all this education for if it makes you ashamed of your family? Where is my little girl that I loved so much? I have lost her."

Despite my Vassar degree, I had much to learn.

FOURTEEN

Maktoub!

T HE PSYCHOLOGICAL and emotional journey from Selwa Carmen Showker of Kingsport, Tennessee, to Mrs. Archibald Bulloch Roosevelt Jr. of Washington and New York was a long one, but I never doubted for a minute that a benevolent God had planned it all.

How can I think otherwise, when I reflect on the complex events leading to the most wonderful moment of my life—my meeting Archie?

It was literally love at first sight for both of us. We met on a Saturday, Archie asked me to marry him on Sunday, and three months later, on September 1, 1950, we were married.*

To summarize his first thirty years: He was born in Boston, at the end of World War I, the grandson of President Theodore Roosevelt. He had an establishment upbringing and a Groton-Harvard education. At a young age his brilliant and versatile mind was drawn to foreign cultures and languages, particularly those of the Middle East.

Archie married right out of college and with his first wife headed west to Seattle, where he started life as a journalist—a career soon aborted by World War II. He tried to enlist but was

---

*Archie has described our meeting in his own autobiography, *For Lust of Knowing: Memoirs of an Intelligence Officer* (Little, Brown, 1988), with the humor and class that characterized everything he did.

turned down because of poor eyesight, however he finally got into military intelligence and found himself in the North African invasion. The war years were spent in intelligence activities in Morocco, Algiers, and Tunisia, and then he became assistant military attaché in Iraq, where he wrote a definitive study on the Marsh Arabs.

After the war, because of his knowledge of Persian he was sent to Teheran as assistant military attaché. He became fascinated with the history and culture of the Kurds and studied their language as well. He also participated in the American decision to help Iran resist the Soviet takeover of Azerbaijan.

Finally he grew restless in the military, and at a critical juncture in his life pondered four career paths—*New York Times* correspondent in the Middle East; a field job with the Arabian-American Oil Company; the State Department, where he had just completed the Foreign Service exams with the highest grade then ever recorded; or the Central Intelligence Agency.

He chose the CIA and was immediately sent off to Beirut to set up shop there. But while his professional life was in orbit, his private life was in shambles. His wife hated his career and the Middle East, and wanted a divorce. They had one son, Tweed, and Archie would settle for nothing less than joint custody.

Fortuitously, he was offered a job back home, setting up Voice of America broadcasts to the Middle East and to the Soviet Eastern nationalities—a revolutionary concept at the time. Today, of course, discontent in Soviet Armenia, Azerbaijan, etc., is a constant front-page story.

Taking a leave of absence from the CIA, he came to New York—where the Voice of America then had its headquarters—to accept the new challenge, and to settle his unhappy private life.

Meanwhile, some months before my Vassar graduation I started job hunting, looking particularly at journalism and the State Department. The Voice of America seemed like the perfect combination of both. Edwin Wright, who interviewed me at the State Department, suggested that I go to see one Archie Roosevelt at the Voice of America.

My parents were coming to the end of their financial rope, and I had exhausted my savings. In late February I wrote a letter home, pleading for money to finance my job hunting: "Instead of giving me any sort of graduation present . . . I'd rather have carte blanche to do some of the things which seem very important to my future . . . I want to go to New York to see Archie Roosevelt, who works with the Voice of America."

Just before graduation I requested an appointment with Mr. Roosevelt for Saturday, May 20. His secretary relayed the message to him. "Absolutely not," he said. He used Saturdays to catch up with the backlog that had accumulated during the week.

"But, Mr. Roosevelt, she has such a nice voice," said his secretary, my unknown champion, who was intrigued by my Southern accent. Reluctantly, he agreed to see me.

Wearing my prettiest outfit, a red wool dress and matching jacket, and a tiny black hat with a veil demurely covering my eyes, I set off for New York with my senior thesis, "Communism in the Arab World," under my arm.

I wrote my mother this description of our meeting: "I walked into his office and there was this very attractive young man—Archie himself. He was very impressed with my thesis [according to Archie, he only pretended to be] and of course, he knows a great deal about the subject himself . . . he was so impressed that he asked me to have lunch with him, which he later told me was against all precedent. After lunch he took me to a bookstore which has all kinds of Arabic books. Archie is amazing. He speaks Arabic, Russian, the Kurdish dialects, and of course French and all the more prosaic languages. After that, we went to the Metropolitan Museum . . . to see the Vienna Collection. He asked me to go out with him that night, but I already had a date . . . so then he asked me to spend Sunday with him. Sunday morning he drove me to Poughkeepsie, we had lunch here and spent the afternoon hiking along the river and he left last night about 10:30.

"The whole thing has been like a dream. He keeps saying I am too good to be true! . . . Incidentally, he is 32 years old . . . he has a mustache and goatee for business reasons. He may be sent by the State Department to the hinterland and he wants to look as Arab as possible."

This was a somewhat censored version. I didn't tell Mother that on Sunday morning when Archie came to pick me up at Ruthie Pratt's apartment I was not quite ready, so I threw on Ruthie's negligee to open the door—a glamorous blue confection trimmed with a feather boa. "I declare," I said, as I opened the door, "I look like a whore"—pronounced "ho-wah" in my Southern accent. Both he and Ruthie still tell this story as the reason Archie was so smitten.

I also didn't dare tell Mother that he was divorced and had a child, and that we had decided we were destined for each other and would get married. I waited until they had received my first letter and then broke the news. Daddy was not pleased.

"I know about New York playboys," he said. "He's already left one wife and son and now he wants to marry you because you are younger and prettier. After you have some children, he will leave you for a younger girl—and you will have to raise the children. Yes, miss, you think you're so smart, but I know about playboys."

Daddy was so far off the mark I could only laugh. Archie had not wanted a divorce; his wife had left him to pursue another way of life. Actually, Archie was an endangered species—an old-fashioned scholar and gentleman, with a British sort of wit, shy and modest about his prodigious intellectual achievements, and a man of enormous charm. He was adorable, and I loved him the moment he first smiled at me. But a boulevardier he was not. He made no attempt to impress me. Indeed, he told me right away that he was broke because of his divorce, and took me on my first (and last) subway ride. He also drove me to Vassar in a terrible old jalopy.

"Please don't judge him yet, Daddy," I begged. "Wait till you meet him. And he speaks Arabic."

"Humph," my father replied. "He's just saying that."

I could understand my father's skepticism, but actually Archie had a more profound knowledge and understanding of my antecedents than any Lebanese or Arab-American I could have married.

There was no way to explain that sense of recognition—of knowing that this was the man I wanted to spend the rest of my life with. I had so often heard my parents remark that certain events were *maktoub*—written in the book of God. Here was the ultimate proof that God was always with us and had carefully structured both our lives so that we knew immediately we were meant for each other.

While the news of my imminent marriage did not sit well with my father—I would be the first member of my family to marry outside the Druze religion—surprisingly enough, on the Roosevelt side there was universal approval.

Archie's mother, who was appalled when I greeted her with a Southern "Hi" instead of the more formal "How do you do," decided to overlook this, and wrote me:

"Archie's happiness means everything to me . . . I do not lose sight of the difficulties for you—the fact that he is divorced, very little money—a son—no wedding presents, etc. I know your courage is high and that you are wise beyond your years. I felt a relationship with you right away and knew we could rely on and trust each other always and that we will be very close. I also believe that you and Archie love each other very dearly and in a true marriage this grows deeper and stronger with the years . . . God bless you, dear."

Archie's was the first divorce in the Teddy Roosevelt family, and this was a great sadness to his parents. Mrs. Roosevelt wrote my mother: "As parents I know how hard it must be to have her marry a divorced man, with all the resulting responsibilities and financial strain, but given Lucky's courage and unusual intelligence and perception, I feel sure she can handle the situation with wisdom and tact. She must have a very wonderful mother. On my side, I can tell you Archie is honorable and sweet in character and highly gifted in mind. His faults have always been those of omission, not of commission, and I can honestly say that I think he will take good care of her and make her a good husband."

Mrs. Roosevelt's brother, Dunbar Lockwood, was Archie's godfather and favorite relative, and he wrote Archie: "I loved your little girl, thought she was properly humble and self-effacing when the Lords of Creation talked together. . . . Her scholastic record is good enough so that she must know how little she knows. So I think you are lucky."

Years later Cornelius Roosevelt told me that word of our engagement sent his mother, Auntie Eleanor (Mrs. Theodore Roosevelt Jr.), and all the clan rushing to the encyclopedia to look up "Druze." When she, a true grande dame, pronounced her approval, everyone followed her lead.

I knew so little about Washington and New York society that I did not yet understand just what my marriage meant in those circles. I had heard vaguely about a famous Washington hostess, Alice Longworth, but had not realized that she was Archie's aunt until a letter came from her signed "Auntie Sister"—the way she was always referred to in the family.

Mrs. Longworth did not care for Archie's parents, but she liked Archie enormously. When she heard that he was marrying a Druze, she announced in Washington, "That's splendid and will be very good for that pompous brother of mine." But to Archie she wrote more decorously: "I long to meet Selwa . . . everyone says how lovely she is—even the press photographs couldn't obscure her charm and beauty. What fun that you are going to be in Washington."

Archie's three sisters—Theodora, Nancy, and Edith—joined in the chorus of warmth and affection, and the nicest remark of all came from Margaret, the eighty-year-old black cook who had been with the family forever. "Mister Archie," she told him, "you done got yourself a honey-wife."

But there were problems too. Archie's ex-wife spoke rather disparagingly of his "somewhat exotic marriage." And my new little stepson asked his mother if I was going to be like the stepmother in "Cinderella."

To avoid an expensive wedding, and because this was Archie's second marriage, we decided to have the ceremony in New York at 9 Sutton Place, the home of Auntie Belle Roosevelt (Mrs.

Kermit Roosevelt), a perfect setting with a garden extending to the East River. (Later, it became the residence of the Turkish ambassador to the United Nations.) My parents, proud to the end, insisted on having a nice supper after the wedding, and took out a bank loan to pay for it. A cousin of mine, who owned a dress shop in Virginia, gave me my wedding dress of Chantilly lace.

A Methodist minister performed the ceremony that hot September day, and then we left for a brief honeymoon at Virginia Beach. I found the hotel room filled with roses, and a note which I still cherish: "To my honey-wife— If I were a Sultan, I could strew the bed with rose petals to make it soft and sweet and fragrant for your beauty—but as it is, here is my poor substitute— like your man, complete with thorns, but I hope both will do."

Archie and I had promised that on his next free weekend we would go to Kingsport, where Mother and Daddy would give a reception for the local gentry in the afternoon, and another for the A-rabs (as Archie irreverently called them) from the scattered Druze communities in the area.

Not accustomed to ebullient Southerners, Archie found the receiving line tough going—especially as no alcohol was served. When he protested, I said, "No, you can't have a drink—they'll smell it on your breath."

Friends filed through the line, poking Archie in the stomach or clapping him on the back and saying, "I declare, you sure do favor your granpappy," or "Son, you got yourself a nice little girl here. I remember when Selwa was just a baby and S.L. was so proud of her," or "I'm mighty glad you belong to the Oyster Bay Roosevelts—I got no use for those Hyde Park Democrats."

Archie's eyes began to glaze over. I jabbed him in the ribs and whispered, "Smile, honey, and stop acting like a Yankee."

Archie's final hurdle in this unusual marriage of his was meeting my family living in Lebanon. In a 1951 letter to my in-laws, I described our first trip to Beirut after our wedding:

"You should have seen the way Archie handled my relatives. . . . They all thought he was wonderful, and no one took after him with a knife for not being a Druze. (Remember how he used to tease you about that after we were married.) He astonished them with his knowledge of Arabic and managed to make his typical Archie witticisms even in Arabic.

"Their main concern now is for me to produce a son. All the toasts seem concerned with that subject—either 'to the birth of a son,' or if you have a son, 'to the marriage of your son,' or if your son is married, 'to the birth of a grandson.' "

I am so grateful that Archie was able to meet and know my Lebanese family long before that country became a universal metaphor for anarchy and chaos. The last time we were to see my grandmother and uncles was in December 1964, when we were living in London and went to Beirut for our winter holidays.

Soon, the collective memory will be unable to recall that delightful other Lebanon; no one will believe it existed and it will slip into the realm of fantasy. The land of my ancestors and their way of life is finished, and if war and religious strife can destroy that ancient country, then none of us should be overly complacent. The lesson of Lebanon is how precarious civilization can be.

FIFTEEN

The Honorary WASP

WHEN THE QUINTESSENTIAL WASP marries the ultimate ethnic, it makes for a rollicking marriage. Ours was full of love and laughter thanks to Archie, and full of drama, thanks to my Mediterranean temperament.

Early on we faced the fact that I was the grasshopper and Archie the ant. Archie warned me that he had been brought up with a New England conscience and this motto: "Eat it up/wear it out/make it do/do without." He recited this in doomsday tones, just to tease me. But he meant it.

In my culture, the "bella figura" was everything. Like most insecure people, I was a lavish tipper; Archie insisted that was vulgar and ostentatious gifts also were to be avoided—"it's the thought that counts." While ethnics indulged in hyperbole, WASPs were given to understatement, such as calling a palatial estate in Newport a "cottage." Shabby genteel was desirable; shiny new was not.

I was shocked when we dined with Archie's family or his rich friends. The last person served emptied the tray. And it never came back replenished. That, to my family, would have been a disgrace. We offered our guests an abundant table, pressing food on them and feigning insult if they did not take seconds.

Although in Archie's world the food was paltry, the table settings were elaborate. My mother-in-law always used the finest china and finger bowls, even when we were just family. The damask napkins were enormous, handsomely monogrammed by Mrs. Theodore Roosevelt and used in the White House almost a hundred years ago.

WASPs had magnificent linen—exquisite blanket covers, a luxury new to me, linen sheets, and the thickest towels I had ever seen, all monogrammed of course.

For my first Christmas with the Roosevelts, I bought expensive presents for everyone. Likewise, my parents sent extravagant gifts, not to be outdone by those rich new in-laws of mine! Archie insisted his family never spent more than ten dollars for a gift, but I paid no attention. And I couldn't believe it when a WASP friend carefully unwrapped her present, saving the paper and ribbon to use again.

Some of our wedding presents amazed me, especially one from the famous philanthropist Mrs. August Belmont, who was godmother to Archie's father. It was a small wine-colored sack, of ordinary fabric, which might have been used by a European housewife to fetch food from the market.

When Archie was a little boy and lost a tooth, he would find a dime under his pillow from the tooth bunny. But once, Archie lost a tooth while visiting his grandmother in Boston, and found only a penny had been left. When he complained, his father showed no sympathy. "What do you expect?" he said. "That's the stingy old New England tooth bunny."

Archie and his friends talked about how much things cost, which to me was a no-no. It took me years to realize that a mortgage was not something to be ashamed of. My in-laws talked freely about their wills and what was being left to each child. With us, the subject of death and inheritance was taboo.

In Archie's world it was assumed that everyone knew how to ride a horse and shoot a gun—neither of which I could do. The urban poor never come near a horse, and in the South women did not have guns for sport. (I thought only poor folks ate rabbit and birds.) I remember at Vassar being surprised at what a small allowance my friend Sis Hanes had—and yet her parents cheerfully paid for boarding her horse at school.

One of Archie's old college chums was Claiborne Pell, like

him, a scion of the establishment, later U.S. Senator from Rhode Island. He and Archie bragged about wearing their fathers' shirts and twenty-year-old shoes. They paid a sewing woman to turn their shirt collars, a practice I only learned about after my marriage. They competed in driving the oldest, most beat-up car. I think Archie won. Our first car, a VW bug, lasted about fifteen years; then we splurged on a VW Rabbit in 1976, which we still have. Recently, I threw caution to the winds and bought a 1989 Honda Civic!

Personal relationships and expressions of affection were another area of difference. In my world, the extended family was everything; they were judge and jury on all aspects of one's behavior. But more important, they could be counted on in sickness, in death, and whenever needed. I never knew anyone who had been to a psychiatrist until after I married.

Archie's family and friends valued their privacy; no one dared drop in without an invitation. When we were returning to New York following our Kingsport reception, my mother politely said, "I hope you will remember me to your aunts." Archie said he would be glad to, but didn't expect to see them. It was inconceivable to Mother that we would not routinely call on Archie's relatives every time we were in New York.

All of my tribe were demonstrative—much kissing and hugging, but also much shouting and temper over the most trivial matters. This was a normal way to cope with stress. WASPs, however, seemed to find emotional excess a sign of weakness. They were wary of propinquity and kept both a physical and psychological distance from everyone. Archie found the noise and gesticulations disturbing at first; he naturally assumed that so much passion meant people were seriously upset. In his world, clenched lips and cutting remarks were signs of anger—and equally effective.

Stoicism and the stiff upper lip were tenets of the WASP creed. I observed that the Astors and Rockefellers were less likely to complain about poor service, or waiting in line, or any such momentary hardship. Ethnics tended to complain loudly to make themselves seem important.

Despite an outward puritanism, WASP men, I discovered, were very sensual; however, they often seemed to repress their sexuality. Most of them married comfortable women who looked like their mothers and sisters, let their hair go gray early, cultivated splendid gardens, and rode horses into old age. I could never understand how their sexual chemistry kept going, but if they had mistresses, they certainly were discreet about it.

In my family, we were never ashamed to show sentimentality, and we wept copiously at movies, the opera, and even at weddings. Early in our marriage Archie and I saw a production of *Showboat*, and I can never hear the music without getting teary, remembering how happy we were! Archie, though secretly pleased, pretended this was a bit *de trop*.

Like most ethnics, I worried endlessly about "doing the right thing." I wanted to avoid anything that might reveal my ignorance. But marrying Archie liberated me from that tyranny. Archie's attitude was "Whatever we do is right." That sounds arrogant, but in fact he was simply laid back. And, of course, it reflected his deep sense of security in social matters.

I came to appreciate much about my new environment. Today I admire the Eastern establishment as a citadel of taste and restraint in an increasingly vulgar world. They set high standards of integrity and many are the embodiment of the founding fathers and the qualities that made America great.

In the end I became an honorary WASP—thanks to Vassar, to the warm welcome of the Roosevelts, and to the husband whose gentle humor and loving heart saw me through the metamorphosis.

Acquiring a famous name was a mixed blessing. I learned to my delight the pleasure it gave both Theodore and Franklin Roosevelt fans to meet a member of the family. I constantly received letters requesting autographs and photos. Headwaiters recognized me, and people always returned my calls. On the debit side were all those folks out there who hated the rich, the establishment, and any and all politicians.

Archie's family were low-key about their lineage, and

thought it bad form to exploit it in any way. Shortly after my marriage, I was offered $1,500 to do an ad for Pond's face cream— a series with the theme "She's lovely, she's engaged, she uses Pond's." I wanted to do it, to augment our finances. With trepidation I approached my in-laws. Their answer: "You must use your own judgment—it's your name now." I did pose for the ad, and had my first experience of being photographed by a world-famous photographer, Louise Dahl-Wolf. But thank heaven, the ad did not run in the United States. They decided my looks were too Latin and would be more effective in South America.

My mother-in-law, Gracie, whom we called Hoo-hoo, was a slim, birdlike woman, bright and wickedly funny. Her world was bounded by Boston, where she grew up, the Colony Club and an apartment on the Upper East Side in New York, a house on Long Island, and in her later years, a winter residence in Hobe Sound, Florida. She was famous for her absentmindedness and grasshopper mind. Typically, she once asked her husband, "How old were you when your father was born?"

Archie senior, a curmudgeon and terrifying to most people, was, underneath that brusque exterior, a sentimental man who longed for his ideal world which existed before World War I. He and his brothers had been valiant in war, and one, Quentin, had given his life. Among our most cherished possessions is a letter Theodore Roosevelt wrote on July 21, 1918, to Archie senior, who had just been wounded in France.

"Dearest Archie," he wrote. "On Tuesday, the 16th we heard rumors about Quentin; but it was not until today that we were absolutely sure of his death. Poor little Flora [Quentin's fiancée] is broken hearted, but very brave; and Mother suffers as much and is even braver; for Mother has the true heroism of heart. Well, it is very dreadful; it is the old who ought to die, and not fine and gallant youth with the golden morning of life still ahead; but after all, he died as the heroes of old died, as brave and fearless men must die when a great cause calls."

Although he lived well into his eighties, Archie senior never came to accept our contemporary culture, with its compromises and vulgarities. Once, after visiting us, he wrote me this bread-and-butter letter: "I was so proud to see what a wonderful hostess you were and what a wonderful host Archie was. So much 'breed-ing' and no 'side,' if you know what I mean. There is lots of 'side' now and very little 'breeding.' "

After Gracie died tragically in a car accident, my father-in-law was inconsolable, but he came to rely on me a great deal. He called me "the General" and allowed me to run his house and organize his last years in Hobe Sound. His thanks were profuse: "Selwa, my dear, you must have a headache due to the weight of your halo and your shoulders must be sore where the wings have begun to sprout."

Remembering my in-laws, I am amazed at how much atten-tion those aging parents devoted to us, at least in their thoughts. I had become discouraged and depressed in the late 1960s—I had finally to face the fact that I could never have children, and two books I attempted to write had been thwarted. To console me Gracie wrote, "You must remember that as far as Archie goes, you help him every moment by just being his beloved wife—a good housekeeper, a wonderful hostess and a perfect companion. You both have so much to be grateful for."

I was indeed fortunate. Through all the years Archie loved me uncritically, and every day, no matter how difficult, had elements of joy. He shared with me his fertile mind, his encyclopedic knowledge. I never knew anyone so widely read, so curious, so catholic in taste and scope. He had infinite tolerance and was only intolerant of bigots and fanatics.

Archie was pure of heart, utterly self-forgetful, unaware of his own treasured qualities, and throughout our forty years to-gether he never lost the deviltry and humor of youth alongside the profound and provocative mind of a sage.

SIXTEEN

CIA Wife

A FEW WEEKS before our wedding, as Archie and I were having lunch in New York at an outdoor restaurant in Rockefeller Center, I noticed he seemed preoccupied, and kept looking nervously over his shoulder.

Finally, after the waiter was a safe distance away, he leaned forward and said, "Lucky, I'm afraid there is something terribly important I haven't told you yet."

The conspiratorial voice, the furtive look, were so unlike Archie. What on earth could it be?

"I'm not really in the Foreign Service—I'm just on loan to the Voice of America for a year. I'm actually an officer of the CIA."

"What's that?" I asked.

"The Central Intelligence Agency," he replied, surprised that a Vassar graduate, with a major in international relations, would ask such a question. But in 1950 this agency, created at the end of World War II as an outgrowth of the OSS (Office of Strategic Services), was very low-key. The press honored a gentlemen's agreement to keep a veil of silence around the supersecret outfit; its employees were always referred to by their cover jobs, even if the reporter knew their real identity. They and their families were under a discipline never to reveal their true mission.

I looked at Archie with new eyes. Here was a man I had thought utterly without guile, a straight arrow, incapable of telling a fib, who was in fact leading a complicated dual life that I would now share.

As he explained to me what we could look forward to—years of anonymity, discretion, mental strain, and maybe even physical danger—I scarcely paid attention. It was thrilling. My husband a spy—a front-line soldier in the Cold War! (Archie would later explain to me that he was an intelligence officer, not a spy. A spy or agent works clandestinely, often in hostile territory, and reports to an intelligence officer.)

I began college as a liberal, but left Vassar a militant anti-Communist, revolted by revelations of Americans who betrayed their country to the Soviets. Whittaker Chambers' *Witness* and Jan Valtin's *Out of the Night* had had a great effect on me.

I saw how European intellectuals of the post–World War I era had contributed to the climate of cynicism and despair which preceded the Nazi takeover in Germany. I wanted to be a part of the intellectual current of our own postwar era which might contribute to a forceful new patriotism, to a resurgence of free enterprise and belief in the American dream.

In California, a Hollywood actor named Ronald Reagan was going through the same intellectual process. Certainly no one in those early 1950s recognized that he would be the leader who would give expression to the sentiments we cherished. And that that same leader would later have the strength and courage to work with Russia's Mikhail Gorbachev to bring about an end to the Cold War.

Meanwhile, fate had placed me in a role I was destined to play for the next two and a half decades, the wife of a senior official of the CIA. Six months after our marriage we were on our way to Istanbul. This was at the height of the Cold War, and Turkey's location on the Russian border, and sandwiched between Eastern Europe and the Arab world, made it a very significant post.

We had a well-rehearsed cover story, and I had no trouble assuming the role of the wife of a consular official in Istanbul. But I almost blew it over a matter of protocol. In those days it was customary for a new consular wife to make calls on the official wives who outranked her, both American and foreign. Of course, not being versed in State Department protocol, and Archie being blissfully ignorant of these niceties, I did no such thing. I couldn't understand why everyone seemed cool to us—we were not asked places, and none of the wives were friendly. Finally one of them took pity on me.

"Mrs. Roosevelt, are you aware that by ignoring protocol and not making calls you have offended everyone? No one will invite you until you call on them."

The Roosevelt name apparently caused people to assume we were snobs and had no desire to make friends with them. Of course, I immediately rectified the situation. But it made me realize early in our marriage that, on matters of protocol, I was on my own.

Our ambassador, George Wadsworth (later succeeded by George McGhee), had a special fondness for Archie and took a paternal interest in me. We always stayed with him when Archie had business in Ankara, and I learned by observation how a major embassy was run.

Istanbul was a learning experience in every way. I decorated my first house, hired my first servants, trained my first cook, gave my first dinner party, and had my first taste of living the diplomatic life. I loved it.

It was also in Istanbul that I attended my first Soviet party celebrating the October Revolution. I was sure that thanks to the KGB something sinister would happen to us, but in fact, we arrived at the ornate Russian consulate, a holdover from Czarist days, to be greeted by officials in gold-trimmed diplomatic uniforms—a formality we Americans eschewed because we thought such trappings undemocratic! The invitation called for white tie and tails and I wore my grandest ball gown. The Russian ladies, rather huge hulks, were in ill-fitting government-issue dresses. They gathered around me and one poked my arm commenting with obvious distaste on how thin I was!

In those days the representatives of Iron Curtain countries talked only to each other, afraid to mix and mingle. The Turks, Americans, and others of the diplomatic corps banded together, and the Russians were divided between those who seemed fairly civilized and the more thuggish-looking who we assumed were KGB. We observed this pattern in almost every Soviet reception we attended over the next thirty-five years.

I hoped that in Istanbul we would have our first child. In a humorous letter to my mother, Archie wrote about me:

"I have every expectation that she will not only soon be famous [as a writer] but that she will be able to support your grandchildren. I suppose you are wondering when the first of these is due to arrive, and I am afraid I can give you no encouraging news. It is a problem I am working very hard on, and your child is assisting me every way she can; in fact we devote a lot of our spare time to it—but so far, even our most concentrated efforts have borne no fruit. The best I can promise you is that I shall continue to give the matter a great deal of attention, and anyway, it is not so much of a chore as one might suppose."

(That was not to be. Only years and many doctors later would I discover that I could not have children.)

That first year in Istanbul, I got to know Archie's nine-year-old son, Tweed, who came from boarding school in the States to spend the summer with us. At the age of twenty-two, I found it hard to imagine myself a stepmother, and I wanted so much for this child to love me. We formed a warm bond which has lasted to this day. Perhaps one of the most touching moments was when I heard him tactfully referring to me as his "other mother."

Archie and I had to be separated for weeks at a time, when he went on secret missions, but he took me with him as often as he could. I took my first trip to Saudi Arabia when it was still a primitive kingdom. They did not allow paper money, so we hauled a huge sock full of silver coins to pay our hotel bill.

Archie was the boss, but almost all his employees were older than he, and I was viewed as a child. I had a long way to go to earn their respect. I also had to be the morale officer. CIA wives are often very lonely—they cannot discuss their husbands' work; they cannot explain to their children why Daddy is away so much and works such dreadful hours, or why Daddy never seems to get promoted, or why, no matter how brilliant he may seem, Daddy never becomes an ambassador.

The CIA is made up of America's finest and brightest, and the players are as varied in ethnic and educational backgrounds as our country itself. As a group, however, they have in common a felicitous mixture of imagination and discipline, courage and intellect.

The CIA officer must know languages, he must be in contact not just with the elite of the country, but with a broad spectrum of the population. Archie already knew Arabic, Persian, Hebrew, Russian, French, and a dozen other languages when we went to Turkey, and as a matter of course he set about learning Turkish.

(Right after our wedding, when Archie was still at the Voice of America, I came home one Friday to find him buried in a book. He explained he was learning Uzbek. "What's that?" I asked. "A Turkic language spoken by millions in the Soviet Union," he explained. "I have to interview an Uzbek on Monday for a program we are starting and I want to be able to communicate with him in his own language.")

I often teased our smug journalist friends who assumed a certain moral superiority vis-à-vis the Agency. "A CIA officer and a journalist do exactly the same thing," I would point out. "They seek the truth—the intelligence officer does it for his country; the journalist does it to sell newspapers, keep his editors happy, and win Pulitzer Prizes."

What Archie most liked about the Agency was the intellectual freedom he enjoyed. He had no public image to worry about. He could, indeed was obliged to, report the facts as he saw them. But much as he liked his work, Archie eventually would resign at the age of fifty-six, after thirty years in the government. He saw that intelligence gathering was a young man's game. There were no public honors to store up for middle age; no ambassadorships, no future invitations to join boards of directors or to head foundations.

Now that the Cold War is ending, it is easy to forget that we had such a sinister enemy. We still do not live in a perfect world;

terrorism and totalitarianism, though receding, still threaten our freedoms. And the CIA's men and women must continue to toil and die and are no less heroes than our military men.

We spent the first twenty-five years of our marriage with the CIA. And although I had to give up several careers, move a dozen times, and assume burdens for which I was never paid, I know that CIA wives are often as important to the success of a mission as the officers themselves. I am proud to have participated in their great cause.

Because Archie was in the CIA, I was never able to indulge in political activity, but letters exchanged with my mother over those years show consistent interest. I was always a political animal.

I wrote in February 1952, "I am getting more and more conservative . . . even tho I think Taft is all wet about a lot, a little Taftism wouldn't hurt the U.S. should the Republicans make the foolish mistake of choosing him over Eisenhower. No one who works for the government can doubt there is too much government and too much squandering of the government's money. (Not for quotation, by the way, since we are employees of this gargantuan spending machine.) . . . It's a national disgrace—the waste and total disregard for the taxpayer."

Eisenhower's win was not so certain in 1952, Mother wrote. "Too many people . . . are thinking of nothing but their pay checks. They think the Republicans will bring on a depression and they will lose their jobs."

I was delighted with Ike's nomination and wrote Mother: "Are you going to help in the Eisenhower campaign? You should . . . I want very much to see Tennessee go Republican." And when Ike won: "What a joy to have a Republican in the White House . . . it just goes to show what widespread discontent the people have felt."

We were stationed in Spain during the 1960 elections. I wrote Mother: "I envy you, watching the conventions on TV. I still think Kennedy will win [the nomination] . . . I certainly pray they won't nominate Stevenson, but of course, Nixon could beat him with his hands tied behind him."

In September 1960 I wrote: "Naturally I want the Republican Party to win and would vote that way, but while I hate the Democratic Party and its platform, I think Jack Kennedy has a lot on the ball and will be a good President, if he can dominate his party. . . . Still, we will all be better off if Republican financial policies can prevail. Don't you agree?"

After the Nixon-Kennedy debates, I wavered, and almost was convinced that Kennedy would make the better President, even though "I realize that the Democrats mean inflation, higher prices, pie in the sky and all the rest of their platform."

When the election was over, I observed: "I really don't think Kennedy will be a bad President—he might even be a great one. I haven't written Jackie yet, but I am thrilled for her."

SEVENTEEN

From Copy Girl to Columnist

*F*OUR SUMMERS of working at the *Kingsport Times* had given me the equivalent of a year's experience as a reporter. I thought I was pretty hot stuff when I arrived in Washington after two years in Istanbul and immediately started looking for a newspaper job.

It took only a few tries to realize that getting to any important Washington editor would be impossible without a sponsor. I asked Mark Ethridge, editor of the *Louisville Courier-Journal*, for help and he sent me to Ed Tribble, city editor of the *Washington Star*. Treating my previous experience with the disdain it probably deserved, Tribble said he could only offer me a position as copy girl.

I grabbed it. I knew damn well I would not stay a copy girl for long. In fact, it took me six months to go from fetching coffee and answering the phone to writing my own column.

In the beginning I was regarded with some suspicion; my colleagues were dubious about a woman who was married to a State Department official with a famous name and who wore Balenciaga suits to the office. (We were broke, but the suits were couture hand-me-downs from my smartly dressed mother-in-law.)

The first day, when I answered the phone a tough old newshen, the society editor of the *Washington Times-Herald,* demanded, "Who the hell is this?"

"It's Mrs. Roosevelt," I replied primly.

"Oh, yeah? Well, this is Mrs. Woodrow Wilson."

I learned after that to identify myself as Selwa or Lucky Roosevelt.

Gradually, my colleagues came to regard me as one of the girls. I became part of the "lunch bunch"—a group dominated by Mary McGrory, a true friend and marvelous writer with whom I disagreed on just about every major political issue. Jerry O'Leary, a handsome young Irishman, was a pal who went on to a distinguished journalistic career in South America and later at the White House. Another buddy was the fashion editor, Eleni, a diminutive Greek who was married to Sidney Epstein, longtime executive editor of the *Star*. Eleni and I were look-alike Mediterraneans, and when either of us sashayed through the pressroom the guys would yell, "There goes twitchy butt."

Jackie Kennedy was responsible for my big breakthrough. She had only recently married Senator John F. Kennedy and moved to Georgetown. When we lunched together, she was full of happiness and joy. I remember her saying to me, "Lucky, isn't it wonderful to be married and in love." She hated the publicity surrounding her marriage, and even then was shy with the press, but she made an exception for me. To help me launch my career, she agreed to give me an interview—something every reporter in America was dying for.

Months later, I was unable to return the favor and I still feel guilty about it. Jackie called me on behalf of her sister, Lee Bouvier, who worked for one of the fashion magazines. Lee was doing a series on interesting young Washington couples, and Jackie and Jack had agreed to participate.

"Would you and Archie agree to be photographed for the series?" she asked. Of course I wanted to do it—not only to oblige Jackie, but also because I thought it a great compliment. But Archie was under CIA discipline and any publicity, even favorable, was frowned on. I had to say no, and couldn't even say why. I don't remember what silly excuse I gave Jackie, but I felt I had let her down.

Jackie's generosity to me immediately changed my life. My

editors took notice, and during the next few months I managed to get more exclusive interviews and stories. After analyzing the women's section I realized there was a place for me. No one was mining the rich ore of the diplomatic world, and few reporters had my contacts. So after a six months' apprenticeship, the *Star* made me a columnist.

We called the new column "Diplomatically Speaking," and my beat was the State Department, the diplomatic corps, and state visits—the same "beat" that Ronald Reagan would assign me to some thirty years later.

At the time, Betty Beale was the *Star*'s famous society columnist. A tall, imposing woman always accompanied by a tiny Chihuahua called Pogo, she was much too exalted to come to the office, except occasionally to drop off copy. I was worried that Betty would regard me as youthful competition and a threat to her own position. But just the opposite occurred. Betty was my greatest champion. She threw stories my way, she encouraged me, she introduced me to all her friends; in short, she behaved with enormous class.

On the theory that the route to success was to build a better mousetrap, I approached the reporting of social events differently. Until then, society reporters simply described the food, flowers, decor, clothes, and entertainment, and gave a complete list of guests. They did not look for the political or international implications of who was there and who wasn't, who spoke to whom and who didn't. But being married to Archie and having served abroad in a diplomatic post gave me a broader perspective on these events.

I usually wrote a Sunday feature as well. One of my earliest stories was a full-page article on Mrs. Woodrow Wilson, whom I discovered alive and well, but more or less a recluse. I talked her into an interview, which was considered quite a scoop. And from our files I selected five portrait shots which showed her from a young girl to the present—a nice layout. I later received a pained letter from Mrs. Wilson complimenting me on the story but adding, "more in sorrow than in anger," that the earliest photo was not of her, but of the first Mrs. Wilson.

My editors did not let me off lightly on that one. But gradually I improved, and wrote home: "Got a nice compliment from my boss recently—said I was a real credit to the *Star* and that I had made more progress, faster than anyone he had ever seen."

I even made the front page from time to time. Ambassador Joseph E. Davies called me one broiling June day to say he had an exclusive story he wanted to give me. He had decided to leave his palatial estate, Tregaron, to the U.S. government to be used as a residence for the Vice President. He wanted me to come to his house immediately.

"But, Ambassador Davies," I wailed. "I can't come now. I look so tacky!" I was dying of the heat and had worn an old cotton dress to work, knowing I had no outside engagements.

The entire office had heard about my reply even before I got off the phone—and between the ribbing and the chastising for not reacting like "Brenda Starr, reporter," I thought I'd never hear the end of it. Anyway, tacky dress or no, I went, and my story made the front page—with a two-column headline above the fold. (Alas, the government turned down the offer, and instead put the Vice President in the inadequate house at the Naval Observatory.)

I worked for the *Star* during the Eisenhower era, and my columns form a chronicle that makes an interesting comparison with the Reagan administration, thirty years later.

Eisenhower and Reagan were the only two-term presidents since Franklin Roosevelt, and both were Republicans. Their presidencies were popular and relatively tranquil. Both were detached administrators, and both had a sense of the importance of the ceremonial and traditional. But the atmosphere was quite different.

In Eisenhower's day, we seemed to have good relations with almost all the countries of the world, except for those behind the Iron Curtain and China. The countries of South and Central America, usually right-wing dictatorships, were stable; there were no Cubas or Nicaraguas, no drug-plagued Colombias or Perus. The African nations—both the French-dominated ones of North Africa and sub-Saharan, black Africa—were emerging, and we greeted their independence with applause and hope. The Arab states were becoming prosperous; the Middle East had not yet seen anarchy and terrorism. Europe had recovered from World War II, Japan as well, and Indochina was not yet devastated by the Vietnam war that would also destroy the fabric of American society. The hints of what was to come were undoubtedly obvious, but as a reporter in the fifties, I was far removed from Vietnam, drugs, civil rights turmoil, the sexual revolution, and the women's movement.

It was in retrospect a "kinder, gentler world." And it was a kinder, gentler journalism we practiced. We were not playing "Gotcha"; we were not investigative reporters manqué; we were not looking for sexual revelations; we did not regard all public servants as rogues waiting to dip their hand in the till.

It was an era of famous hostesses and *salonières*, and one of them was Alice Longworth, Archie's aunt. We had a tacit understanding that I would never report anything about Mrs. Longworth's dinners, but thanks to her I came to know the Washington establishment. Even Presidents came to her parties, and her stamp of approval meant that Archie and I were also persona grata in the salons of the "three B's"—Mrs. Robert Woods Bliss, Mrs. Robert Low Bacon, and Mrs. Truxton Beale.

Mrs. Gifford Pinchot was yet another of these ladies who were old world and old money, and had seen many a politician and parvenu come and go. They never gave a damn about big money or flashy parties, but people would kill to get into their good graces.

We must have dined with Mrs. Longworth dozens of times, and the menu was always the same—crab soup, roast filet of beef with tiny potatoes and a vegetable or two, miniature biscuits, salad and cheese, and the best crème brulée in the world. Delicious French wines always accompanied the meal, and the long table was laid with a lace cloth, enough silver to stock Tiffany's, and the finest Baccarat glasses.

Daisy Harriman, who by that time was in her eighties, still had a political salon for Democrats. But it was not easy to compete with Mrs. L. and the three B's, who were all Republicans. (It would be decades before another Harriman—the beauteous Pamela—would take Daisy's place.)

Another breed of hostess—Perle Mesta, Gwen Cafritz, Polly Guggenheim, Mrs. Marjorie Merriweather Post—were also making their mark. In contrast to the old-world ladies who avoided publicity and thought it unseemly, this new type courted the press.

I did not care for Mrs. Mesta; she was tough and had a mean streak, but she gave a helluva party. Mrs. Post was another cool customer, admirable, but not very lovable. She preferred square dances with handsome young boys brought in to amuse the septuagenarian ladies or incredibly grand and pretentious dinners. Polly Guggenheim (now Mrs. John A. Logan) was and still is the nicest, a really generous and sweet woman. But the one who amused me most was Mrs. Cafritz, with her Zsa Zsa Gabor accent and quick wit.

I covered a party at Mrs. Cafritz's the day the Russians sent up Sputnik, the first earth satellite. "What do you think of that?" I asked her.

In a flash she said in her throaty voice, "Vell, dahlink, I'm not too upset about it. After all, the Russians have so many satellites—it's just one more." (She was referring, of course, to the countries of Eastern Europe.)

As a columnist, one learns quickly about the power of the press. Determined social climbers never let up on the courting, the invitations, the compliments, and even the gifts, many of which I returned. I had the power to hurt people, even to ruin their lives, but instead, the job made me more conscious of human frailty, and I made the extra effort to be fair. I had no personal vendetta, and tried not to let my likes and dislikes show.

Today most ambassadors and state visitors arrive in Washington by plane, but in the 1950s I spent a lot of time at Union Station covering the arrival of VIPs. Official visitors always stayed at Blair House, the only exception being the Queen of England and Prince Philip on their first state visit in 1957, when they stayed in the White House.

1

2

1 and 2. My mother's grandfather, Mohammed Dweik and her great-uncle Najib Choucair, a leader in the Arab
Nationalist movement.
3. A proud papa shows off his firstborn in
front of his store in Kingsport, Tennessee.
4. My parents' favorite photo of me and
my younger sister, Kay.
5. At age 20 with my mother and grandmother during a visit to Beirut.

3

4

5

MAURICE TABET

6

7

6 and 7. My mother and father, Najla and Saleem Showker.
8. Sweet sixteen and a junior in high school.
9. In the Lebanese mountains during Vassar's summer break.

8

9

10

10. Archie, the first time I saw him, May 20, 1950.
11 and 12. Grace and Archibald Roosevelt, Sr., my mother- and father-in-law, during World War Two.

11

12

TWO PHOTOS: WALTER SCOTT SHINN

13

13. Our wedding day September 1, 1950.
14. Posing for a Pond's ad at age 21.
15. At thirty.
16. At forty.
17. At fifty.

14

LOUISE DAHL-WOLFE

15

16 TWO PHOTOS: AMER–VENTOSA

NORMAN PARKINSON

17

18

18. At the Williamsburg Economic Summit, I run to catch up with France's President Mitterrand and Japan's Prime Minister Nakasone. Behind Mitterrand, his ubiquitous interpreter, Christopher Thiery.

19. Receiving instructions from Secretary of State Shultz during the celebration of the centennial of the Statue of Liberty.

19

20. President and Mrs. Reagan with Archie and me at a White House reception, July 1986.
21. A tea break at Winfield House, the American ambassador's residence in London, provoked this inscription from the President.

Dear Lucky – Hurry! The King is almost here!
Warm Regards Ronald Reagan

22

23

22. Secretary Shultz and I watch Soviet Foreign Minister Eduard Shevardnadze sign the President's guest book in the Roosevelt Room of the White House. Directly behind me are Deputy Foreign Minister Aleksandr A. Bessmertnykh and Soviet Ambassador Yuri Dubinin.

23. Canadian Prime Minister Brian Mulroney and his wife, Mila, with whom I shared many happy moments.

24. That woman holding the flowers was not Mrs. Gorbachev, as most television viewers thought.

25. The Vice President and Mrs. Bush at a white-tie gala at the National Gallery of Art honoring Paul Mellon.

24

25

26

27

26. The President could reduce me to stitches.
27. With David Rockefeller at a Malcolm Forbes party in New Jersey.
28. President Reagan and a special visitor, the late President Napoleón Duarte of El Salvador.

28

29 and 30. Two of my favorite monarchs—King Juan Carlos with Queen Sofia of Spain arriving at Andrews Air Force base and King Hussein of Jordan in the Roosevelt Room, with Teddy's portrait in the background.

30

31

32

31. The Chief of Protocol in her office.
32. Malcolm Forbes, Astrid Forbes, Secretary Shultz, myself, and Kip Forbes, wearing the Forbes tartan, at a party honoring Malcolm at Blair House.
33. On the front steps of Blair House, the President's guest house, with the decorators, Mario Buatta (standing) and Mark Hampton.
Flying in style! 34. On *Air Force One,* en route to the United Nations General Assembly in New York. 35. With Barbara Bush on *Air Force Two*.

33

34
35

38

39

36. The Queen and Prince Philip visit California. Mike Deaver and I escort them.
37. An intense moment with Chief of Staff Don Regan and Vice President Bush.
38. With Chinese Premier Zhao Ziyang on a carriage ride in Williamsburg, Virginia.
39. Our tall president welcomes an even taller visitor—the six-foot-eleven President Diouf of Senegal.
40. Showing the flag at the launching of the USS *Theodore Roosevelt*, as guest of Defense Secretary Caspar Weinberger.

40

To Ambassador Selwa Roosevelt.

Dear Lucky: What a superb
job you have done with Lasting Thanks
Dec. 15, 1988
George Bush

41

41. A gracious goodbye from the new president.

Presidents Kubitschek of Brazil and Sukarno of Indonesia, Prime Ministers Eden of Great Britain, Menzies of Australia, and Mollet of France, the Sultan of Morocco, and the Emperor of Ethiopia all came to Washington, and I covered their visits.

In the fifties Washington had no Kennedy Center, hence almost no opera or ballet and very little theater. The cultural life of the city generally revolved around certain embassies and private homes where dinners were followed by musicales, one of the most memorable being a recital by Maria Callas at the Italian Embassy. Many embassies had ballrooms which they actually used for their original purpose—the Spanish, Italian, Brazilian, Colombian, Venezuelan, Cuban, to name a few. I recently ran across a headline which I'm sure could never appear today: "Residential Society Attends Gay Ball."

On my beat I also interviewed many celebrities—Margot Fonteyn, Cantinflas, Rosalind Russell, Sophia Loren, Lady Nancy Astor, Dame Edith Sitwell, the Maharani of Jaipur, and countless others.

Everything I learned as a journalist would later stand me in good stead as Chief of Protocol. Shortly after assuming office, I received an inquiry from Senator Claiborne Pell, asking for guidance on how to wear a certain decoration. The only reference I had at hand was an article I had written on the subject in 1957.

Being married to a CIA official and writing a column were not very compatible. However, Archie's cover was the State Department, so to the outside world our careers seemed synergistic. Early on we made a pact. He would tell me no secrets, and I would tell him nothing about what I planned to write. Thus, if I learned something legitimately from one of my own sources, he could not be blamed.

Most of the time this worked, but I almost got Archie fired when I revealed an ambassadorial appointment before the White House was ready to make the announcement. It was a front-page story and when Secretary of State John Foster Dulles saw it, with my byline, he immediately called his brother, Allen Dulles, head of the CIA, and demanded Archie's scalp. Of course, I could not reveal my source, a senior State Department official very close to Foster Dulles. To protect Archie, I asked the officer if he would confess to Dulles that he was the source. I shall always be grateful to him for bailing me out.

Three decades later it was tit for tat. My job as Chief of Protocol required me to be discreet; Archie, liberated from the CIA, wrote his autobiography and could say what he liked, within security bounds. We were asked to give a joint interview in connection with his book's publication. I should have smelled a rat—but since my journalistic colleagues had always treated me honorably, I had no reason to think we were stepping into a trap.

In any case, the interviewer started off by asking Archie the two questions that were sure to cause embarrassment: one about Israeli intelligence and another about the Soviet KGB. In both cases I interrupted to head off his answers because I knew that at about the time the article would appear, I would have as visitors Israel's Prime Minister Shamir and Russia's Eduard Shevardnadze. The reporter became exasperated and did a number on me, and I doubt if I will ever live down the bitchiness of that article.

Archie's job took him overseas frequently, and I often had trouble explaining his absences. I wrote Archie, "You know, it's getting a little embarrassing to tell people you're away all the time—people must think we've had a quarrel or something."

I also worried about his safety. Riots and revolutions seemed to follow him; he flew in dangerous airplanes held together by luck and by God. During those years he led a charmed life—he never picked up strange illnesses on these trips, and somehow managed not to get arrested nor have his true missions exposed.

Archie's CIA career always took precedence over my own. I would have had it no other way. But after four exciting years in Washington we were assigned to Madrid, and reluctantly I had to abandon journalism.

Leaving the *Star* to follow my husband to Madrid was one of the sadnesses that came with our CIA life. No one who worked for the *Star* ever forgot the fun and camaraderie of that newsroom. I had to accept the end of this happy interlude, knowing it would never be recaptured. We sailed for Spain on a liner departing from New Jersey, and in our stateroom I found the following telegram:

"Lunch bunch in mourning. All balls cancelled. Buffets draped in black. Feel Hoboken hopelessly unsuitable launching platform our top-drawer diplomatic correspondent. It's tacky, that's what. Fondest love and warmest wishes. Mary McGrory."

EIGHTEEN

Spain—the Love of My Life

S PAIN, WITH ITS DRAMA and passion, was the great love of my life. I was seduced almost from the day we arrived in Madrid, and my ardor has never abated. The four years in Spain— where I found my real roots and discovered with joy the Spanish language and culture—were probably the best preparation I could have had for being Chief of Protocol. And it almost didn't happen.

Archie came home one day to tell me that our next assignment abroad would be Madrid. He was not happy about it, and wanted to turn it down. "Imagine sending me to one of the few countries where I don't speak the language," he said, baffled and disgusted. "I've spent so much of my life studying the Middle East—what do I know about Spain?"

But I was delighted. "Archie, you will learn the language in three months [which he did], and everything you know about the Arab world and other Middle East cultures is a great preparation for Spain. After all, the Arabs ruled Spain for eight hundred years."

The CIA was not so stupid after all, and this assignment tied in with my thinking completely—Archie and I should avoid being identified with only one part of the world. Archie needed to broaden his scope so that no one could accuse him of being parochial or heavily influenced by his marriage to me.

I also saw Spain as the intellectual and emotional bridge between my own world and that of my ancestors. Arab civilization reached its zenith in Spain; and it was from Spain that the discovery of America and the conquest of the New World began.

That omniscient and kindly God was hard at work again, and who were we to question this strange new turn in our lives!

We arrived in Madrid in the spring of 1958. Archie was to be a special assistant to Ambassador John Davis Lodge. The ambassador and his wife Francesca, unlike some of our State Department colleagues, believed in Archie's mission and gave him strong support. We made great strides in getting to know the Spanish and immediately plunged into the thick of Madrid life.

These were probably the happiest and most carefree years of our lives. Being a second and younger wife has many advantages. Archie looked upon me as his child and loved to indulge me. It took very little money to live well in Madrid, and we did.

We found the perfect apartment on the tree-lined Calle Velázquez—double drawing room, study, dining room, four bedrooms, five baths, servants' rooms and bath, kitchen, pantry, and a flower-filled terrace winding around three sides of the apartment.

Once the apartment was furnished, we decided to give our first grand dinner, complete with a small orchestra for dancing. We invited several ministers of the Franco government, and several grandees—the haute aristocracy of Spain.

The future Chief of Protocol did not have an auspicious beginning as far as Spanish protocol was concerned. A few days before the party I discussed the seating with my newest best friend, Madrid lawyer Gregorio Marañón, son and namesake of one of Spain's most distinguished intellectuals. When he saw the list of acceptances he shook his head and with typical Spanish hyperbole said, "*Es un desastre.*"

"What do you mean, disaster? It isn't often so many distinguished people come to dinner with a fairly junior embassy official," I said.

"Aha! But we Spaniards take matters of protocol very seriously, and there is no way you can seat this dinner without half of your guests leaving in indignation."

Gregorio explained that a protocol battle was being fought out between the ministers appointed by Franco and the titled aristocrats—those dukes, marqueses, counts, etc., who had been given by the Spanish kings the highest distinction of the nobility— "grandee of Spain." The aristocracy guarded their prerogatives jealously. They were never fond of Franco but simply tolerated him, waiting for the King to return. And to show both their independence and their contempt for the Franco regime, they refused to accept being outranked by politicians.

Into this controversy I had innocently plunged. How would I save the evening? I remember the words of a French diplomat who told me, "When you see a protocol disaster looming, never run away—just walk around it."

My "way around it" was to write in gold ink on chic black matchbook covers the name of each female guest. I threw them all in a silver bowl and the men then drew one for their dinner partner and the number of their table. No one had ever done such a thing in protocol-conscious Madrid, but the evening was a great success and other hostesses began copying me.

Spain was the most exciting learning experience of my life. Within three months we both were able to speak Spanish— Archie's grammar perfect, and mine decidedly imperfect, but valiant and voluble.

Archie's job required him to travel and meet people all over Spain: Segovia, Ávila, Salamanca, Mérida, Valladolid, Seville, Granada, Cordova, Málaga, Santiago de Compostela, Santander, Bilbao, Pamplona—names that roll off the tongue, cities as beautiful as they sound.

We found a marvelous pretext for our journeys. Each weekend we chose four or five castles to visit—based on information from the Amigos de los Castillos de España, an organization dedicated to preserving the two thousand castles that dot the Spanish landscape. Thus we would find ourselves in a small village, where no strangers ever came, climbing over the ruins of an ancient castle—Fuensaldaña, Torrelobatón, Peñafiel.

Usually the *alcalde*, the mayor of the village, would drape his ribbon of office with its gold medallion over his peasant work clothes and come to greet us. Some villagers had never seen a large American car before, and our driver, puffing up his own prestige, liked to inform them that we were *"extranjeros muy importantes."*

In these villages we learned the meaning of Spanish pride. They always offered us hospitality—food, wine, whatever they could. They never apologized for their modest homes, their threadbare clothes, or their ignorance of the wider world—some were not exactly sure where America was. Their manners were perfect; their carriage erect; they spoke with the same accent as the duchesses and marqueses for whom many of them worked. In one village a portly red-faced character insisted we sample several glasses of wine from the *vendimia*, the grape harvest. As I expressed effusive thanks for his hospitality, he made a short bow, kissed my hand, and said, *"Señora, nosotros somos los servidores de la humanidad."*

Although we saw much poverty, we also witnessed the economic miracle in progress that would take Spain from a backward agrarian economy to one of the largest industrial powers in the world even before Franco died.

Archie was in touch with most of the opposition, though his primary job was to deal with the government. Through monarchists such as the late Count of Fontanar, we met the exiled King in Portugal and came to know his son, Prince Juan Carlos. Thus, we were not strangers when we saw King Juan Carlos many years later. The very tall, slightly awkward young Prince had grown into the handsome, self-assured monarch who kept Spain's fledgling democracy from disintegrating in its first tentative years.

We also came to know some of the socialists, whom we saw and entertained less publicly since their liberty depended on their discretion.

The pain of the Civil War had permanently seared every Spaniard's psyche, no matter where their sympathies lay. Some of the giant intellects of Spain, such as Dr. Gregorio Marañón—who had spent much of the Civil War in exile in France—had finally been allowed to return.

Dr. Marañón's *cigarral* (country house) in Toledo was a magnet for intellectuals from all over the world, and his son invited us early in our stay to spend a Sunday in Toledo—the city that is, above all others, the essence of Spain.

Toledo had been a center of Christian, Moorish, and Jewish civilizations, all blending happily and seamlessly together until religious bigots expelled the Moors and Jews from the city beginning in the twelfth century. Slowly Toledo declined as a cultural and financial center, the mosques disappeared, the synagogues fell into disrepair. (They have been restored under the present regime.)

We wanted to meet Dr. Marañón more than any person in Spain, and we were not disappointed. Meeting him, I felt I had wasted all my life. "How lazy most of us are!" I wrote in my diary. "Dr. Marañón practices medicine in the morning, writes his books in the afternoon, maintains a vast correspondence, reads prodigiously, and still has time for callers from all over the world. He was so relaxed, so genuinely glad to receive us. He has the kindest eyes—eyes reflecting the compassion that comes with wisdom and the forgiveness which comes with real tolerance."

The *cigarral* dated from the 1600s and was restored by Dr. Marañón in the 1920s. Today it is a national monument. After that first visit I wrote, "From the terraces of the Marañón house one gets a tremendous view of Toledo, with those same El Greco clouds hovering over the city. As the sun sets it seems to fall just on the city, as if to highlight some rare jewel. And when the sun reluctantly departs, it leaves behind a blue sky the color of lapis lazuli—a sky I've never seen before."

We spent many leisurely Sundays there with Dr. Marañón and his family—for whom I felt a deep love and a special affinity.

"I am sure that you and I played together as children here four hundred years ago," his son Gregorio once said to me. I knew what he meant. They had discovered the remains of an Arab structure which once stood on the spot.

In Toledo I was not a stranger; I had found still another home.

NINETEEN

London

AFTER JOHN F. KENNEDY became President, Archie began to feel restless in Madrid; all his friends from Groton and Harvard were now running the government—Kennedy himself had been a classmate at Harvard. The New Frontier was for our generation. The new First Lady was my contemporary and friend.

Archie asked for an assignment in Washington, and in the summer of 1961 we were back in America. I decided not to seek another job in journalism, so, hoping to expand my horizons, I went to see Roger L. Stevens, the newly appointed head of the National Cultural Center (later to become the John F. Kennedy Center for the Performing Arts). I carried a letter of recommendation from Senator Claiborne Pell, a Democrat and an old friend.

Roger hired me as his special assistant to help with fundraising for the new center. At that time, detractors produced a thousand reasons why the philistines of Washington did not need a cultural center. Traveling around the country, I encountered strong resistance to funding a Washington project. "We have our own local arts groups in desperate financial straits. Why should we send money to Washington—it should be the other way around!"

Roger was a great boss, and it was a challenge to be in on the ground floor of a project which in ten years changed Washington from a cultural desert to a fertile and blooming garden of the arts. I had found a new career.

But not for long. I was in Dallas, on a mission for Roger, when I got a call from Archie.

"How soon can we pack up and be on our way to London?" he asked. It never occurred to him to ask if I wanted to go. The London station chief is the most important overseas job in the Agency and global in scope. For Archie, only forty-four at the time, this was an enormous opportunity.

For me it was a heartbreak. We had not been home a year, I had just gotten settled into our house, and I loved my job. Once again, I would have to move and start a new life—the sixth time in a dozen years.

"When must we leave?"

"The sooner the better. The present station chief is too ill to continue, and John McCone [Director of the CIA] wants me there yesterday."

This time I thought my guardian angel had deserted me. But he was taking good care of Archie, so I couldn't complain.

The gloomy gray days that greeted us on our arrival in Britain did nothing to gladden my Mediterranean heart. It was a wet spring, even for London, and the circumstances of our assignment were particularly sad. Archie's predecessor was too ill to leave his house, which we were to take over, so we camped out in a dingy furnished flat, cold and miserable.

My depression was exacerbated when I met the wives of the officials Archie would be in liaison with. With only one or two exceptions (the most notable being Lady Antonia Fraser, then married to the Minister for Aviation), they were a generation or so older than I, then just thirty-three. They seemed proper and middle-class and pinched—pinched from the devastating World War, from socialism and the high taxes exacted to support it, pinched from constantly living on the edge and trying to "keep up appearances." They did not laugh easily, they spoke in hushed voices, and I had the feeling—for the first time since leaving Tennessee—that once again I was "too exotic by half."

Nonsense, of course. It took about nine months for me to realize what a wonderful gift we had been given. Where Spain was a mindless passion, overwhelmingly sensual, London was a serious and lasting love, more cerebral and perhaps more mature. Eventually I would meet many of my contemporaries, and would fall into a circle of writers, actors, and producers, as well as the usual politicians and diplomats. Archie decided to join the fusty-musty Garrick Club, preferring arts and literary figures to the more fashionable aristocrats of Boodle's or White's.

David K. E. Bruce was our ambassador, and Archie's mentor—a prince of a man, a Virginia gentleman, brilliant, cultivated, and witty. Evangeline Bruce—his much younger, beautiful, and elegant wife—became my teacher, and from her I learned how to entertain on a grand scale, how to run a large establishment. And make no mistake about it, being an ambassador's wife is a tough administrative job.

One of London's great hostesses, Fleur Cowles, took Archie and me under her wing. The wife of lumber tycoon Tom Montague Meyer, Fleur excelled as a painter, writer, editor, decorator, gardener, philanthropist, and patron of the arts. Her "chambers" in Albany, an elegant eighteenth-century building that had once been the home of Lady Caroline Lamb, in the heart of Piccadilly, and her enchanting country house in Sussex were magnets for the literati and glitterati.

Fleur taught me that a great hostess must be a catalyst, bringing together people whose paths might not otherwise cross. Herself an American and formerly married to media mogul Gardner Cowles, Fleur specialized in Anglo-American cross-pollination. Politicians met actors, writers met diplomats, royals met talented young musicians and painters Fleur was trying to help.

Prime Ministers Edwin Heath and James Callaghan were frequent guests. Lilli Palmer and her husband, actor Carlos Thompson, became friends of ours thanks to Fleur, as did King Constantine and Queen Anne-Marie of Greece.

One weekend, Rebecca West gave me a lift down to Fleur's Sussex house, where she and I were the only guests. She kept up a running commentary, and she was not shy about her opinions.

"If I could delicately desecrate a few graves," Dame Rebecca said, "Nehru's would be my first choice." She found him arrogant and supercilious. She liked Allen Dulles and Adlai Stevenson, but thought the latter would have been a terrible President. She feuded with the Liberal establishment and mentioned that the beautiful British hostess Pamela Berry had seduced Gaitskell, "just before the end."

From the intelligence point of view, London was gripping. Archie and I were fascinated by the British upper-class Soviet spy syndrome. Guy Burgess, Donald Maclean, and Kim Philby had all been unmasked. Eleanor Philby had sought out Archie as an old friend when she returned from Moscow, and tearfully told him that her husband was having an affair with Mrs. Maclean. We knew that among the men Archie saw frequently were more traitors, still to be exposed. My own suspect was Sir Roger Hollis, the head of MI5, the British equivalent of the FBI. Since our stay in London, books have been written on the subject, and facts have been marshaled to support either his innocence or his guilt.

My suspicions began when we were invited to spend a weekend with the Hollises in Wells, the site of one of the most beautiful cathedrals in England. Sir Roger's antecedents were eminently respectable—his father had been Canon of Wells Cathedral and later Bishop of Taunton.

Sir Roger and his wife, a frumpy no-nonsense type, were generous hosts, plying us with good food and especially good red wine. I remember noting, as Sir Roger refilled our glasses, a mocking look in his eyes, a certain smugness.

We talked quite a lot about spies. And I ventured the opinion that men who lead double lives in the end expose themselves, if only the people around them cared to observe.

He seemed intrigued, but guarded. I cannot remember just what he said that sent up signals, but as we returned to London that Sunday I said to Archie, "That man is hiding something. Be careful. He could be the spy you are all looking for."

This was before any word had leaked about him. My reaction was pure intuition and observation of character. Shortly thereafter, Sir Roger retired and ran off with his secretary, whom he later married. Archie was convinced that what I had sensed was a man involved in extramarital dalliance rather than espionage. And Archie's view was supported by Prime Minister Thatcher, who told Parliament that an official inquiry had cleared Hollis of all charges of espionage.

I never understood the spy novels that characterize master spies as frightened and full of self-doubt. Actually, to be a successful spy one has to have an actor's aplomb, the mental adroitness of a trial lawyer, and the hypocrisy of a sinning evangelist.

When Roger Hollis was confronted by some of his colleagues with their purported evidence that he was a Soviet agent, they hoped that he would crack and confess. On the contrary, he is reported to have said, "Well, gentlemen, I suppose this means that you think I am a spy?"

Yes, they answered.

"Hmm, that's very interesting," he said, and glancing at his watch, added, "Now, if you'll excuse me, I have another engagement."

Despite the spy scandals, the relationship with the British was an excellent and productive one for both sides—for example, during the Cuban missile crisis in 1962.

One day Archie informed me that he had received instructions to proceed with Ambassador Bruce in the middle of the night to a remote air base and await the arrival of an important colleague from Washington. If Archie had any idea what it was about, he did not tell me, but naturally I was apprehensive. Anything that hush-hush had to be cosmic. And it was. The CIA had irrefutable evidence that the Soviets were placing offensive missiles in Cuba, and the proof was being hand-carried to London to brief our allies, so that we would have their support for whatever action we might take—even war.

Ambassador Bruce informed the British government, and Archie briefed the intelligence community. But, Archie pointed out, it was also important to brief the opposition Labour Party leaders and the press. I remember Hugh Gaitskell and George Brown coming to our house the next evening, and leaving pensive and serious. The usually jovial Brown, who was at times in his cups, was dead sober. The British stood by us through the crisis, both Labourites and Conservatives, and David Bruce and possibly Archie helped bring this about.

We were almost five years in the British capital, the most sophisticated city we would ever live in. "Swinging London" in the sixties set the pace in theater, opera, and ballet—and even in rock music (the Beatles) and television (*That Was the Week That Was*). Sir Laurence Olivier headed the National Theatre, and we saw him in many famous productions, most memorably *Othello*. Some twenty years later, shortly before his death, I helped persuade the Reagans to give a dinner in his honor at the White House.

At Covent Garden, Margot Fonteyn and Rudolph Nureyev were the most charismatic dance duo of our time. And I can never forget Maria Callas' devastating Tosca, with Tito Gobbi as Scarpia, in the Franco Zeffirelli production that would make operatic history.

I came to love everything about England except weekends in the country. Archie had a passel of relatives there, each with a country place, and each determined to have us visit.

Our first foray took us to the Cotswolds, to see a cousin, Sir Humphrey Clarke, and his mother, Lady Clarke, in their Elizabethan manor house. What with socialism and taxes, the Clarkes kept only one corner of the house going—maintained by a few creaky and ancient retainers.

Even in June the house was bitter cold, heated only by fireplaces. We welcomed the hot-water bottles in our beds until they cooled down, making the clammy sheets seem even damper. And to visit the loo meant a trip down a dimly lit icy corridor. The food traveled a long way from the kitchen, so there was no way it could arrive hot, and the wine was served at room temperature— meaning the burgundy, though superb, had a nice chill!

Humphrey, with his portly figure, florid face, protruding teeth, and upper-class stutter, could have been the original Bertie Wooster. His charming and rich French mistress, Arlette, shared his passion for horses, and was the subject of volumes of erotic poetry composed by Humphrey and privately printed. ("Ope thy thighs" was one of the more forgettable lines.)

That first experience soured me on country weekends, but finally by late August Archie had persuaded me to accept an invitation from Lady Manvers—a Roosevelt relation who had a Victorian "medieval" castle, Thoresby Hall, near Sherwood Forest in Nottinghamshire.

Shortly after our arrival we joined Lady Manvers in her drawing room, lured to the roaring fire. I was still in my tweed suit and a polo coat, which I could not bring myself to remove. Unaware that my teeth were chattering, Lady Manvers threw open the windows, allowing arctic winds to sweep through the enormous room. "It does get so stuffy in the summer," she muttered.

Dear Lady Manvers could never understand why we refused all future invitations. But we did enjoy weekends with an American cousin, Mrs. Mervyn Herbert, and made friends with her neighbor Auberon Waugh, a writer as iconoclastic as his famous father, Evelyn Waugh.

Many years later, on a return visit to London, Auberon Waugh and his wife, Lady Teresa, invited me to Somerset for the first weekend in October. His father had died and Bron had inherited his enormous eighteenth-century country house, Combe Florey.

On the train down, Bron said, "Lucky, I know how you Americans feel about the cold—you'll be happy to know that we have recently installed central heat."

Music to my ears. As we walked into the house and the familiar damp cold assaulted my senses, Bron said, "Oh, I forgot to mention. We don't turn on the heat until October fifteenth."

We were in England during one of the greatest national tragedies of our time—the assassination of President Kennedy. Archie and I, that fateful Friday, had left for Bonn to visit our ambassador to Germany, George McGhee, and his wife. It was their twenty-fifth wedding anniversary and they had planned a white-tie ball. We were staying in the embassy, and that evening, as we came down in our fancy clothes, the first reports started to come in from

Dallas. For George McGhee, it was a particularly bitter and cruel evening—he and his family were from Dallas. Soon Germans from all walks of life were gathered outside the embassy, some leaving messages of condolence, others just standing in silent vigil.

We returned to London the next morning, and a few days after that I wrote Mother: "These days have been so heartbreaking that I don't know how we shall ever laugh again . . . I have suffered every moment for Jackie and those two adorable little ones—her magnificent courage, in the end, gave us all some hope."

We attended the memorial service for the President in St. Paul's Cathedral. We were also comforted by the extraordinary outpouring of sympathy and a shared sense of loss from so many British friends.

Another three years passed. Soon it was time to leave London and once more put down roots in Washington. I told Archie that I didn't feel I could ever get up the energy and courage to serve overseas again—and luckily I was not put to the test.

TWENTY

Washington and New Paths

W<small>E RETURNED</small> to Washington for good in the late 1960s. It had been ten years since I last worked on a newspaper, and I felt a great nostalgia for my years as a journalist. The *Washington Post* was now the most important paper in town, and they were willing to let me do features at my own pace. No more daily deadlines, no more going to the office. I could travel with Archie whenever I wanted.

I found a special champion in the editor of the women's section—she liked my work, but thought I needed a friendly nudge. "Lucky, can't you be a little . . . well, *bitchier*," she asked me one day. I knew what she meant. My stories had no edge, no bite. I wasn't a disciple of the "new journalism," in which the writer becomes part of the story.

I remember once comparing notes with the *New York Times'* Charlotte Curtis and she said, not altogether in jest, "I would walk over my own grandmother for a good story." I kept my thoughts to myself, but I had to face the fact that I did not have fire in my belly.

Also, after all those years of writing a column and then another year with the *Post*, I felt I could never again crank up the enthusiasm to write about Washington society, diplomats, entertaining, etc. To me, it was all passé, a language made obsolete by new imperatives—Vietnam especially. I wanted to pursue subjects that would teach me something and help me to grow.

Years before, I had sold my first magazine article to the *Saturday Evening Post* for $2,000. They didn't change a word of it, so I decided, "This is a breeze." However, beginner's luck was a cruel teaser. When I tried again, it took many attempts before I found my niche.

My great good fortune was meeting up with Frank Zachary of *Town & Country* magazine, where I became a contributing editor. Frank was a legendary editor-in-chief who governed by instinct—he trusted his writers and gave them their head. If I said, "Frank, it's the twentieth anniversary of the Russians' departure from Vienna. Let's do a story on what that means to the city now," he, instead of asking for an outline or worrying about the cost, would simply say, "Do it."

I might spend a month in São Paulo or Mexico City, and come back with a twelve-page color spread. I wrote pieces on Mallorca, Madrid, Belgium, the United Arab Emirates, Morocco, and Egypt including a cover story on Mrs. Sadat—wherever Archie's job or my wanderlust took me.

Still, something was missing. Although I was active in many charities in Washington and helped found the Children's Hearing and Speech Center (because of my own partial deafness), I felt it was time to pay some dues.

My father had died of cancer in 1958, and subsequently many of my cousins were also cancer victims. One close relative was diagnosed with cancer in both breasts, and without so much as a second consultation, this woman in her mid-thirties had her breasts, as well as some surrounding tissue, removed.

This shocked me. How was it possible that so brutal an assault on a woman's body could happen without a second thought? Was this necessary? Was a radical mastectomy the only answer to breast cancer? Were there degrees of surgery, depending on the stage of the cancer? And was it possible to have reconstructive surgery? And so began a two-year quest for the answers.

Today, these matters are freely discussed between doctor and patient. But in 1972 the doctors I interviewed told me my questions were frivolous, that I was a dangerous amateur, that I would be responsible for women losing their lives if I persisted in this meddlesome nonsense.

But not Dr. George Crile of the Cleveland Clinic. I flew to Ohio to see him, and with his encouragement wrote a major piece for *Family Circle* magazine, which appeared in November 1974, just at the time when First Lady Betty Ford was diagnosed with breast cancer. Art Hettich, the editor of *Family Circle*, had bought my article after reading the lead, which began: "If cancer of the penis were as prevalent as breast cancer, would our male surgeons so readily lop it off?"

Meanwhile, I had come to the attention of doctors at the Duke University Comprehensive Cancer Center, and was invited to join their advisory board. And so began a phase of my life which would lead me to many hospitals and doctors, working on a variety of articles about cancer and cancer research. Nothing I've ever done has been more rewarding, and while I never wanted any recognition, I was thrilled when the Susan G. Komen Foundation of Dallas presented me with their Betty Ford Award for the advancement of breast cancer research.

This was on October 23, 1985, and President Reagan was hosting a reception in New York City commemorating the fortieth anniversary of the founding of the United Nations. More than twenty heads of state or government were to attend. I had made my commitment to be in Dallas months before, and was scheduled to speak at a sold-out luncheon in my honor. That morning I flew to Dallas, gave my speech, accepted the award, and flew back to New York in time to assist the President with a 7:00 P.M. reception.

I came to see my medical interests as God's way of restoring balance to a life filled with glamour and riches. This medical "education" would also help me deal with the toughest challenges of my life, when Archie, not once but three times, almost died in a series of bizarre medical mishaps.

My medical interests reinforced a strongly held conviction ever since my Vassar days—that a woman's right to a safe and legal abortion was simply not negotiable. I had seen too many women's lives ruined by illegal abortions. And even though I was not a bra-burning feminist, I found it appalling that male legislators and judges all over the country could impose their antediluvian attitudes on the solid majority of women who favored legal abortion.

I lobbied hard for pro-choice positions, and when the *Roe v. Wade* decision was handed down by the Supreme Court in 1973, making abortion legal throughout the United States, I felt that at last the issue had been put to rest.

However, the anti-abortion forces began to marshal their troops, so I decided to join NARAL—the National Abortion Rights Action League—and became a member of their advisory board. In June 1976 I appeared before the Republican platform committee and said, "The reason I am a Republican is the same reason I am for a woman's right to have an abortion. It is because the Republican Party has always taken the lead in upholding individual freedom and personal rights. . . . We do not believe the state has the right to impose either an economic order, philosophical tenets or religious dogma on anyone."

I urged the committee to take abortion out of the political arena and make no reference to abortion in the platform at all. Sadly, I and like-minded Republicans lost that skirmish—and all subsequent platform battles over abortion rights. In addition, a certain stigma became attached to the abortion rights issue. The viciousness of the anti-abortion forces made many women fear risking their careers in government and certain professions, and they began to moderate in public their strongly held private views.

As a medical writer I am dumbfounded by the recent return to the dark ages, as seen in governmental decisions forbidding the use of fetal tissue in medical research and preventing the introduction of important new birth control methods already in use in Europe. It is no surprise that our brightest doctors and scientists reject careers in the National Institutes of Health because they refuse to meet the litmus test of being anti-abortion.

The abortion issue and cancer research took up much of my energy in the seventies. But it is government, and especially foreign policy, that has fascinated me all my life.

I remember even in high school being inspired by the founding fathers, and many who came after them, who articulated noble concepts, framed by minds well schooled in history, philosophy, ethics, religion—men with broad vision, soaring intellects, and a true world view. Men such as Alexander Hamilton and Thomas Jefferson, and a century later Abraham Lincoln, set the tone of our national and international discourse, and we became that beacon to the world that Ronald Reagan so often talked about.

Living in Washington, of course, one gets a ringside view of how government works, how foreign policy is formulated. Alas, it has not always been edifying.

I was often troubled by the amateurishness and ham-handedness of modern-day politicos who dealt with foreign policy. The idea that anyone can frame or execute a coherent foreign policy—his only qualification being loyalty to a political party coupled with a hefty campaign contribution—appalled me. I was amazed that we often sent boobs and boors to foreign countries as ambassadors, while those countries sent us their top people.

Worse still was the increasing encroachment by Congress on the prerogative of the President to conduct foreign policy. Congress had become a debating society in which the participants postured for the benefit of their constituencies without regard to the greater national interest.

Somewhere along the way, we stopped talking about the true greatness of America—somehow we stopped believing it. But two hundred years ago, the American dream was born, and nurtured from generation to generation by those like me who are its beneficiaries.

And so, when Ronald Reagan came on the scene, he struck a responsive chord—I believed in that shining City on the Hill—and when he asked me to join his administration, I was grateful and ready to do my small bit to illuminate the American dream.

PART THREE

The Cast of Characters

TWENTY-ONE

Ronald Reagan

D ON'T LET ANYONE tell you differently. Having the President of the United States to dinner is a big deal.

After I had worked for the President for three years, I finally screwed up my courage and said to him, "Mr. President, I'm dying to have you and the First Lady come to my house for dinner."

"Well, why don't you ask us?" he answered in that refreshing and direct way of his. (One reason I hadn't asked sooner was that I had only recently found time to have curtains made for the living room. I knew the Secret Service would not want him in a room at night without the curtains drawn.)

We scheduled a summer date, when the work load would be lighter. Then came the bad news of his cancer operation and, of course, the date was canceled. But Ronald Reagan never forgets a promise. As soon as he recovered, the dinner was rescheduled for October 14, 1985.

I wanted to keep the party small—a luxury the President was not often permitted—so I decided to have sixteen in all, two round tables of eight. With the Reagans and ourselves, this meant asking only six other couples.

How do you decide whom to ask? To avoid offending all our Washington friends we limited our guest list to out-of-towners— the David Rockefellers, the Willard Butchers, the James L. Fergusons from New York, the John de Bragancas from Winston-Salem, North Carolina, the Nicholas Gages from Boston, and Vane and June Ivanovic, who would fly over from London.

The menu? The Reagans were easy. The President did not like tomatoes, but otherwise they had almost no food taboos. After consulting with Fiona Charlton-Dewar, my party chef, we came up with this: lobster with truffles, followed by quail stuffed with chestnut purée, angel hair pasta, and mushrooms. Dessert was a glorious chocolate and raspberry confection, a specialty of Fiona's. A butler and two waiters were reserved for the night, the centerpieces were ordered—salmon-colored floribunda roses—and I thought I could relax.

Well, not quite. Several weeks before the big event, I had a call from the White House advance office. Shelby Scarbrough, a lovely young woman who later came to work for me in Protocol, was on the line. "Ambassador Roosevelt, could we come to your house to make plans for the President's dinner with you? We would be about twenty people—the Secret Service, White House Communications, etcetera."

And so it began. They inquired about our neighbors. They checked the windows in every room where the President would be, and told me just which curtains should be drawn (in case a sharpshooter was lurking outside). They installed telephone lines for instant communication with the entire world. My two-car garage became the Secret Service outpost, and the downstairs guest room became the holding room for the doctor, the President's military aide, and others who had to be available if needed.

I did balk, however, when the Secret Service wanted to attach an awning with side flaps onto the front of my house which would engulf the President and hide him from public view as he left his car and walked the fifteen feet to the front door.

"That awning will attract so much attention you will have all of Georgetown crowding onto this street, wondering what's going on," I told them. I won this point, and the President and Mrs. Reagan arrived and departed relatively inconspicuously.

By relatively, I mean that about sixty-five people came in his motorcade—several limousines disgorging White House aides and the official photographer, an ambulance carrying both nurse and doctor, Black Marias with Secret Service men armed with assault rifles, the Washington police to keep back traffic and pedestrians, and the ubiquitous press pool known as the "death watch," who ghoulishly follow the President everywhere he goes. Our neighbors tried not to gawk, but I could see them discreetly watching from their windows or front stoops.

Everyone in the presidential entourage, especially the Secret Service agents, were my colleagues; we worked together continuously, and I had enormous respect and affection for them. I couldn't have them in my house, even on duty, without offering them something. So I instructed Fiona to prepare food and drink for an additional forty to be served in the garage.

It was only three months after the President's cancer operation, and Mrs. Reagan was keeping a watchful eye on him. I was asked to keep the evening on schedule so that he could leave at ten thirty.

Dinner went off without a hitch. The President, as always, sang for his supper. A great raconteur, he soon had a circle of guests around him, not wanting to miss a word. The upcoming Geneva summit, his first meeting with Gorbachev, was on everyone's mind, and guests later told me how impressed they had been—that the President showed a much greater command of detail on arms-control issues than they had expected. About SDI, Reagan said, "Doggone, I wish Teddy Kennedy hadn't called it Star Wars. It gives the wrong impression. It's a defensive system, and I've offered to share it with the Russians."

Mrs. Reagan made a beeline for Nick Gage, telling him how much she and the President had loved his book *Eleni* and discussing current Greek politics with him. Later, the President quizzed him about certain details in the book. "Does your sister still have a scar on her foot?" Nick's mother had burned her daughter's foot with a poker, maiming it so that she would not be conscripted by the Greek Communists for their army.

The Reagans had recently returned from California, where the President had been resting and recuperating. He had even gone horseback riding.

"Mr. President," I told him, "you certainly gave everyone a scare—going riding so soon after your operation."

He looked at me more sternly than he ever had. "Lucky, I *had* cancer; I do not have cancer now."

That attitude was the essence of Ronald Reagan. The incurable optimism, the jauntiness not only in his walk but in his heart, drew everyone to him like a Pied Piper. To those who came under his spell, Reagan was magic—a man of such grace and generosity of spirit that one could forgive his failings. Indeed, in him they were endearing. If that sounds fatuous, so be it.

I find it difficult to be objective about the President—in my eyes he did little wrong. His sins, so far as I can fathom, were sins of omission; he was much too tolerant of subordinates who let him down and caused him embarrassment. I disagreed with him strongly on several issues—the most important being abortion and the Middle East—but somehow this did not color my perception of him as a person.

In retrospect, I wish I had been more courageous and raised the abortion issue with him. I, like a lot of other Republican women, was very complacent, and I thought *Roe v. Wade* had decided the issue. The majority of the women appointees and administration wives, if they told the truth, were pro-choice. But I knew that Reagan sincerely believed that abortion was murder.

I wish I had said to him, "Mr. President, I respect your views on abortion, but I beg you to respect mine. I grew up in the years when abortions were illegal. In college, I knew women who had back-alley abortions; I knew a woman who committed suicide rather than have an illegitimate baby; I know women made sterile by botched abortions; and I have seen women blackmailed by sleazy characters from the underworld of illegal abortions.

"We who are pro-choice believe we know what murder really is. Murder is allowing AIDS babies and crack babies to be born, only to die the most painful deaths. Murder is drinking so much that a baby is born deformed. Murder is bringing unwanted children into the world who will die of neglect or from beatings and molestation. Murder is women who will die if abortion is made illegal again.

"Murder is withdrawing funds for birth control as well, from starving Ethiopians, Brazilians, Indians, Egyptians, and millions of others around the world who reproduce themselves at such a rate that they cannot possibly survive. That is murder."

Yes, I wish I had said all this and more. But truthfully, I could not imagine ever raising an unpleasant subject with Ronald Reagan.

One of my most rewarding duties as Chief of Protocol was escorting world leaders to meetings with the President. Over the seven years I did this hundreds of times. I also brought at least fifty foreign ambassadors a year to present their credentials to the President. I rarely saw a world leader or ambassador who did not succumb to the President's charm. In fact, the only one I can remember who seemed impervious was Prime Minister Robert Mugabe of Zimbabwe. He entered the Oval Office with a gloomy expression, and after lunch with the President departed with an even sadder one. This was in 1983, and he never came back. (I later learned that Mugabe and National Security Adviser William Clark had had an unpleasant exchange at lunch, which brought the meal to an abrupt halt.)

I always presented guests to President Reagan at the state dinners, and there again, the guests unfailingly responded to his charisma. But when I first learned that receiving-line introductions were part of my duties, I panicked. I have been totally deaf in my right ear since a bout of measles in childhood, and I knew the President was also deaf in one ear. What if I couldn't hear the names? But it turned out the President and I both favored our left ears. Thus the receiving line was always organized so that the military aide whispered the name in my left ear and I in turn announced the name to the President in *his* good left ear. (I don't think the Reagans were ever aware that I had this handicap.)

The President had that special quality—call it presence for want of a better word. When he entered a room, he dominated it.

His physical presence was commanding—he was six foot one and weighed about 185—but he also exuded authority and success. (He is the only man I ever knew who could look elegant even in a brown suit!)

Much has been made about his being an actor, as if that explained why he was so successful. If so, then he was a much better actor than he was given credit for. He never seemed to be acting to me. My view is that with Ronald Reagan, what you see is what you get. He did not have the enlarged ego one associates with actors—and curiously, he did not exude a sexual awareness that most screen stars seem to have.

He did not "think queer"—an expression my mother-in-law always used to describe people who looked for hidden agendas and ulterior motives. The President had infinite trust in people—obviously too much in some cases, as witness the way he was let down in the Iran-Contra scandal. He was lucky to have Nancy Reagan to protect him from his own guilelessness.

Nothing annoyed me more than those who dismissed him as an "amiable dunce." He was rather canny and had an agile mind; he seemed to me fastidious and organized.

He was not an intellectual, he did not agonize over decisions. Nor did he hang his soul out on the line to dry; he conserved his emotions. I confess, however, that I was surprised that a man who came from soulless Hollywood could actually believe in the literal truth of the Bible, even to the Book of Revelations and the coming of Armageddon.

The President always telephoned to thank me for a birthday or Christmas gift—and the first time it happened, it produced quite a dramatic effect in my office. "Ambassador Roosevelt, it's the President on the line," my secretary Dee Lilly breathlessly announced.

"Which country?" I asked absentmindedly.

"Ours," she said. "President Reagan."

I, who am rarely at a loss for words, always became tongue-tied when talking on the phone with the President. I just couldn't chat, thinking how the leader of the free world had taken time off to express thanks for some modest gift!

Books were my favorite gift to President Reagan. His reaction to Edmund Morris' biography of Theodore Roosevelt tells much about Ronald Reagan. Because of his appreciation of Morris as a historian and writer, he agreed to allow Morris to become a modern-day Boswell, with virtually unlimited access. To write a biography of Reagan, Morris observed him almost daily in the White House, at the Geneva and Moscow summits, and debriefed him after every important event. This reveals to me a President very much at ease with himself. Morris is an acute observer and a writer of integrity. He will not write a puff piece. Yet I feel sure Reagan had no worries or second thoughts about giving Morris such unprecedented access.

When my husband wrote his autobiography, *For Lust of Knowing*, he sent the first copy to the President. A few days later Reagan told me, "I'm halfway through Archie's book and I really am enjoying it." A week after that he told me, "I read every word of Archie's book. Contrary to what most people think, I do read!"

Archie's book appeared just as he celebrated his seventieth birthday, and I asked the President and Mrs. Reagan if they would stop by at a party given by the dean of the diplomatic corps, Swedish Ambassador Count Wilhelm Wachtmeister and the Countess, to mark both the birthday and the publication of the book.

The President told me they would attend. I wanted to surprise Archie, so kept it a secret. But just a few days before the event, I had a call from Deputy Chief of Staff Kenneth Duberstein telling me the legal eagles in the White House had decided that the President should not be in the position of promoting a book. Therefore, the President would not be attending the party.

"Lucky, you know how the President hates to break a promise, so instead of going to the party, he wants you and Archie to come and have tea with him in the Oval Office on the afternoon of Archie's birthday," Ken told me.

So we did. And the President talked mostly about Archie's book—he had been particularly fascinated by Archie's early run-in with the Communists who controlled the American Youth Congress and his attempts to expose them. The President likened this to his own struggle against Communist domination of the Screen Actors Guild. Later he sent Archie a photo of the occasion inscribed "Happy Birthday, Kid."

The President was always very touched by examples of personal courage and suffering, particularly under Communist tyranny. He was really excited about meeting Mme. Nien Cheng the night she was to be his dinner partner at a state dinner. She had just written her extraordinary account of her years of imprisonment in China and the murder of her only daughter during the Cultural Revolution. "What a brave woman," the President commented, full of awe at what she had endured.

To mark my first year with the President, Archie and I decided we wanted to give him some memento of Theodore Roosevelt, whom he very much admired. So we took from our collection a small bronze buffalo skull by the sculptor James L. Clark (1883–1969) and presented it to him. I put the sculpture on his desk along with a letter explaining its provenance. Either the President loved it or he was too tenderhearted to move it. It stayed in that location for several years and appears in most of the photos taken in the Oval Office over that period of time.

Of course, this thrilled us. The President kept very few things on his desk, and we took this as a sign of great attachment to our gift. Then one day I noticed the buffalo head was gone. I asked his assistant Jim Kuhn—one of the nicest men who ever worked in the White House—what happened to it.

"Mrs. Reagan decided to reorganize the President's office," he said. "It was moved, but I'm not sure where to." I never saw it again.

No one, except possibly Nancy Reagan, knew the President's innermost thoughts. He understood that a bit of mystery—a bit of holding back—was both tasteful and wise in a President. Only when he looked at Nancy did one see the barriers drop away. The sight of her made him happy, and there was only tenderness and love in his treatment of her.

Before every arrival ceremony on the South Lawn of the White House, we would wait in the Diplomatic Reception Room for the signal that the visitor was on his way from the hotel or Blair House. Invariably while waiting, the President would envelop the diminutive First Lady in his protective arms, by way of reassuring her before all the pomp and protocol began.

She was equally protective of him. The President objected to wearing his overcoat for these outdoor ceremonies. (Why do so many American men seem to think that no overcoat is a sign of manliness?) But on one occasion Mrs. Reagan's wifely concern almost caused the President to make an embarrassing mistake.

On a cold December morning in 1984 we were waiting inside for the arrival of the President of Venezuela, Jaime Lusinchi. President Reagan was looking his usual dapper self in a dark suit, when an aide stepped forward with his black chesterfield. He waved the aide away.

"Ronnie," said Mrs. Reagan, "it's really cold out there. You've got to wear your overcoat." Mrs. Reagan had on a fur coat and fur hat—something she herself rarely wore.

The President, with an exasperated "Oh, golly, do I have to?" put the coat on to humor his wife, and they walked outside to the ceremony.

I stood behind the reviewing stand, so I had a direct view of the two presidents as they watched the troops march by. Then Reagan stepped up to give his welcoming remarks. He reached in his coat pocket and pulled out the index cards containing his speech. I noticed that he paused a brief moment; I heard him mutter in a low voice, "Uh-oh." Then I saw him put the speech back in his coat pocket, reach under his coat to his suit pocket, and pull out another set of index cards. All the while, he was ad-libbing the first pleasant words of welcome.

After the ceremony, as the two presidents and I walked toward the Oval Office, the President just couldn't contain himself.

"I probably shouldn't tell this," Reagan said to Lusinchi, smiling broadly, "but I just can't resist."

It seems that three weeks earlier, during the visit of the Grand Duke and Duchess of Luxembourg, Nancy had also insisted that the President wear his overcoat. He had not worn it again since that day.

"When I pulled out my speech from the pocket and started to read, it began, 'Your Royal Highnesses.' Thank God I realized in time."

Lusinchi was delighted with the story. And as soon as we got to the Oval Office, I heard him say to his aides in Spanish, "Imagine, how wonderful that the President of the United States would tell this story on himself."

The Reagans' deep concern and protectiveness toward each other showed in so many ways. I will never forget the night of the state dinner for El Salvador's President José Napoleón Duarte. President Reagan knew that Nancy had been diagnosed with breast cancer and would be going in for an operation in two days. Instead of being gloomy he was unusually animated and forthcoming, I later realized, for Nancy's sake.

And what patience the President had! Even in stressful moments he did not show his anger—for example, on the day in June 1982 when he fired Secretary of State Alexander Haig. We had scheduled a credentials ceremony at 1:30 P.M. to present six ambassadors, one right after the other, to the President. I arrived early to see that all was in order—and found the West Wing awash with tension. Presidential aides scurried around, grim-faced and self-important, and one whispered to me that there had just been a dramatic meeting between Haig and the President, who had accepted Haig's resignation as Secretary of State. Haig was drafting his formal resignation letter. Now all that remained was for the President to make the announcement.

"Should we postpone the credentials ceremony?" I asked Charles Tyson, the executive director of the National Security Council.

I was only three months on the job, and didn't realize the President never would have canceled. When I walked into the Oval Office with the first ambassador, Juan Agurcia of Honduras, the President was as genial as ever. No sign of the harried expression everyone else was wearing. He had made his decision, and after the credentials ceremony he went to the White House briefing room and announced Haig's resignation.

Another time, I had a group of ambassadors in tow, when his lovely secretary, Kathy Osborne, warned me that the President had just taken an important phone call and might be a few minutes late. After twenty minutes, I went back to her. "The President is never late, Kathy. What gives?"

"It's his son Michael on the phone." A family crisis. The next day a story appeared in the papers about a wrenching phone call concerning Michael's book, which had deeply upset the President. Nonetheless, when I went in with my first ambassador, the President seemed totally unperturbed.

While waiting outside the President's office, I noticed that often Kathy was typing letters, transcribing them from sheets of yellow legal paper covered with the President's neat handwriting.

"Kathy, why on earth are you typing those letters?" I asked. "Most people would kill to get a handwritten letter from the President of the United States."

"I know," she said. "But the President thinks his handwriting is not very legible, and he wants to make it easier for the recipient."

Years later, I was reminded of this when I read Don Regan's memoirs. He was offended because the President's farewell letter to him was typewritten and, he thought, drafted by staffers. Kathy told me the President had personally composed the letter on the usual yellow legal pad and she had typed it.

One October day in 1987 President Reagan met with Rajiv Gandhi, Prime Minister of India, who had the sensual good looks of a movie star. The stock market had just plummeted some 500 points, and Mrs. Reagan had just had cancer surgery; the President had every reason to appear preoccupied or worried. Not at all. As the two heads of state sat for the inevitable photo op, three waves of American press stormed in, demanding answers to questions about the economy—"Is this the beginning of another 1929?"

Finally, the fourth wave, the Indian press, came in. One of the female reporters announced in a loud voice, "You are the two most handsomest men in the world."

It cracked up the meeting, and the President, loving it, quipped, "Why doesn't our press ever say things like that?"

The President also didn't mind a cheeky retort from others. When I took Prince Bandar of Saudi Arabia to present his credentials as ambassador, the President said to him, "Prince Bandar, I remember the first time we met in 1978. You were in charge of a Saudi team sent to me, as a former governor, to marshal support for the sale of the F-15s to Saudi Arabia. You were just a young air force major. You've come up in the world!"

And Prince Bandar shot right back. "You haven't done so badly yourself, sir. When we first met, you were just an unemployed governor!"

Reagan often used humor to dispel tension, as he did the day that Secretary Shultz came to a meeting in the cabinet room to discuss new initiatives in our relations with the Soviet Union—at that time headed by Yuri Andropov. According to a staffer present, Secretary Shultz began with a stern admonition to the assembled group. Not a word of the discussion was to leak out and swift retribution would come to anyone who did. He cast an intimidating look around the room, and everyone began to feel uncomfortable.

At that point, Reagan looked down, under the table, and said in a warning voice, "And that goes for you too, Yuri." The laughter that followed changed the atmosphere completely.

The worst expletive I ever heard Reagan use was a gentle "By golly"—even when television correspondent Sam Donaldson was at his most rambunctious. Often after the President and his visitor had made departure statements in the usual South Lawn ceremony, Sam would shout impertinent questions at the President. I think the President had a real weakness for Sam. Sometimes he would answer, other times he would pretend or actually not hear (I wasn't sure which), and as we walked into the White House he would shake his head, amused, and say, "That Sam!"

I couldn't imagine swearing in front of the President. And

once when I needed to tell him that a seemingly harmless gesture he had made in a photo was actually an obscene gesture that could start riots in South America, I asked one of the men to tell him.

He probably loved his role as commander-in-chief of the armed forces more than any other, and after every ceremony he would wave to the troops and say, "Thanks, men. You were marvelous as always."

The President was courteous to everyone, but his natural courtliness caused one of the few protocol flaps that ever landed on the front page. It was during the London arrival ceremony with the Queen. As they started to review the troops, he motioned the Queen and Nancy forward and dropped back with Prince Philip. Of course, the heads of state should have been walking together, and the British papers had great sport making the American president look like a boob.

Most of the time, the President's instincts were perfect. He could give a big *abrazo* to a Latin visitor, without any awkwardness. With other nationalities he was more reserved, but always warm and smiling. His firm handshake and strong eye contact seemed to embrace his visitor. Socialist prime ministers Felipe González of Spain and Robert Hawke of Australia got just as warm a reception as Margaret Thatcher or Jacques Chirac, whose politics were closer to his. Indeed, Samora Machel, the late Communist president of Mozambique, was euphoric and bouncing with excitement as we rode back to the hotel after his lunch with Reagan.

But even for so polished a performer as Ronald Reagan it was not always easy to keep his aplomb—for example, when the ambassador from Swaziland, Peter Helemisi Mtetwa, presented his credentials. The ambassador was wearing "ceremonial" dress—a leopard skin covering a bit more than a loincloth, but exposing one shoulder and breast, with feet bare—and carrying a lethal-looking spear in his right hand. I had not been forewarned, so I had no opportunity to send a message to the President's aides. The Secret Service immediately declared that no one, ambassador or not, could take a weapon into the Oval Office. We negotiated that, and I delayed our entrance long enough for someone to go in and warn the President. But I could see the amazement in his eyes, and I'm sure he wondered, as did I, how the ambassador managed to avoid pneumonia on such a chilly November day.

I often thought how much more difficult the protocol job must have been for some of my predecessors, but I can truthfully say that never in the seven years did I have an embarrassing moment because of some gaffe of Ronald Reagan's.

On the contrary, the President's personal diplomacy was an important ingredient in our foreign policy. He came across as a man of honor and clarity of purpose, and he felt the most important contribution he could make was to get to know his visitor as a human being. He was able to establish rapport with a wide variety of leaders—and actually almost dominate relationships with people of greater intellectual complexity. There was nothing Byzantine about Ronald Reagan. Because he himself was not complex he often outfoxed those who were not acute enough to understand his extraordinary empathy.

Once he established a personal affinity with a foreign leader, then he felt he could try to sell his message. He also knew that he could fall back on this personal rapport in moments of emergency or crisis between the two countries.

I remember during a 1985 visit of President Hosni Mubarak of Egypt, when the President's personal diplomacy saved the day. It was a working visit, so no White House dinner was scheduled. Instead, Vice President Bush was giving Mubarak a big dinner at the State Department. Then Soviet General Secretary Chernenko died, and the Vice President headed the delegation to the funeral. Normally, the Secretary of State would have subbed as host, but the Secretary was also going to Moscow.

I told the Secretary, "We have a real problem. The visit is a disaster and Mubarak is upset, especially since the dinner has no host. As a head of state, he cannot agree to have an official dinner given for him by someone of subcabinet level. And furthermore, the Egyptians always measure what we do for them against what we do for the Israelis. There is only one way to save the situation. I have checked President Reagan's calendar—he is free that night. Could you ask him if he would be willing to come to the State Department and substitute as host?"

Shultz was taken aback. The idea was clearly unorthodox, but I could see his eyes light up as he thought about it. He asked Reagan, and with no hesitation the President agreed. So, instead of a dissatisfied Mubarak, he was one of the happiest visitors we ever had. (I might add, it was quite a feat for my staff to quickly change menu cards and place cards, and many other details. When the President is entertaining, we must use the Presidential Seal, not the Great Seal normally used by the State Department.)

The press often made fun of President Reagan's need for cue cards. This was just prudence on Reagan's part. No one can understand the variety and breadth of what goes to the President in a day. He saw far more people than I did—but I always had cue cards for myself. It was impossible to memorize dozens of foreign names, and in addition remember every important issue he might wish to take up with a visiting statesman. In fact, the President was said to have a prodigious memory. His aides often lamented, "Don't tell the President anything you want him to forget."

After the assassination attempt, the cancer operation, and other illnesses, I was always amazed at how quickly the President recovered his natural ebullience. I usually walked behind him when a chief of state was with him, so I had many opportunities to observe the spring in his step. Even as he approached his seventy-eighth birthday, he never slowed down or shuffled like an old man. The President strode briskly, shoulders erect, head high—and that was the way he said goodbye to us as he left the White House following one of the most successful presidencies in our history.

TWENTY-TWO

Nancy Reagan—an Enigma

A T A NEW YEAR'S EVE party in London some twenty-five years ago, a fortune-teller looked into her crystal ball and told me, "Beware of women born in July!"

That is the only time in my life I have had my fortune told by a genuine medium, and I never forgot her admonition. Strangely enough, a certain number of interesting women in my life, including my late mother-in-law, have July birthdays—Nancy Reagan, Jackie Onassis, Arianna Stassinopoulos Huffington, to name a few.

All these July women share certain qualities of mystery and glamour, but none is a greater enigma to me than Nancy Reagan. I observed her for almost eight years, but I would not presume to say that I know her or understand her. And I never knew whether to embrace her or, as the soothsayer advised, "be wary."

I often thought about her predecessors and how they are remembered. Edith (Mrs. Theodore) Roosevelt was noted for her stern dignity; Eleanor Roosevelt for her compassion; Bess Truman for her honesty; Jackie Kennedy for her style; Ladybird Johnson for beautifying the environment; Pat Nixon for her grace in adversity; Betty Ford for her courage; Rosalynn Carter for the strong support she gave her husband.

But how will Nancy Reagan be remembered? She combined

many of those qualities in some degree, but her greatest contribution was her effort to mobilize America to fight the drug epidemic among our young people. In many ways, she was an outstanding First Lady, and yet she, more than any negative press or carping critics, undermined her own reputation and place in history by writing an autobiography that barely mentions her most important contribution. This has caused people to question —unfairly—the sincerity of her efforts.

Here is a woman who was an exceptional chatelaine of the White House. She worked hard, she entertained beautifully, she always looked attractive—her clothes appropriate to the occasion. Her public demeanor—with a few exceptions, such as letting Raisa Gorbachev get her goat—was usually beyond reproach, and she and the President even managed to show their affection for each other without appearing smarmy.

Mrs. Reagan had discipline and self-control. I never saw her lose her temper—though she could make strong men quake. She was a perfectionist, and I often heard that hint of exasperation in her voice when things weren't exactly as she wished. (Being myself a perfectionist, I recognized the frustration!)

But Nancy Reagan was not an easy person. She often appeared cold and secretive, uninterested in most people, yet she had a curious vulnerability, and valued uncritical loyalty above all things. "You are either with her or agin her," said one friend. And an aide explained, "Anyone she felt competitive with or threatened by, anyone she felt could one-up her, gave her social insecurity." I found this hard to believe. How could anyone compete with the First Lady?

Mrs. Reagan obviously loved fine clothes, but not as a topic of conversation. She never complimented or noticed what others were wearing and never encouraged compliments on her own outfits. In fact, she seemed embarrassed when praised about her appearance.

When I first went shopping after my appointment I went to Adolfo to buy some suits, and made him promise that he would not sell me anything that Nancy Reagan had already bought. Well, he did, and the first time I wore my new Adolfo to the White House, Mrs. Reagan said, "Oops, we almost wore the same outfit. I have that one too."

She was very good-natured about it. But I could just imagine appearing at the same function with Mrs. Reagan dressed like her twin. The attention would not be on the important visitor from abroad; the news story would be Mrs. Reagan and the Chief of Protocol in the same outfit. Thus, my care about such details was not frivolous.

I would like to put to rest one canard. Both Barbara Bush and I have been asked if Mrs. Reagan told us not to wear red when appearing at an event with her. I can assure you that Mrs. Reagan never mentioned the subject either to Mrs. Bush or myself. But I would not have worn red in any case. It seemed to me that all the color and attention should be on the First Lady.

And incidentally, Barbara Bush always played the role of Second Lady in low key, even though she is by nature a lively, feisty woman. But Mrs. Bush also has perfect manners, and instinctively knows what is good taste.

There is no question that Nancy Reagan was on guard, suspicious of anyone she thought was trying to use or manipulate her, and very few got close enough even to try. Her true friends, with few exceptions, were those outside of government and not involved in palace politics.

While I was waiting for my security clearance, I went to have tea with Mrs. Reagan in the private quarters of the White House. I wanted to thank her and the President for giving me such an exciting opportunity. Queen Beatrix of the Netherlands was due to arrive in a few days, and I explained to the First Lady that I could not be sworn in or begin my official duties until the FBI investigation was completed.

"I don't understand why it has taken so long," she said, annoyed by the bureaucratic holdup. Actually, it had only been six weeks, and most clearances took months, but Nancy Reagan was a woman after my own heart. She picked up the phone and called Attorney General William French Smith and laid it on the line.

"Bill, we want Lucky Roosevelt to greet and accompany Queen Beatrix on her state visit, which begins this Saturday. She must have her security clearance immediately. Can't you get them to hurry it along?" (It worked. A few days later my clearance came through.)

As I left Mrs. Reagan, I gave her an affectionate hug and said, "I hope that I will never let you and the President down."

"I'm sure you never will, Lucky. After all, you were my first defender."

That was probably as unguarded a moment as I ever had with her. After that day, I never felt comfortable calling her Nancy, even though we had been on a first-name basis before my appointment. Now, such familiarity seemed disrespectful.

Some months later I accompanied her to the British Embassy to see Princess Alexandra, who was on a private visit to Washington. On the way I showed Mrs. Reagan a beautiful silver box designed by Williamsburg silversmiths as an official gift for her to give. She liked it and told me to order at least a dozen.

Then she mentioned a member of my staff and told me, "Lucky, get rid of that person." I was flabbergasted. It was not easy to fire anyone in government, and one had to have grounds. I was still new, and the employee in question had not been given a chance. Wisely, I did not argue with Mrs. Reagan but later appealed to Mike Deaver and asked him to give me time to do the fair thing. I don't know what he told the First Lady, but the matter went on hold and eventually the person resigned.

This probably did not endear me to either Mrs. Reagan or Mike Deaver. Perhaps I was a bit too independent. One day I asked Mike if Mrs. Reagan was unhappy with me. Mike looked at me sternly and, I thought, even a wee bit sympathetically.

"Lucky, there's one thing you have to understand about Nancy," he said. "She doesn't really like dealing with women— she prefers to deal with men. Don't eat your heart out worrying about how Nancy feels about you or what you are doing. If you don't get any complaints, you can assume you're okay."

I took Mike's advice and stopped worrying. However, I did not listen to another piece of advice he gave me.

"Call Nancy and chat with her on the phone from time to time," he said. "She likes to know what's going on and likes to hear from people such as yourself who are well plugged into the Washington and New York scenes."

I did not call often. I felt it was unprofessional and an imposition to telephone such a busy woman—although when I did call she was always pleasant and never gave me the impression I was intruding.

The best description of our relationship would be "cordial and correct." I felt she did not want us to be close, and I respected that and did not presume. If Mrs. Reagan ever criticized me, I am unaware of it; and I never said a critical word about her during my tenure. While she never complimented my work or that of my staff—even when I paid my farewell call on her—she was punctilious in writing thank-you notes, by hand, for any thoughtful gesture—a social occasion in her honor, a small gift, even a basket of cookies.

After Mike Deaver left the White House, Don Regan inherited the "Nancy" portfolio, and if ever anyone was destined to come to grief it was poor Don Regan—a gruff, hard-charging, extremely effective person in the masculine business world he knew. The nuances of palace intrigue were not for him.

He treated me well. When I had anything important to tell Don Regan that might impact on the President or First Lady, I asked to see him. We went through the agenda quickly, his no-nonsense answers were usually on the mark, and I left assured that my concerns or problems would be presented accurately to the Reagans.

Although Regan was invariably helpful to me, I agree with Nancy Reagan that he should have departed the minute Iran-Contra became a *cause célèbre*. He was not personally involved, but he could have spared the White House and the country much grief if he had resigned immediately. In his own book, Regan clearly thought his personal honor was at stake, but I think he should have viewed it as a British cabinet minister would have, and resigned as a matter of form. In other words, he should have fallen on his sword.

(For example, Peter Lord Carrington resigned as foreign secretary at the beginning of the Falklands crisis. In his memoirs* he explains why. "It was not a sense of culpability that led me to resign," he wrote. "[It] was my sympathetic understanding that the whole country felt angry and humiliated . . . it is right that there must be a resignation. The nation feels that there has been a disgrace. Someone must have been to blame. The disgrace must be purged. The person to purge it should be the minister in charge. That was me." And Lord Carrington added, ". . . the Government was in for a hard time and my presence would make it not easier but harder. . . . My departure would put a stop to the search for scapegoats. It would serve the cause of unity. . . .")

I remember speaking to Mrs. Reagan at the time. The President was recovering from prostate surgery, and she was concerned for his health with this storm swirling around him. She told me, in effect, that she was trying to protect the President and Regan was trying to get him to take on more than she thought he should.

Donald Regan's revelations about Mrs. Reagan's use of an astrologer were a shock. To me, it still seems totally out of character for Nancy Reagan. I had no inkling, but simply a sense of frustration from time to time over what I thought were arbitrary decisions. Now incidents that once puzzled me fall into place.

I was bewildered, from the very beginning, when dates for state visits had to be confirmed with Mrs. Reagan before they could go forward. I assumed it had to do with checking their social engagements and public commitments, but the reasons were always a bit murky. So much so, I wondered if Mrs. Reagan understood the foreign policy implications of some of her decisions. I thought it a bit *outré* that she could overrule the State Department and the NSC with regard to the dates and the desirability of a visit.

Mrs. Reagan had some genuine blind spots in my areas of responsibility. For example, she did not seem to understand the importance of the diplomatic corps and of making an effort with

* *Reflecting on Things Past* (New York: Harper and Row, 1988).

them. At the annual White House diplomatic reception, she insisted the President leave as soon as the receiving line finished,
giving him no chance to converse and mingle with the envoys—
their one time to see President Reagan. (Once I actually heard the
President protest as she pulled him away from the party.)

The first time this happened, Secretary Shultz was as troubled
as I was. We could not understand why they went to the trouble
of preparing an elaborate party only to leave early.

Traditionally, the White House diplomatic reception had been
one of the most important social events on Washington's official
calendar. Until 1955, the entire corps was invited, but the numbers increased so dramatically that by the 1980s only the chiefs of
mission could be asked. The ambassadors looked forward to this
party enormously.

Also, until Reagan, it had been the custom for the President
to welcome the ambassadors and say a few words—perhaps a brief
tour d'horizon—something the envoys could later wire back to their
governments. The dean of the diplomatic corps would respond on
behalf of the diplomats. This never happened with the Reagans,
and I had a hard time finding a graceful explanation, particularly
for the Swedish ambassador, Count Wachtmeister, who was the
most articulate and gracious dean imaginable.

In contrast, Mrs. Reagan went to great lengths to assure the
success of the state dinners—the food, the flowers, the atmosphere
perfection. There were about ten a year, and they were paid for by
the State Department and given for foreign policy reasons. Mrs.
Reagan tended to regard these with a proprietary eye, putting her
best effort into them.

I went to each one of them in my role as Chief of Protocol
(which meant about seventy) and they were flawless, with one
exception—the entertainment. The word was that President Reagan did not like opera or heavy classical music. So our foreign
guests were often subjected to has-been popular singers and other
marginal performers who were not up to White House standards.
Even when they had a great opera star such as Sherrill Milnes, they
asked that he not sing opera! I felt that the White House should

showcase our finest musicians and dancers, regardless of the personal tastes of the First Couple.

One matter struck me as strange. Neither Jimmy Carter nor Gerald Ford was ever asked back to the White House for a social event during the Reagan years. I don't think the Carters were surprised, but I do think it must have hurt the Fords.

Just after the 1988 elections, a protocol flap occurred that I never understood. The last White House state dinner given by the Reagans was in honor of Britain's Prime Minister Thatcher. Dan Quayle was now the Vice President–elect, and I alerted Secretary Shultz's office that we should immediately invite the Quayles to his luncheon for Mrs. Thatcher. They agreed and instructed me to extend the invitation by phone on behalf of the Secretary. Then I telephoned the White House and told Mrs. Reagan's staff that I thought the Reagans should include the Quayles in the state dinner. They did not, and so, of course, the big story the next day was the "snub" the Reagans had given the Quayles.

Mrs. Reagan took a lot of flak for interfering in personnel matters, but many times she was right. Take, for example, Helene Von Damm's appointment as ambassador to Austria. Mrs. Reagan thought it a mistake to send this Austrian-born former secretary of the President to Vienna, and refused to attend her swearing-in.

One of the duties of the Chief of Protocol is to swear in new ambassadors. I was asked to administer the oath, which I did, but I also disapproved of the appointment because I am strongly opposed to ambassadorial appointments based on ethnic origins.

As the American ambassador, Helene promptly got involved in a love affair with a handsome and prominent Viennese, and she divorced her husband to marry him. At that point she should have resigned, but she stayed on. The Austrians were horrified; their ambassador here spoke to me at length about it, and George Shultz was beside himself. If Nancy Reagan did force her resignation, as Helene says in her memoirs, then she did the right thing.

Until recently, it was U.S. government policy never to send a diplomat to the country of his national origin. I think it would be inappropriate, for example, to send me as ambassador to Lebanon or any other Arab country. The key question is how would the receiving country perceive me—would they think of me as belonging partly to them?

The Reagan administration repeatedly ignored this wise stricture, and the Bush administration has done no better. They have sent an Italian-American to Italy and a Greek-American to Greece (both of whom are said to be doing excellent jobs—but that is not the point).

Mrs. Reagan deserves particular tribute for the way she handled the assassination attempt on the President, his cancer, and her own struggle with cancer. Despite the physical and emotional toll such illnesses take, both the Reagans faced their trials with great courage.

In particular, I will never forget Nancy Reagan's heroism the day she learned the President's colon tumor was cancerous. The scene was the South Lawn of the White House, where a concert was about to begin celebrating the 100th anniversary of the Boston Pops orchestra. Following the concert, Mrs. Reagan was due to receive all the foreign ambassadors and their wives at the annual event for the diplomatic corps. It was mid-July, the heat was overwhelming, and she had just received the pathology report. Somehow she steeled herself for the ordeal of shaking over four hundred hands; she gave a gentle, almost consoling, smile to everyone who came through the receiving line. Every ambassador returned to his embassy that evening confident the President would pull through. Her demeanor had reassured the world.

TWENTY-THREE

George Shultz— the Beloved Buddha

W ITH ALL DUE RESPECT to President Reagan, the most important man in my life, professionally, was Secretary of State George Pratt Shultz. Where I might see the President once or twice a week, I saw the Secretary almost every day unless he was traveling. And familiarity bred anything but contempt.

Shultz was a giant of a man, and I adored him—as did most of the people who worked closely with him, especially the women. He could be formidable when angry and very stubborn when crossed, but he was my mentor and inspiration—an old-fashioned gentleman and a true patriot, a man of integrity and honor who, despite his impressive achievements in academe, industry, and government service, managed to retain a delightful humanity and a surprising innocence.

The Secretary and I worked together in great harmony and developed a shorthand between us as we perfected the business of receiving the nation's important guests. His standards were high, and he felt the greatest nation on earth should not go second-class; we must treat our visitors with the same graciousness that they showed our top officials when they went abroad.

Before a visit, he would outline his foreign policy goals; it was my job to provide the best setting for achieving them. He kept a careful eye on expenditures, but he also felt that the many luncheons, dinners, and other events he gave were an aspect of his public diplomacy—that is, a public relations effort on behalf of our diplomatic objectives.

He would often say to our visiting VIP—simultaneously teasing and complimenting me: "My advice to you is do whatever Lucky Roosevelt tells you to do—that's how I stay out of trouble!"

Shultz needed little coaching from me. He was instinctively a gracious and perceptive host—his quiet manner the perfect rebuttal to the stereotype of the insensitive and brash American. As we stood at the entrance to the White House waiting to greet a visitor, I often briefed him about any observations my staff and I had made—for example, tension among members of the delegation; annoyance with press coverage, or lack of it; matters of personal pique sometimes expressed by the visitor at a lower level in hopes it would reach the Secretary's attention. (I was careful to keep my back to the waiting press, for if they had been able to read my lips they might have picked up a sexy item such as, "The aide accompanying this VIP is actually his mistress.")

We generally took our foreign dignitary into the Roosevelt Room, where he or she signed the President's guest book. President Reagan was usually punctual, but if we needed to mark time Secretary Shultz had a little routine he did with me.

"Contrary to what you might think," he would say, "the Roosevelt Room was not named after our Chief of Protocol. Actually this is the only room in the White House named for a President. That's because there were two Roosevelt presidents—Theodore, a Republican; and Franklin, a Democrat. Thus, no matter which party wins an election, they never change the name or decor of the room."

Shultz would also point proudly to the Nobel Peace Prize, in a glass case adorning the mantel, which was awarded to Theodore Roosevelt in 1905 for arranging the treaty ending the Russo-Japanese War. The first Nobel Prize ever won by an American in any category, it was presented to the Reagan White House by the Theodore Roosevelt Association. Aside from being a history lesson, Shultz's little diversion subtly enhanced my prestige and thus the level of welcome being accorded the visitor.

• • •

Because Shultz did not have a lean and hungry look, many had the notion that, while he kept things calm, he was not creative and did not initiate ideas. Nothing could be farther from the truth. From the beginning he emphasized that the technological revolution—the new world of computers and instant communications—would make it impossible for the Eastern European countries to stay authoritarian and under iron control. He also realized that the Soviets were going to have to face a basic truth: that without the free flow of information they were doomed to third-world status. Thus he began to shape a policy toward the Soviets based on these assumptions—which of course proved more prescient than anyone could have imagined.

He anticipated the dramatic emergence of the Far East economically; he put on the table the best plan ever advanced for a Middle East peace settlement—the initiative of September 1982—which failed, but not from a lack of imagination; he was a power behind the Canadian-American free trade treaty.

George Shultz proved every day that diplomacy was the art of the possible, but he never seemed afraid to dream impossible dreams.

Beneath Shultz's stolid, Germanic exterior lurked the heart of a bon vivant. In the office he was all business, but he enjoyed parties and social life. (Waiters all over Washington had to relearn the formula for a manhattan, his favorite drink, which went out of fashion in the fifties.) Despite his portly appearance, he was a graceful dancer and a fine athlete—he had been a varsity lineman at Princeton and was still an avid golfer, swimmer, and tennis player.

With women, Shultz was positively debonair. He admired and respected the senior female officials who worked for him, giving them some of the toughest jobs in the department. We all felt comfortable working with him; he treated us as intellectual equals.

He also liked our femininity. I noticed this with his female staffers, his woman doctor, his interpreters, and his preferred tennis partners (Kay Graham and Cynthia Helms). My protocol officers lived to please him and we all made a special effort to look good—he often noticed and complimented a new dress or hairdo, just as he was quick to notice and compliment a job well done. We usually received a letter of appreciation from him after every major event my staff orchestrated.

Women seated at his table at his lunches or dinners invariably gushed with enthusiasm about him. Otherwise levelheaded and sensible women—and gorgeous ones such as Anne Getty or Teresa Heinz—would declare, "I'm in love with George Shultz."

Nancy Reagan also appreciated the Secretary and seemed downright coquettish around him. She saw to it that at state dinners a glamorous movie star or celebrity, one who could be counted on to wear a revealing dress, sat on one side of Shultz (on the other he usually had the wife of a visiting foreign official). He had no trouble recognizing the likes of Ginger Rogers or Claudette Colbert, but when it came to current stars such as Joan Collins or Raquel Welch he was at a loss.

"Who is Brooke Shields?" he asked me, before one White House dinner.

"She's a famous model and movie star, Mr. Secretary, but just talk about Princeton—she's a student there."

He did, and afterward commented, perfectly deadpan, "She's a very intelligent girl."

The Secretary had his little vanities. He loved to wear a red cummerbund and red bow tie, a reminder of his Marine Corps dress uniform. On the Fourth of July he sported a loud candy-striped red-and-white shirt, on St. Patrick's Day a bright green silk tie. And he especially liked his white brocade dinner jacket, made for him by a Hong Kong tailor. "I like it because women always want to stroke the fabric," he said, eyes laughing.

A woman head of government, such as Margaret Thatcher or Corazon Aquino, brought out the playful in Shultz. He might spend hours in heavy meetings with these women, but he always had a lighter touch for them on the social occasions.

He showed up at his big dinner for President Aquino with a "Cory" doll pinned to his dinner jacket. And people are still talking about the last luncheon he gave for Prime Minister Thatcher shortly before he left office. Shultz presented her with "The Order of the Handbag"—a handsome black leather purse—in recognition of her talent for pulling just the right statement from her handbag at meetings of allied leaders. While they were searching for the correct stand to take, Mrs. Thatcher would produce a perfect compromise statement from her purse, "like a rabbit out of a hat," said Shultz, who then quoted several examples.

Mrs. Thatcher seemed taken aback at first, but his speech was so graceful she loved it. Later I complimented him on his surprise toast. "I didn't tell you about it ahead of time," he answered, grinning, "in case you might think it was undignified."

In most cases, Shultz was so dignified he was awesome, but he was never pretentious. No one called him anything but "Mr. Secretary" to his face, but behind his back we referred to him affectionately as "Shultzy" or, when he was in a bad mood, "the Sphinx" or "the Buddha." We also had an early warning system as to his moods—if his faithful secretary, Lora Simkus, saw him come in with "the Shultz scowl" on his face, we knew to give him a wide berth until it disappeared. His essential good nature would not permit him to stay angry long.

He was a curious mixture, both sophisticated and unworldly. Simple things gave him great pleasure—a thoughtful gesture, an appreciative word. He liked to entertain with great style in the State Department's elegant diplomatic reception rooms and often monitored every detail. At the same time, he felt quite comfortable inviting a head of state to have a barbecue dinner at his house—with himself the chef. Once he had us arrange a meal of hamburgers, hot dogs, coleslaw and chocolate sundaes for Shevardnadze and his Russian entourage, and for entertainment he wanted to show a movie and pass around the popcorn.

Shultz made a valiant effort to get a permanent house for future Secretaries of State—something sorely needed for security reasons alone—but Senator Jesse Helms successfully mounted a campaign to oppose it.

Shultz was both cerebral and physical; he was totally secure in both his masculinity and his intellect—a professor comfortable writing his books and economic studies, but also supremely proud of having served his country in the Marine Corps. I saw him finish off more than one formal dinner at the State Department by stepping to the podium and saying, "Okay, folks, that's all there is. As they say in the Marines, let's stack arms and get the hell out of here!" (The interpreters sometimes had trouble translating this.)

He received dignitaries in an imposing ceremonial office, often with an inviting fire burning in the fireplace. But he preferred working in a tiny, uncluttered office nearby, looking slightly rumpled in the heavy blue-and-white sweater he usually wore. He was a "clean desk" man, each piece of paper to be read and disposed of in an orderly fashion, and the desk reflected the neat and organized mind of its owner.

No one enjoyed and appreciated his charm more than his wife of more than forty years, Helena Shultz—known to everyone in Washington as "O'Bie." (The nickname came from her maiden name of O'Brien.) Shultz treated her with a thoughtfulness and affection any wife would envy. Infinitely serene, she was a welcome and comforting presence on all his trips abroad, never interfering but keeping a benevolent eye on the Secretary, his health and needs. Although today a motherly figure, she still loves him with the passion of the young nurse he met and wed during World War II. And she was a lioness if anyone attacked him.

The Shultzes loved going to the theater and to dancing parties, especially those that featured big-band music reminding them of their courting days. I noticed she was always amused by the flirtatiousness he provoked in women from seventeen to seventy, as evidenced in this exchange between her and Betty Beale, the doyenne of Washington social columnists.

"O'Bie, how do you feel about all these pretty women making eyes at the Secretary?" Betty asked, rushing in where most reporters would not dare to tread.

"I don't mind at all," said O'Bie, the mother of his five children and grandmother of six. "After all, I'm the one who goes home to bed with him."

And when rumors circulated around Washington that our

taciturn Secretary of State had a tiger tattooed on his tail, a memento of his Princeton salad days, it was O'Bie who laughingly confirmed it to the press.

O'Bie endeared herself to me from the very beginning. "Lucky, there cannot be two bosses in this matter of our official entertaining," she stated. "I don't have time to give these events the meticulous attention you and your staff must devote to them. Also, if something goes wrong, you will be responsible, therefore you must be the sole manager of these affairs. I will not interfere unless there is something I don't like or feel needs change or improvement. Otherwise, you are on your own. George and I trust your judgment completely."

Well, almost. George Shultz was also responsible for one of the most embarrassing episodes in my career with him.

When he became Secretary of State in July 1982, he laid down some guidelines about his official entertaining. He liked round tables of ten; and no press at his table, so as not to inhibit conversation. He personally designed a menu card, as a nice souvenir for visiting dignitaries to take away with them. His only food bans were veal, because it is so often served, and squash, because he hated it.

Shultz had a special aversion to tall flowers in the center of the table. He felt they interfered with conversation and made it impossible for him to eyeball his guests. Of course, we respected his wishes and kept the arrangements low. But once, before I got back from vacation, my assistant decided to try a compromise. She ordered handsome vermeil vases three feet high and as slim as candlesticks, with late summer flowers spilling over from the top—well above the sight line.

The occasion was the state visit of President António dos Santos Ramalho Eanes of Portugal. When my enthusiastic assistant proudly showed me the Thomas Jefferson Room all set up for the luncheon, I had to admit it looked lovely, but I was apprehensive.

There were eight tables of ten each, and on my right was the smooth Portuguese chief of protocol, Ambassador Helder de Mendonça e Cunha. We had just started comparing notes on our respective jobs when I heard a tinkling of glasses—a signal that someone was about to speak. This was not in the scenario, but I saw Secretary Shultz stand up, as if to propose a toast.

"Ladies and gentlemen," the Secretary said, "I hope all of you have had a chance to admire the beautiful flower arrangements in the center of each table. However, these luncheons are designed for good conversation, which flowers impede. Therefore I ask the waiters to remove the centerpieces so we can get on with the luncheon."

An awkward silence magnified the sound of the waiters moving among the guests, leaving bare tables in their wake. How I longed to disappear—especially when I saw the bemused expression on my Portuguese counterpart's face.

(The next day, at Defense Secretary Weinberger's luncheon for Eanes, he noted that he liked flowers and had them on the luncheon table. The Pentagon, he said, was negotiating with the State Department to acquire the beautiful vases that Shultz had banished from his luncheon.)

After Shultz's lunch I telephoned Raymond Seitz, the Secretary's executive assistant.

"Did you hear what happened at lunch?" I asked.

"Indeed I did." Ray sounded grim. "But there's something much worse than the flowers, Lucky. Take a look at the menu card."

I looked, and I saw the *absolute* no-no. Shultz's name was spelled "Schultz"—an unpardonable sin in *this* State Department. Also, the event was described as a dinner instead of a luncheon. Three strikes. I was surely out!

The next evening, as luck would have it, I was seated next to the Secretary of State at a dinner dance. As I took my seat I said, "Mr. Secretary, why don't you fire me now and get it over with so that we can both enjoy this party."

His eyes twinkled, and I knew he had already forgiven me, but he said with a devilish chuckle, "I got your attention, didn't I?"

Thus I learned, as did most of my State Department colleagues, not to trifle with George Shultz. He liked people who were straightforward and honest with him. If any of us made a mistake and owned up to it, he was forgiving and understanding. But if someone lied to him, he never forgave—and it stayed in his mental computer forever.

I was sometimes an extra set of eyes and ears for Shultz—especially in the Washington social world that was so much a part of my life. He hated gossip and the rumors of sexual shenanigans that went around from time to time. He wanted to know the latest political stories, the books and articles he might have missed, and interesting people who might enhance his knowledge and vision. And although he had his feuds with various members of the administration over policy, especially Secretary of Defense Weinberger and National Security Adviser William Clark, he never let it spill over into personal vendetta. I never heard him utter a malicious personal remark about anyone.

Usually, when I had a meeting with him I had so much to cover that I prepared a detailed agenda, and it was a challenge to get through it in the time allotted. A typical agenda in the summer of 1985: "The Chinese visit, matters concerning President Li and Li Peng; Secretary and Mrs. Shultz's entertaining at the U.N. General Assembly—plans for the President to attend the 40th anniversary celebration, division of responsibility between my staff and his; Blair House briefing book prepared for Anne Armstrong, organizational meeting scheduled; method of selecting state visits out of control [I did not know then about the astrologer]; explain how we coordinate food decisions with White House; problems with White House staff; Geneva summit, letter from Bourguiba, Peruvian author Mario Vargas Llosa coming, urge Shultz to see him."

After every important visit, I briefed the Secretary. Much of what we discussed involved personalities—the sort of information beloved of columnists and the "Style" section of the *Washington Post*. I insisted on seeing him alone, with no note-takers. If I sent a written memo, it was personal and private and "not for the system." As a result, nothing that he and I discussed ever leaked.

Meg Greenfield, editor of the *Washington Post* editorial page, once wrote, "Shultz has the self-assurance of an honest man."

Indeed, I think he valued personal probity above all other virtues. This explains in part his intense opposition to lie-detector tests. The idea that the State Department was populated with scoundrels to be flushed out by the lie detector was deeply offensive to him. The implication that his honor should be tested on this machine so offended him that he swore he would resign before submitting to such an indignity.

His was not just an emotional reaction. He had studied the matter in depth. He had little faith in the efficacy of the polygraph and was troubled by the large potential for damage to innocent people. He learned that in England the Thatcher government had come to the same conclusion. The more he came to know, the more he found the polygraph fallible. Thus, his decency and sense of fair play made him opposed to the tests. He warned, "If you try to manage people by fear you will lose."

As the wife of a former CIA official, I had never shared Shultz's feeling about the lie detector. My husband thought they were necessary in the case of CIA security clearances, and I was influenced by his opinion. But Shultz challenged this. He had a deep suspicion of too much authority in the hands of agencies that operate in secrecy.

During all the years my husband was in the CIA, the rivalry and suspicion between State and the Agency was a fact of life. Naturally, while a CIA wife, I was sympathetic to their point of view, but after joining State I found myself much more understanding of the department.

Once Shultz made up his mind about a person or a policy, it was almost impossible to turn him around, but he did not arrive at conclusions frivolously. The process of study and consideration, in keeping with his professorial background, gave weight to his opinions and judgments. He projected such gravitas that few in the department dared to argue with him and if they did, they were well advised to have their facts in hand or he would nail them.

My tasks usually did not involve arguments over substance, but I did have to tangle with him occasionally over form. I learned that he did not like to be stampeded, and was best approached in a quiet and deliberative manner—he could be amused by emotion, but rarely swayed.

I was the only one in the department who dared tell Shultz that his speeches—usually written by others—were sometimes boring and often too long. When I blurted this out, expecting him to get red-faced, he just laughed and said, "You know, that's what O'Bie says."

He hated to give his toasts after dinner; he liked to get them over with at the beginning, so he could relax and enjoy the party. Shultz's preference sometimes upset the chef—long-winded toasts ruined more than one soufflé or roast beef—but he was determined. And he sometimes began with this anecdote:

"In Roman times they tell of the disappointment Nero experienced when the lions refused to devour one particular Christian, in contrast with the zest with which they had consumed the martyrs offered earlier. As each lion dashed at him, the Christian whispered something to him. The lion skidded to a halt and slowly trotted away. After the hungriest and fiercest of the lions had refused to eat, a frustrated Nero ordered the Christian unchained and brought before him. Nero said, 'If you tell me what you said to the lion, I will set you free.' To which the Christian replied, 'It's a deal. All I said was "After dinner, there will be speeches." ' "

One time, we were planning a party for a hundred Latin-American heads of state, foreign ministers, and delegates attending the United Nations General Assembly. Malcolm Forbes's yacht was to take us on a dinner cruise around Manhattan.

"Lucky, I don't see how I am going to deliver my remarks after dinner—the guests will be dispersed around the yacht," he said, looking concerned.

I couldn't resist. "Mr. Secretary, believe it or not, the Latinos will not regard this as a tragedy. This party will be a smashing success. For once, an American Secretary of State will not lecture them!"

Sometimes when Shultz threw away his prepared remarks he could be very entertaining, but the State Department did not take kindly to improvised speeches from Secretaries of State!

The "Department" however, did take kindly to George

Shultz, and I think he was one of the most highly regarded Secretaries of State in history. Various conservative members of Congress and some of the White House staff complained that Shultz was a "captive" of the State Department's Foreign Service—as if these officials belonged to a foreign country. On the contrary, Shultz respected the Foreign Service and used them wisely, co-opting them rather than excluding them. Thus if anyone was "captured," it was the Foreign Service and not the other way around. And he never let them forget that setting foreign policy was the President's prerogative.

Shultz's departure from the department was one of the most moving events I have ever witnessed. Everyone who could crowd into the vast main lobby of the State Department had gathered to give him a surprise send-off. As Secretary and Mrs. Shultz appeared at the top of the stairs leading down to the lobby, the band struck up the Marine Hymn and everyone started singing. The Shultzes descended the staircase, somewhat overwhelmed, and I saw the normally imperturbable Secretary of State almost on the verge of tears as longtime aides and friends gave him and O'Bie one last embrace. Guiding O'Bie protectively through the crowd, Shultz walked her to their waiting car to the strains of "California, Here I Come," and then they headed back to their home on the Stanford University campus.

TWENTY-FOUR

A Plague of Courtiers

BEING CHIEF OF PROTOCOL to Reagan, Bush, and Shultz was challenging, satisfying, and fun. But, as is often true in life, the people at the top are the easiest to deal with—it is the courtiers and aides, puffed up with self-importance by their access to power, who create the problems. And in the Reagan White House, alas, bigshotitis was rampant.

As columnist George Will wrote in *Newsweek* recently, "Washington . . . has too many self-important people doing unimportant work, people with serious-sounding titles who know they are not serious but want to be seen as busy making history. . . . Washington has a small elite and a single obsession, power, which is scarce. So Washington's many non-grown-ups scramble for gratification from Washington's evanescent substitutes for power, one of which is the appearance of being important."

I was an innocent. My mentors were men like my husband who regarded serving their country as a privilege, a higher calling—something you elected to do rather than make money. Or they were men like former secretary of the treasury C. Douglas Dillon or the late Ambassador David Bruce, who had all the material rewards the world could offer but felt drawn to government service out of a sense of noblesse oblige.

Even though I had lived in Washington for most of thirty

years and reported on successive administrations, I never saw much of the breed who help get presidents elected—the advance men, the media manipulators, the dozens of men and women who create a successful political campaign and then expect to be rewarded through the "spoils system" of political appointments.

These types often end up on the White House staff and form the trappings of a court. For many, this is their first encounter with real power, and for an increasingly large number, it is their stepping-stone to big money in the private sector. They also mistakenly think that the conduct of foreign relations is simply an extension of the political campaign.

The White House staff seems to divide and reproduce itself as rapidly as rampaging cancer cells. Theodore Roosevelt, at the start of the century, had a staff of thirty-five. Today, it is well over three thousand.

In this mélange, one finds both heroes and bums. There were a lot of heroes, and I had many good friends in both the East and West Wings of the White House. But this chapter will focus exclusively on those we referred to inelegantly as "the little shits." Others called them "the Munchkins"; a later group was known as "the mice."

My troubles with them began almost the first day on the job. I got a call asking me to place as assistant chief of protocol a young woman they needed to relocate. Although she was qualified, it meant putting her in over Gahl Hodges, one of my most competent employees. (Later, Gahl would become Mrs. Reagan's social secretary and marry Richard Burt, Chief Arms Control negotiator in Geneva.)

When I refused, they started using muscle. Mike Deaver himself telephoned. I still said no. Next came a call from a well-meaning White House official, who was a friend of many years.

"Lucky, let me give you a piece of advice," she said. "If you want to get along in this administration, just do what those people tell you to do. You make a big mistake to take them on, and they will make you pay for it."

I thought she was being overly dramatic. Little did I realize how sound her advice would prove. But meekness and humility were not my strong suits. I would not be bullied; I preferred telling them to take the job and shove it. I also felt that when the chips were down I would always have the backing of the Secretary of State—and should I ever have to go to the President, he too would defend me.

Michael K. Deaver, the deputy chief of staff and one of President Reagan's closest friends and advisers, was my designated liaison with the White House. He wielded enormous power, and on balance his influence on the President was positive and often wise. I will never forget the day I came to Mike's office shortly after he had persuaded Reagan to call Israel's Prime Minister Menachim Begin and demand that the Israelis stop bombing Lebanon.

Mike Deaver was often described as the ultimate advance man, but he was more than that, even though no detail was too small for his attention. Mike liked to create the scenario, set the scene, and then let the actors come on stage and do their thing. He was a genius at programming the Reagans.

Mike had excellent political instincts, and he was tireless in his devotion to the Reagans. He was the only person who could translate Mrs. Reagan's wishes into effective action and keep her hand from showing. No one ever doubted that Mike dealt from strength, but as time went on he seemed more and more inundated and often gave his subordinates too much rein. They took actions and gave orders in his name—and by implication that of the President or First Lady.

They created enormous ill-will toward Mike, much of it unnecessary. They thought of themselves as extensions of the First Family and issued commands using the imperial "we"—a word I would forbid anyone in the White House to use if I were Chief of Staff. They were unctuous around the President, but they also threw the Reagans' names around as if they were on an intimate footing with them. "The President wants this," they would say, or "Mrs. Reagan insists that you do that." Such commands could even intimidate cabinet officers!

Sometimes, the moral myopia of these young appointees was disconcerting. For example, one man, who actually was rather nice, insisted that my office should let him purchase one example of every official gift selected by the Reagans for heads of state. Many were monogrammed or otherwise personalized by the President, and this vastly increased their value as presidential mementos. One day, they would have historic significance as well.

"But I can't do that," I said, pointing out it would be unethical and possibly illegal.

"I will pay for them," he insisted. While he could certainly go into a store and buy any item off the shelf, the shop would not put the Presidential Seal on it or inscribe it without my permission.

"That's not the point," I told him. "These gifts are selected by the President for specific purposes. If he wants to give them to you, he can do so, but not out of our inventory." (Of course, the President knew nothing about this. I don't think this man ever understood the impropriety of what he proposed.)

Throughout my seven years with the White House, no one on the Bush staff ever gave me a problem. Either the Vice President maintained a tighter discipline or his associates had a different ethical compass—maybe both.

However, just as soon as *President* Bush moved into the White House, the men who helped elect him started to throw their weight around. One in particular, who has since departed, called a meeting after the election to inform me that the President-elect and Mrs. Bush did not wish any of the ten Reagan political appointees in Protocol—most of whom were Bush people—to participate in the inaugural activities. That was so arbitrary and so unlike Barbara and George Bush, I didn't believe him. Sure enough, when I checked, I found that the Bushes had issued no such instructions.

The first time I ever heard the expression "advance man" was during the Eisenhower administration. Archie was stationed at the embassy in Madrid, and Ike was coming on a state visit. The entire embassy was thrown into chaos by the arrival of the advance team, come to make preparations for the great man.

They ignored the ambassador and State Department people, ordered around the host-country officials, and so upset Archie's normally smooth relations with the Spanish security services that it took a long time for everyone to recover from the havoc. I heard similar stories about the high-handed approach of the Kennedy advance teams when Archie and I were stationed in London.

It's interesting that while advance men brought out the worst in everyone, the Secret Service, who can be very demanding at times, manage to do so without causing so much heartburn. They are a remarkable group of men and women—brave, incorruptible, discreet, good-natured, and always totally professional.

The campaign trail does not provide expertise in foreign affairs, nor is it a recommended course in diplomacy. Once when we were preparing for Corazon Aquino's visit, one advance type asked me, "Will Mr. Aquino be coming?"—apparently unaware that Cory had become President after her husband's brutal assassination.

Another time, I was asked by a White House official to tell a group of Gulf Arabs, who were calling on the President, not to wear their national dress. When I pointed out that this would be a terrible insult, he immediately backtracked. The media experts were only worrying about the domestic political impact of the photo op!

In previous administrations, the Chief of Protocol usually headed the team preparing for the President's trips out of the country. By the time I took over, the Reagan administration's patterns had already been established. Mike Deaver and his selected advance team made all the arrangements abroad. Protocol was a part of that team as a matter of form, but in truth Mike ran the show. He negotiated the meetings, some of the protocol, and all the logistics, security, and communications. Mike did his part well. It was after his initial work that our troubles began—with the staff.

Simply stated, they were immature and insecure, and exercised their power in petty ways. Everything to them was a turf battle. They were insensitive and had little understanding of foreign customs and protocol. For example, in the Middle East and in much of South America it is extremely rude to talk business

until you have been offered a cup of coffee and exchanged pleas-
antries. But our people would sometimes barge into meetings
with the attitude "Let's cut the crap and get down to business."

When Irish Foreign Minister Peter Barry, who had been appointed Reagan's official escort in Ireland, came to Reagan's hotel
the first morning to pay his respects, the White House aides ignored him. They had made no provision for the Reagans to receive Barry for a few cordial words before starting on the official
program. We, of course, corrected this.

Another time, in New York, the advance team failed to check
menus with Protocol, and ended up offering prosciutto (made of
pork) to King Hassan of Morocco. They also strong-armed the
King's tea-makers, harmless fellows who always accompanied the
King, causing quite a scene in the Waldorf-Astoria, where Hassan
was lunching with President Reagan. After that Protocol handled
the President's meetings with foreign dignitaries in New York.

Probably the most unpleasant part of dealing with the White
House staff in the early years was the constant personal humilia-
tions they took pleasure in inflicting. Not just on people at my
level, but even on the Secretary of State.

Alexander Haig was their prime victim when I began my job.
He had offended the White House staff and Mrs. Reagan when he
announced just after the assassination attempt on the President that
he was "in charge." In fairness, Haig maintained that he never
meant this the way it was interpreted, but nonetheless his relations
with the White House went from bad to impossible.

Still, it shocked me to see staffers treat Haig so cavalierly. As
long as he was Secretary of State, it was their obligation to show
respect for the office. On our trip to the Versailles summit, they
deliberately kept Haig off the President's helicopter, so that he
could not arrive gracefully with the President. The Haigs were
relegated to a cargo helicopter which landed in the middle of a cow
pasture. They were so far back they had to run in an undignified
manner to catch up with the presidential party and find their car in
the motorcade.

I suffered for lovely Patricia Haig, one of the nicest and most self-effacing women alive; through it all she kept her dignity and charm even though she was rarely included in any of Mrs. Reagan's activities. Such violations of protocol norms send messages to the rest of the world, and foreigners, especially the *protocolaire* French, could not understand why the President of the United States would allow his Secretary of State to be so humiliated.

Our ambassador to France, Evan Galbraith, also got fed up with being pushed around by the advance men. And when they tried to exclude me from the historic Versailles gala that wound up the summit meetings, Galbraith put his foot down. He insisted that as a member of the official delegation I had to be included or he would protest to the President. He also pointed out that staffers and advance men had no business attending the dinner at the expense of the official delegation.

But this sort of thing continued throughout the trip, directed not only at Haig, and sometimes myself, but at most of the State Department and Treasury contingent. I put up with it—after all, this was my first trip abroad with the President. I naïvely believed that when I got back, if I told Mike Deaver all that had happened he would straighten things out and see that it did not happen again.

But it did. After I had been on the job awhile I decided to go on an advance trip to learn how they were done, and find out why my staff dreaded them so much. The trip I chose was to South America, where I had a silly, unsettling experience.

We were visiting many cities and sites in preparation for a presidential trip—maybe a country a day. I shared a car with two senior White House officials. One of them, whom I had never met before, barely spoke to me during the entire trip. He hugged his side of the car and stared out the window. I had the impression that he was embarrassed to be assigned to a car with the Chief of Protocol—and a woman at that. Someone might think we were equals. He might lose face. All of this he managed to convey in body language and by pointedly addressing any conversation to the other man in the car. Later, I could never pass that man in the White House corridors without wanting to stop him and say, "Tell me—here was I, a woman you had never met before, who might have been interesting to talk with, had you bothered to explore. Why did you behave so rudely?"

Thinking that perhaps being a woman was the problem, I decided to send my male deputies on future advance trips. After a few trips, even the men got discouraged and refused to go.

(When I came on board, I had heard that at the Cancun conference the advance team's concept of protocol's duties was to have the deputy chief of protocol drop off jars of jelly beans in each delegate's room.)

When the 1983 economic summit was held in Williamsburg, Virginia, my office, under the direction of the White House, was heavily involved in the preparations. The same little White House coterie tried their best to rattle me, but I didn't want to fall into their trap the way Secretary Haig had done.

I arrived in Williamsburg to find that the special White House phone in my hotel room was dead. (This was hooked up to the White House switchboard and was vital for communicating with my staff scattered about town.) After investigating, an innocent communications fellow told me, "One of the White House staff told us to cut off your phone."

"Why?" I asked.

"Sorry, ma'am, but they don't have to give us a reason."

That night I had dinner with Secretary Shultz and recounted some of my problems.

"Lucky, if you let them get your goat, they will win," the Secretary admonished. "If you protest, if you go public, they will do to you what they did to Al Haig. They will turn everything around to make you appear the petty one, worried about your perks."

I remembered an old Arab saying, "Be patient and the funeral procession of your enemy will pass in front of your tent." And that's what happened. But not without a lot more grief.

Shultz would have his own problems with them. As was revealed in the Iran-Contra hearings, one of the mice was always giving him a hard time over requisitioning the planes he needed for his many missions abroad. To show his power, the staffer would simply hold up the paperwork until Shultz finally had to protest to Don Regan to break the impasse.

On the President's trip to China, during a photo op in Xian, an advance man shouted to the Secretary of State in front of the accompanying Chinese officials, "Mr. Secretary, would you move away from the President, so that we can get a clean photo."

This mania for "clean photos" went to such extremes that cabinet officers, ambassadors, and other important officials were ordered to deplane by the back steps from Air Force One, instead of simply waiting on the plane until the President and Mrs. Reagan had descended the stairs.

Occasionally, the Reagans would invite a guest—a foreign minister, an ambassador—to travel with them on Air Force One. Instead of being given an honored seat, the guest would have to go to the bowels of the plane, walking past White House staffers who were sitting up front.

Jim Rosebush, Mrs. Reagan's very able chief of staff, observing my problems, sent me a note of encouragement just after Williamsburg. Jim, a Christian Scientist, referred me to the Bible, Psalm 35. I looked it up, and loved what I read: "Let them be as chaff before the wind: and let the angel of the Lord chase them. Let their way be dark and slippery: and let the angel of the Lord persecute them."

He cautioned me that bringing these issues to Mike's attention would be counterproductive. "I say let God chase the unjust man and his acts," Jim wrote. "You can rest secure in the knowledge that you are performing great service for your President."

Of course, the longer the Munchkins lorded it around the White House, the more hated they became. I was fortunate that the late Ed Hickey, special assistant to the President in charge of the military office, the planes we traveled in, communications, etc., finally lost patience with the juvenile delinquents and became my protector. On the summit trip to Ireland and London in 1984, he warned me to be careful—that I was being set up.

Ed looked after me, but that trip broke my spirit. I vowed I would go on no more presidential trips overseas as long as this group was running them. And of course, the "angel of the Lord" was busy indeed, for the next summit was Germany, with the flap over the President's visit to the Bitburg cemetery to honor the German war dead there, SS among them, and the dubious purchase of BMWs by some of the advance team. I managed to miss it all.

I also avoided the Reagans' state visit to Spain. Knowing what sticklers the Spaniards were for protocol, I did not want to be associated with the gaucheries that would surely occur. And they did. Apparently three staffers who put themselves on the invitation list for the King's state dinner for the Reagans dropped out at the last minute and were seen Tasca-hopping in old Madrid.

I've asked myself many times since what motivated these people and why Mike Deaver allowed them such leeway. Perhaps he simply never realized what was being done in his name. Much later Mike himself admitted to suffering from alcoholism. It can't have helped him to be surrounded by a coterie with the mentality of a college fraternity, who, instead of helping Mike fight for his sobriety and his life, shielded him from the consequences of his illness.

Over the years, Mike Deaver and I have long since put aside our differences. I admire the way he and his family handled themselves in the adversity they faced after he left office and especially the way he has recovered from alcoholism and tried to help others do the same.

When Don Regan took over, he was well aware of the bad morale in the White House. He took steps to see that the outrageous behavior ceased, and any differences between Protocol and the White House staff were ironed out in a mature and collegial way. And later, Howard Baker and Kenneth Duberstein, as well as William Martin, Frank Carlucci, and Colin Powell, were as nice a group of men as I could ever wish for—and they kept their staffs under control.

Toward the end of the President's first term, I had pretty much made up my mind to leave—mostly because I had no stomach for the degrading backbiting.

I had fought a battle with the White House when they tried to force on me another officer, whom, thank God, the State Department rejected. They also tried to get me to take as my deputy a pal of the Munchkins—a security officer—going so far as to ask Undersecretary of State Lawrence Eagleburger to lean on me. I refused and held out for career Foreign Service officer Timothy Towell, who spoke Spanish, French, and Portuguese and was a trained diplomat with knowledge of the bureaucracy—a decision I never regretted.

Then one day, without any advance notice, the White House commandeered Gahl Hodges to be Mrs. Reagan's social secretary. Shirley Moore, Deaver's secretary, was instructed by one of the Munchkins not to tell me about it. But of course she did, pointing out that I was bound to notice when my star officer was no longer at her desk!

In the same sweep they took our best secretary and one of our best visits officers to be Mrs. Reagan's new advance man. Of course, it was a compliment to our training and reputation for excellence, but when I reported this to Secretary Shultz, especially the manner in which it was done, I concluded with a sigh, "I've really been screwed!"

"No, Lucky, you've been raped," he said, adding, "Don't worry, your people are so good, and I have such faith in your management—you won't miss a beat."

We soldiered on, with Bunny Murdock taking on Gahl's job, and doing it brilliantly. But even though I loved everything else about my work, I hated this ugly undercurrent at the White House. It was not my style to complain, but if the President had known he would have been horrified.

One of the enfants terribles went around saying he was going to get rid of "that woman"—meaning me. After this was reported to me several times, I went to Mike and said, "Look, if this is some ham-handed way of trying to get me to resign, no one has to go to these lengths. All you have to do is tell me that the President is no longer happy with my performance and I will leave immediately. I did not ask for this job; I have, by all accounts, done it well. But I had a great life before the White House, and I will go back to a great life when I leave it."

Mike was taken aback. "Don't be silly, Lucky. The President and Nancy are extremely pleased with your performance, and there has been no suggestion that you should leave."

"In that case, call off that guy, or you will be explaining to the Secretary of State and the President—and possibly the press—why I left."

I heard no more rumors, and I think Mike effectively stopped them. But having made such a fuss, I was no longer inclined to leave—and I did not want to give my childish tormentors the pleasure of forcing me out.

The Secretary of State told me he very much wanted me to stay. "In that case," I said, "the President will have to ask me." (At this point Reagan had not yet personally asked anyone, not even his cabinet, to stay on for his second term.)

On November 26, 1984, as I was waiting to take Prime Minister Tariq Aziz of Iraq to see the President, an aide came out of the Oval Office and, thinking he was summoning me and my visitor, we both started toward the door. "No, Lucky," said the aide. "The President wants to see you alone."

I walked in and there sat the President with Secretary Shultz, the latter with a big smile on his face. The President stood up as I walked toward him. Placing his hands on my shoulders, he said, "The Secretary and I think you have done a marvelous job, and I would like you to continue with me in my next term. I hope you will say yes. You see," he added, half-singing, "I've grown accustomed to your face."

That tune from *My Fair Lady* never sounded sweeter.

PART FOUR

*Around the World
with the Chief of Protocol*

TWENTY-FIVE

The Russians Are Coming

THE IRONY OF the situation was not lost on me. I was a forty-year veteran of the Cold War. I was one of those who thought Ronald Reagan quite accurate in describing the Soviet Union as an "evil empire," and I could never understand the hypocrisy of the tut-tutters who decried his bluntness.

And yet here I was, on my way to Andrews Air Force Base to welcome to America for the first time the dazzling and dramatically different leader of the Soviet Union, Mikhail Sergeyevich Gorbachev, and his wife Raisa.

As Ronald Reagan's Chief of Protocol, it was my privilege and duty to greet important state visitors on behalf of the President, and I had done it hundreds of times. But on that day, December 7, 1987, I felt as curious and excited as the first astronaut on the moon.

For two years we had been dealing with a new breed of Soviet leaders, and I had become quite an admirer of Foreign Minister Eduard A. Shevardnadze. I had seen the cordiality and understanding that had developed between him and Secretary of State George Shultz, which now extended to every echelon below them.

Our leaders and our press were only just beginning— somewhat hesitantly—to realize that the Cold War might be coming to an end. But because of what I had observed, I had no doubts. And I couldn't help reflecting on the rapid and unexpected change that had occurred in my own feelings toward the Soviets.

Since my Vassar days, when I had my first unhappy encounters with Marxist dogma and the authoritarian Left, I had had a love-hate attitude toward the Russians. On most campuses in the late 1940s it was fashionable to be leftist; that was the orthodoxy of the time, and I was influenced by my more liberal teachers. But toward the end of my sophomore year, I rebelled. I did not like being yoked to a party line.

It was a declaration of political independence. Only someone who has gone through the idealism and then the disillusionment with the Left can possibly understand the euphoria such a liberation brings. I think that is one of the first things that attracted me to Ronald Reagan—he had been there.

My college experiences made me staunchly anti-Communist, but I was nevertheless fascinated by Russian history, culture, and literature. Thanks to Professor Catherine Wolkonsky, a roly-poly White Russian princess whom we students loved, Dostoevski, Tolstoi, Chekhov, Pushkin, Gogol, Turgenev, Mayakovsky, became a part of my intellectual life.

When I married Archie, an officer of the Central Intelligence Agency, he reinforced my instincts. He was a student of all things Russian, especially the language, and he had a passion for Russian poetry. But he also felt keenly the Communist threat to our democratic ideals, and his CIA career was dedicated to fighting it.

My hatred of Soviet tyranny and love of Russian literature came together for me in the summer of 1958 in an unforgettable intellectual and emotional experience. We were on vacation in Portugal, and I had brought with me the London edition of a book smuggled out of Russia—*Dr. Zhivago* by Boris Pasternak.* After reading it on the beach at Caiscais, I wrote in my journal:

"*Dr. Zhivago* is the hopeful message to all of us who wander through this turbulent century searching for the reason why. To

*Translated by Max Hayward and Manya Harari. I mention the translators because later, when an American version came out in a different translation, it was not nearly as poetic or lyrical, and many of my American friends could not understand my emotional reaction to the book.

give hope in the midst of such cosmic upheavals; to retain a love for humanity in the face of humanity at its most brutal and degraded; to retain a faith in God, when God seems to have abandoned us long ago—this is Pasternak's greatness—for it comes to us from the other side, from behind the Iron Curtain. If he is brave enough to have hope and faith, then who are we to moan in doubt and gloom?"

Now, three decades later, those who had clung to such a vision, those who had never given up, finally would triumph. And the man most responsible for this changing world order was about to land in America.

The giant white Aeroflot bird with blue markings, bearing the General Secretary of the Communist Party of the Soviet Union and his wife, came to a stop in front of the welcoming red carpet. My watch said 4:40 P.M. On time to the minute.

Normally, while standing on the tarmac at Andrews Air Force Base, waiting for yet another VIP to arrive, I mentally reviewed our preparations for the visitor—totally oblivious of the press and television cameras behind me. But not on this blustery December day. Some five thousand reporters and what seemed like an equal number of TV cameras were focused on this first Washington summit between Gorbachev and Reagan, relaying it to the tiniest hamlets around the globe.

I walked down the crimson carpet escorted by Yuri Dubinin, the debonair, prematurely white-haired Soviet ambassador to Washington. We started up the steep stairs. As Chief of Protocol, I would be the first person to shake hands with the Russian leader on American soil.

The Gorbachevs were waiting for us at the top of the stairs. He flashed me his famous smile. "Welcome to the United States," I began. "On behalf of the President and Mrs. Reagan and all the American people we wish you a happy and productive stay in our country."

We descended the stairs together, and I brought him to the welcoming committee headed by the Secretary of State and Mrs.

238 / KEEPER OF THE GATE

Shultz. A young Russian girl presented flowers to both Gorbachevs, but the General Secretary looked a bit surprised; he
turned and thrust his bouquet at me. I clutched it in my arms until
the welcoming ceremony concluded. (The front-page photo that
appeared in newspapers around the world showed Gorbachev and
Shultz shaking hands and me in between them holding a huge
armful of roses. In most of them I was identified as Mrs. Gorbachev.)

The cameras followed Gorbachev to the microphones, where
he and Shultz exchanged remarks, and we then piled into a history-
making motorcade—more than sixty cars, a dozen of which were
black armored Russian Zils, flown in from Moscow.

Shultz accompanied Gorbachev in one car, Mrs. Shultz was
with Raisa in another, and I was in the next with Foreign Minister
Shevardnadze. By now we were old friends. The Russian cars
were luxuriously comfortable, with Oriental carpets on the floor.
They were much easier to get in and out of than our low-slung
limousines. "I wish you would leave this car behind for me," I
told Shevardnadze.

He smiled, and as I looked at his youthful face, gentle eyes,
and distinctive thatch of white hair, I thought of the months and
years he and Secretary Shultz had put into this effort. "You and
the Secretary know what a difficult journey it has been to get to
this day. I believe it wouldn't have happened if it hadn't been for
the special relationship that's developed between you. Secretary
Shultz holds you in such high esteem."

"And I reciprocate that," said Shevardnadze. "There is now
a very warm feeling between us." He then told me that the INF
treaty, banning an entire class of nuclear weapons, was just completed and the documents were being flown in from Geneva that
night.

We escorted the Gorbachevs and Shevardnadze to the Soviet
Embassy on 16th Street, while the rest of the motorcade veered off
for the Madison Hotel. After a brief tea, we said goodnight.

I went home elated beyond measure. Not only was I about to
witness an extraordinary drama from my privileged perch, but I
was involved in every aspect of its unfolding—the backstage ma-

neuvers, the last-minute scene shifts. These three intense and hectic days would change the course of history.

Ronald Reagan had been working toward this moment since 1983, and although he was unequivocal in his condemnation of Communism, the President had a far more open mind about improving relations with the USSR than he was given credit for.

But as Reagan frequently pointed out, Russian leaders kept dying on him—three funerals in three years—so his initial official contact with the Russians came late in his first term, when the Chairman of the Soviet Presidium (and Foreign Minister) Andrey A. Gromyko met with him in the Oval Office.

This was in September 1984, and as I waited for Gromyko at the West Entrance I wondered if time had mellowed the dour and taciturn Russian I had first met thirty-seven years earlier on a field trip from Vassar to study the United Nations. In those days he was Soviet ambassador to the U.N. and the personification of Russian intransigence.

The meeting with the President was cordial if a bit stiff, and afterward I escorted Gromyko back to the Soviet Embassy. Attempting a conversation, I said, "Mr. Minister, I have not seen you for many years but I am impressed with how little you have changed. You and President Reagan both seem to know the secret of staying young."

Pause.

Finally, Gromyko in a thick Russian accent answered, "Is true." End of conversation.

Nonetheless, Gromyko's talk with the President turned out to be crucial to the Soviet decision to resume arms-control discussions at Geneva, and from that frosty beginning I watched Soviet-American relations gradually begin to thaw.

When Mikhail Gorbachev assumed power in March 1985, it was apparent the earth had moved. The new Soviet leader was unlike any other. He courted and won over Margaret Thatcher, a woman not given to misty-eyed sentimentality. He went to Paris and wowed hardbitten correspondents with his performance in a Western-style press conference. And he began to challenge the status quo with tantalizing diplomatic overtures to the United States. Still, few could believe the moment had come to abandon the Cold War.

Ronald Reagan lost no time in arranging a Geneva summit meeting with Gorbachev, in November 1985—a get-acquainted session that allowed the two men to take each other's measure.

George Shultz would be the first to acknowledge President Reagan's effective charting of a new Soviet-American relationship —but no one, including Reagan himself, can underestimate the years of patient slogging by Shultz to make it happen.

It started in Helsinki in August 1985 when Shultz, accompanied by his wife, attended the tenth-anniversary commemoration of the Helsinki Accords on Human Rights. There they met the Shevardnadzes—he had just taken over as Foreign Minister—and Shultz sensed he was dealing with a different breed of Soviet.

In diplomacy, small signals often presage momentous events, and that fall Secretary and Mrs. Shultz made their annual pilgrimage to New York for two weeks of intense social and political activity at the United Nation's General Assembly. It was also the Shevardnadzes' first visit to the U.N. My office was charged with organizing the Shultzes' events, among them a luncheon cruise Mrs. Shultz gave for delegates' wives each year on Malcolm Forbes's yacht, the *Highlander*. We did not know until the last minute if the Soviet wives would attend, and when they did, O'Bie Shultz and Nanuli Shevardnadze reinforced the instant friendship they had felt in Helsinki.

I spent most of my time on that sail around New York harbor diverting other delegates' wives from crowding around Mrs. Shevardnadze so that she and O'Bie could have ample time together. Elsewhere, Russians and Americans were still glowering at each other, but on this friendly cruise something new was happening.

The barriers began to come down. The Shevardnadzes came to Washington the following week, he to meet and lunch with President Reagan, she to be shown the sights by Mrs. Shultz.

With his unfailing instinct for doing the right thing, Shultz invited the Shevardnadzes to his unpretentious house in the Washington suburbs for a barbecue cooked by the Secretary himself.

Years later Nanuli Shevardnadze told me it was then she and her husband recognized the extraordinary human qualities of the Shultzes and developed the trust that carried them through the subsequent ups and downs.

And the downs were not long in coming. The Soviets almost blew it in their miscalculation in the Nicholas Daniloff affair. An American journalist, Daniloff was arrested in the Soviet Union on trumped-up charges of spying, in order to exchange Daniloff for one of their spies caught red-handed in New York.

I am convinced that the civility, trust, and warmth of the Shultz-Shevardnadze relationship, nourished in the 1985–86 contacts, prevented this stupid action by the Soviets from destroying the fragile structure for an arms-control agreement and a summit that the two men had begun to build.

As a signal of their displeasure over the Daniloff affair, the White House instructed me not to greet Shevardnadze at the airport nor at the usual VIP entrance to the White House. He was hustled in the back door. The President did not give a lunch for him. Their Oval Office meeting was one of the stormiest of Ronald Reagan's presidency.

Shevardnadze got the message. I saw he was acutely uncomfortable; he did not relish playing the heavy. He also seemed to feel that his government's actions had made him lose face with Reagan and Shultz.

I admired the way Shultz managed to convey our dismay and at the same time hold out hope to the Russian delegation—if Daniloff was released quickly and without an apparent exchange, then we could resume the search for peace.

Shultz gave a dinner at the State Department for the Soviet group, this time in the Thomas Jefferson Room, one of the most beautiful eighteenth-century drawing rooms in America. Both men were subdued in their toasts—but both seemed determined not to let hope falter. It was a moving evening, and troubling, yet Shultz in a masterly way saved face for Shevardnadze and gave the Russians room to maneuver themselves out of the Daniloff debacle.

I had become so fond of the Shevardnadzes that I forgot my own indignation when they arrived for the State Department dinner. Instead of the cold and correct handshake I meant to give, I embraced and kissed them both. This was photographed by Soviet TV, but luckily no one in our press caught my departure from diplomatic rectitude.

The Shevardnadzes returned in September 1987 for their now ritualized visit to the United Nations and to Washington. The Daniloff impasse was over; the Reykjavik summit, though inconclusive, had advanced the arms-control agenda, and encouraging developments were just under the surface.

The atmosphere was so upbeat I even risked wearing a red dress for the Shevardnadze arrival. That might not seem significant, but anytime I wore red when a Communist country was involved, I got letters and calls protesting "giving aid and comfort to the enemy." I mentioned this jokingly to Shevardnadze and he said, "Ah yes, the Russian word for red, *krasny,* also means beautiful." He added that "Red Square" had no political connotation, but an aesthetic one; it was so named long before the Communist Revolution.

We now were good enough friends to banter, and at dinner the next evening I wore red again and he said to Secretary Shultz, "You not only have a *krasny* Chief of Protocol—but also a most competent one." (I did not let this go to my head, chalking it up to his natural gallantry, but I noticed that Mrs. Shevardnadze pointedly asked where my husband was.)

In truth, the Soviets were becoming familiar to us, taking on human proportions. We were no longer seeing the KGB and the Gulag every time we talked to a Soviet. I noted in my journal: "I have seen in four recent meetings between Shevy and Shultz a growing feeling of closeness and understanding—of mutual appreciation and professional respect. . . .This filters down to the next echelon. Bessie [Aleksandr A. Bessmertnykh, Deputy Minister of Foreign Affairs and now Russian ambassador to the United States] is very genial. Boris [Marchuk] at Russian Embassy reminds me of a nice American yuppie."

I noticed at lunch the way the Soviets and Americans talked about Reykjavik, as if they were alumni of the same university reminiscing about old times. Each tried to top the other with stories of sleepless nights and braving the bleak weather. Bess-mertnykh said that in the midst of round-the-clock negotiations, when everyone was tired and dejected, they decided to take cat-naps. Suddenly an eerie, ghostly shriek awakened them. "We were sure the house was haunted, but it probably was the wind. It was terrifying," he recalled.

As I listened to their conversation, I realized that this cama-raderie, this sharing of their miseries and joys, was a harbinger of momentous changes in our relations with the Soviets.

The last week in October 1987 brought the biggest economic scare in decades: the stock market dropped more than 500 points. And a dejected George Shultz returned from a trip to Moscow, unable to secure a summit date. Then, on October 30, Gorbachev reversed himself and Shevardnadze flew to Washington for one day, met with President Reagan, and together they announced a summit in Washington for December 7, less than six weeks away.

TWENTY-SIX

Arms Control and Apple Pie

THE PREPARATIONS for Gorbachev's visit to Washington were unique. Normally when a state visit was planned I called in the ambassador of the country involved, we worked out the general outlines of the visit, and then our respective staffs saw to all the details.

But not this one. Everyone—Secretary of State Shultz, Colin Powell of the National Security Council, Chief of Staff Howard Baker, and especially Nancy Reagan—got into the logistics act. But still, it was the White House advance team, headed by Frederick "Rick" Ahearn, and my own protocol staff who had to make it happen.

The Soviets, as was customary, also sent an advance team to assist their embassy in negotiating the hundreds of problems that crop up in such a complex undertaking.

On November 7, exactly one month before the summit, I met with Soviet Ambassador Dubinin in my office and hammered out a scenario based on the usual state visit. But after our suggestions had been reviewed by the Reagans over the weekend, they came back with a completely different scenario. I noted that Jack Courtemanche, Mrs. Reagan's chief of staff, seemed tense, and a cocky little guy from the White House advance office was talking very macho.

Implicit in their manner was the message: Nancy Reagan had

decided the schedule. So for the three days there were to be only meetings, meetings, dinner, dinner. Nothing else. Assistant Secretary of State Rozanne Ridgway, an admirable woman—with guts—said, "This is very dull visually."

I noted in my diary: "No contact for Gorbachev with American public . . . I think we have all to gain and nothing to lose by letting him do whatever he likes within reason. I mentioned the Secretary would like to give a lunch—to take care of all the people who want to meet Gorby. Colin said he understood, but added, 'We have some in-house problems we have to work out.' "

I assumed the problem was Mrs. Reagan. Her vision of this visit, understandably, was focused on herself and the President and his place in history.

From the beginning we were told that one item on the proposed agenda with the Russians was immutable—the signing of the INF treaty would be on Tuesday, December 8, at 1:45 P.M. The timing made little sense. Why not have the ceremony be the culmination—the apogee—of the visit rather than the beginning? Everything afterward would seem anticlimactic.

"Do you have any idea why the White House is so fixed on this hour for the signing of the INF treaty?" Shultz asked me, somewhat bewildered. Of course, neither of us realized that this had been designated as the most propitious hour by Mrs. Reagan's astrologer.

Plans called for a formal arrival ceremony at the White House the morning of December 8, followed by the treaty signing. The state dinner would be that evening. Wednesday, Shultz would give a lunch and the Gorbachevs would host a return dinner. Four substantive sessions were scheduled between the two leaders, plus an intimate farewell luncheon on Thursday and an early-evening departure for Moscow. These were the broad outlines.

Colin Powell and Thomas Griscom, representing Chief of Staff Howard Baker, were put in charge of all summit preparations, both substantive and logistical. Although Colin and Tom were delightful to work with, I think their original attitude was "Now we'll show those protocol people how the big boys do things."

By then my deputy Timothy Towell, Assistant Chief Catherine "Bunny" Murdock, and I had handled almost a thousand visits and had negotiated with hundreds of foreign chiefs of protocol. We knew just about all the pitfalls.

Before it was over, those exalted White House officials would appreciate the time-tested reasons for leaving details to Protocol. When negotiated on a higher level, disputes get magnified or even kicked upstairs to the head-of-state level. Usually I dealt with pesky questions directly with the foreign ambassador or protocol chief and disagreements rarely became major ones. Lowly protocol chiefs are of no great interest to the press. Concessions are easy to make if no one is keeping score.

For example, when Ambassador Dubinin came to see me about a concession the Soviets wanted, I gently told him to forget it.

As he departed, he said, "I did not ask you anything, did I?"

"Of course not, Mr. Ambassador. And I did not give you an answer, did I?"

"Absolutely not," he said firmly, both of us understanding that face had been preserved.

The Soviet fourteen-man advance team was headed by their Chief of Protocol, Vladimir Chernyshev—tall, broad-shouldered, and a dead ringer for screen actor Cesar Romero. I had not expected anyone so smooth. But his laconic manner belied a very shrewd mind.

The day of our first meeting, November 11, brought one of those unseasonable snowstorms that throw Washington into a panic. The Russians were amazed that most of our government had shut down over what would be an everyday occurrence in Moscow.

After meeting in the Old Executive Office Building, I invited the Soviet and American teams to lunch at the 1925 F Street Club. An exclusive Washington establishment, the club has a shabby-genteel atmosphere which I thought the Russians would enjoy. The menu included a fish soup, veal piccata, rice, baked tomatoes, salad, four cheeses, pumpkin pie and apple pie. And plenty of bread. Russians don't feel a meal is complete without bread, something weight-conscious Americans tend to avoid.

The lunch was a huge success, thanks also to the wine and champagne which fortified us against the snowstorm outside. I noted in my journal: "We started off on a very high note—full of hope. Will it all be for naught? Will they pull a fast one? Stay tuned!"

The next day Chernyshev seemed testy and wary—not at all genial. We finished the site surveys—the White House, State Department, Andrews Air Force Base, etc. We narrowed the revised schedule to only a few points of difference, such as whether the Vice President would host breakfast for Gorbachev, or vice versa. We preferred the former; they, according to their sense of protocol, insisted on hosting, but asked the Vice President to choose the guests.

The Russians were hung up on the departure time. We wanted them to leave at 8:00 P.M. on Thursday, December 10, so the President could address the nation in prime time, immediately after the summit. They wanted 9:00 P.M., too late for our plans.

They also put out feelers for Gorbachev to address a joint session of Congress, but the State Department discouraged that. We could not be sure of Congress's reaction and did not want to embarrass the Russian leader by having the request turned down. Even if Congress agreed (and the invitation had to come from them), no one could be sure of the reception Gorbachev might receive, particularly from right-wing Republicans.

All these matters were in due course solved after a certain amount of compromise on both sides. But what really caused Chernyshev's furrowed brow was the schedule for Raisa Gorbachev.

We were informed that Mrs. Reagan would not accompany Raisa on her program. Her participation would be limited to one tea and one coffee at the White House. I asked Colin if Mrs. Bush would be accompanying Raisa on the remainder of her activities. "No," he answered. "Only Mrs. Shultz will escort."

Mrs. Reagan normally did not escort the wives of heads of state, so it was not a departure from precedent. What was different was not having Barbara Bush do the honors. From a protocol point of view the Vice President's wife was the appropriate escort, and the Russians knew it. (Later, in Moscow, the wife of the President of the Soviet Union was Mrs. Reagan's escort, not Mrs. Shevardnadze, the protocol equivalent of Mrs. Shultz.)

Over the weekend, we waited for reaction from Moscow, particularly for some guidance about what Mrs. Gorbachev wanted to do. But nothing happened. The Soviets kept hinting they wanted Mrs. Reagan to offer her more. I wondered why Nancy Reagan didn't just make her excuses, citing her recent cancer surgery and her mother's death, and turn the problem over to Mrs. Bush. We were, in fact, at a protocol impasse!

Archie and I thought it might help matters to ask a few of the Russians for tea at our Georgetown house: Ambassador and Mrs. Dubinin, Chief of Protocol Chernyshev, his deputy Igor Sherbakov, and General Mikhail Dokuchaev, the suprisingly affable character in charge of Russian security.

We served tea Russian-style seated around our dining room table. As we put away sinful amounts of chocolate cake and other pastries, Archie steered the conversation to Pushkin, his favorite Russian poet, which he preferred to read in Russian. Instantly the mood changed; delight and surprise at our interest in their literature.

"There's a great English translation of *Eugene Onegin* by Sir Charles Johnston," Archie said, pulling it from his library and reading a few verses in English to illustrate to Ambassador Dubinin the excellent translation.

The Dubinins were impressed, and Mrs. Dubinin said she would like to have the book. In my Lebanese tradition, if a guest admires something, you offer it to him. To my horror, my WASP husband, who obviously loved his books more than his wife, said, "Well, you can't have this copy. It's out of print and I'm afraid I cannot replace it."

I glowered at Archie, hoping he would get the message and gallantly present the book to Mrs. Dubinin. He refused to catch my eye. Thoroughly embarrassed, I babbled something about not wanting to give Mrs. Dubinin such a messy copy and we would send her a pristine one shortly. (The book *was* out of print and it took months to find another, but Archie did finally send her one, receiving a charming letter of appreciation from Mrs. Dubinin.)

To divert attention from that little gaffe, I announced that I had a gift for the Chief of Protocol. "Ambassador Chernyshev, I come from Tennessee, and we are famous for a brand of American whiskey known as Jack Daniel's," I said, handing him a bottle with exaggerated flourish.

Finally, on November 17, Chernyshev had to return to Moscow, still with no answers for us. He thanked me especially for the tea party, saying it was the memorable event of his visit, and sent me a half-gallon of Russia's famous Golden Ring vodka. They planned to return the day after Thanksgiving.

During this ten-day interval, we were not idle. We had less than three weeks to prepare for the most important state visit of the Reagan presidency. Normally we had months of warning.

Arrangements had to be made for the dozen armored cars, hundreds of personnel, and tons of communications equipment the Soviets were flying in. Two hundred special telephone lines were being installed in the Madison and Vista hotels. We set up special protocol headquarters—crisis centers—in the hotels.

The security arrangements were complex. We had a turf battle between the Secret Service and the State Department's Diplomatic Security, and I was delegated to convince the Secretary of State that all security arrangements should be under one umbrella—i.e., the Secret Service. When I discussed this with Shultz, he was annoyed. He thought I was trying to "con" him, as he put it.

Two hours after that conversation with Shultz, he and I were waiting together for the arrival of Prime Minister Shamir of Israel at the main entrance to the State Department.

"How could you accuse me of trying to con you?" I asked.

"That got to you, huh?" he said, looking stern.

"Yes. That hurt. Right here," I said, pointing to my heart.

Then, as we were walking Shamir up to Shultz's office, I

heard him say to Shamir, "This place is being turned upside down for the Gorbachev visit, and much of the burden falls on Mrs. Roosevelt. So I must be very nice to her."

It's easy to understand why, in my eyes, Shultz could do no wrong.

The Saturday after Thanksgiving, Shultz sent for me to go over the guest lists and menu for his lunch party. I recommended an all-American menu: first, a fresh seafood medley of Maine lobster, Louisiana shrimp, Maryland crab, and Alaskan king crab. For the main course we planned Pennsylvania venison, with lingonberry sauce, puree of sweet potatoes, and autumn vegetables.

Shultz nodded his approval, but when I began describing the fancy dessert, he interrupted: "Why can't we have good old American apple pie and vanilla ice cream?"

We talked about the many interpreters needed and the various toasts, with special translated versions that guests could follow. I explained that technically Gorbachev, who was General Secretary but not then chief of state, was not entitled to a twenty-one-gun salute (only nineteen guns), but we had decided to treat him like a chief of state anyway.

By this time, congressional objections to Gorbachev's addressing a joint session had been thoroughly aired in the press, and in the face of so much opposition on the Hill the idea had been scratched. Shultz commented that we would pay dearly for the rejection Congress had given Gorbachev. "They will take it out on the President when we go to Moscow," he said.

Shultz then told me he was about to meet with Deputy Foreign Minister Bessmertnykh and asked me to stay in case I was needed. To my surprise, the nation's top diplomat and this high-ranking Russian spent the next hour and a half laboriously going over every point of the schedule. Not a word about arms control or any other substantive matter. So much for priorities!

In our preparations, especially for the First Ladies, I often thought how much I missed Mike Deaver, who by then had left the White House to start his own public relations firm. When he was in the White House he knew how to channel our concerns to Mrs. Reagan in a way she could accept. Since I did not work for her, I did not feel I should deal directly with her unless she solicited my advice. I was afraid she would regard my trying to persuade her to take one course of action or another as a contest of wills.

But I felt that Nancy Reagan did not really understand the protocol requirements or the importance of her role as hostess to Raisa. I knew Mrs. Reagan did not feel well and was put off by Mrs. Gorbachev's lack of response to her invitations, but I did not want our First Lady to appear petulant or inhospitable. Someone like Mike Deaver could have made her see that it was in her best interests to go the extra mile.

We were getting down to the wire. Less than ten days before the visit, and still no program for Raisa. The two First Ladies were fencing, and we couldn't plan anything. Finally, exasperated, I decided to smoke out Mrs. Gorbachev and force an answer. I instructed Bunny Murdock to prepare a schedule for Raisa. We would make the choices and present this to the Soviet Embassy.

I jotted in my notebook on November 30: "The General Secretary's schedule pretty well done . . . they don't know Raisa's wishes . . . seem scared to death of her. Shultz calls me re plans for Mrs. Bush, re additions to guest lists . . . White House says I can't use anemones for Shultz luncheon because White House will use them for one of their events . . . I switch to pink tulips and rubrum lilies. . . . Soviets now insist on 19 places at State Dinner. White House says no." (We always kept it to fourteen for the foreign guests.)

By December 1 we were frantic. Six days before the visit, and still no confirmation of any event on Mrs. Gorbachev's schedule. Mrs. Reagan was furious because Raisa had not had the courtesy to reply to her invitation to tea; Raisa probably was upset because Nancy was not offering to do more. The Russians felt that Mrs. Bush should be designated as Raisa's official hostess. I was caught in the middle. Once more I asked if the White House would designate Barbara Bush to accompany Raisa on certain events, and once more I was told no—only Mrs. Shultz.

Press interest in the Gorbachev visit was unprecedented. I received hundreds of requests for interviews and TV appearances, most of which I declined. My biggest problem was fielding questions about Mrs. Gorbachev. It was obvious something was amiss, since normally the spouse's schedule is nailed down weeks before a visit. And five thousand curious reporters were keen on rekindling the Nancy-Raisa rivalry.

Four days before her arrival, Mrs. Gorbachev finally accepted Nancy Reagan's invitation to tea, but we still had no general approval of Raisa's schedule. She agreed to visit the National Gallery of Art. She declined an invitation to lunch with wives of the congressional leadership, and turned down a visit to the Library of Congress—a pity, since Librarian of Congress James Billington was a Soviet expert and spoke fluent Russian. We thought it was probably because Congress had rebuffed Gorbachev on the joint session and this was the Russians' notion of tit for tat.

News had leaked out that Pamela Harriman, the beautiful widow of former ambassador to Russia Averell Harriman, and a noted Democratic activist and fund-raiser, would be entertaining Raisa in her Georgetown house. She had invited Raisa at the request of former Soviet ambassador Anatoly Dobrynin. Pamela kept me informed of her arrangements, and I asked her not to confirm anything publicly until the schedule was released. One morning Pamela telephoned me: "Lucky, I called Oscar de la Renta to order a silk scarf to give Mrs. Gorbachev. But Oscar already knew I was entertaining her. Oscar says Mrs. Reagan told him!" So much for keeping a secret in Washington.

While this was festering, I turned my attention to other cosmic matters. "The Secretary wants daily bulletins about his lunch," I wrote in my notebook. "Keeps adding names. Shultz and his apple pie! We sampled three desserts. I thought the chocolate and apricot terrific; he didn't. I rejected the apple pie and apple brown Betty because Design Cuisine's French chefs do not know how to do them American style. I asked our caterer to go back to the drawing board." Arms control began to seem easier than apple pie.

The Secretary of State's luncheon, with over 250 guests,

would be the largest seated event the Secretary had given. We began doing the seating four days before the event. Shultz came to my office, looked at the diagrams of twenty-five round tables seating ten each, and after a few minutes shook his head. "I've had it. I can see this is more complicated than I thought. I'll leave it to you."

Then I spoke to Shultz privately. "I've had a call from the Soviet ambassador's aide asking who will accompany Mrs. Gorbachev to the National Gallery," I said. "I told him Mrs. Shultz, but they feel that proper protocol calls for Mrs. Bush to do it."

Shultz looked uncomfortable. He was fond of both Nancy Reagan and Barbara Bush and also felt protective about his own wife, who was being put in an awkward position by Nancy's decision that Mrs. Shultz should be Raisa's escort. "This sort of silly thing causes the most anguish," I told him.

The day before Gorbachev's arrival—a Sunday—I went to lunch with friends and when I returned home I found two calls from Colin Powell, one from Shultz, and one from the White House social secretary. The reason? Mrs. Reagan wanted to see the seating for the State Department luncheon. I got it to her at once, and called to see if she needed anything further.

Mrs. Reagan was feeling defensive. "It takes most people at least six weeks to recover from major surgery," she told me, "and I was up in a week because of my mother's death. It is a great effort for me to do what I'm already doing. I cannot do more."

She was not exaggerating. She had been looking pale and drawn; I could tell she was exhausted. With the perfect vision of hindsight, I wish I had said, "Then you should relax and let Barbara Bush substitute for you."

When December 7 arrived we still had much to do, but at least I could report to Shultz that the caterer, after three more attempts, had finally produced a perfect apple pie! The all-American menu was complete.

But the Raisa problem would not go away. Bunny Murdock learned that the Soviets had pulled a fast one and called Mrs. Bush themselves to ask if she would accompany Mrs. Gorbachev to the National Gallery. Barbara Bush innocently accepted, not realizing all that had transpired. I told Bunny to let the National Security Council grapple with that hot potato. In the end, Mrs. Bush did not accompany Raisa. Mrs. Shultz did, and as I write this today I still don't understand why.

As the welcoming committee gathered at the airport that afternoon, no one would have believed that organizing the Gorbachev-Reagan summit and completing the INF treaty was duck soup compared to organizing the wives.

TWENTY-SEVEN

"That Guy Is a PR Genius!"

WHETHER IT WAS thanks to Mrs. Reagan's astrologer or to the Good Lord himself, the day chosen for the INF treaty signing was almost perfect. En route to the Soviet Embassy to escort Foreign Minister Shevardnadze to the welcoming ceremony at the White House, I commented to my driver, Eugene Lewis, "Just think, this is the first time during the Reagan administration that the Stars and Stripes and the Soviet hammer and sickle have flown side by side."

Flags festooned every streetlight in the White House area. In addition, for state visits we customarily draped two mammoth flags—ours and the visiting country's—on the façade of the Old Executive Office Building. For the Russians, this almost didn't happen. The White House got worried about how the public might react to seeing this display of the Red flag, but my protocol staff insisted that if we omitted their flag, the Soviets would consider it an affront. We prevailed, and I could only hope the Soviets were as moved as I was by this eloquent symbolic gesture.

And what would I tell future generations about that historic moment in the East Room of the White House when the two leaders signed out of existence an entire class of nuclear weapons? As Reagan and Gorbachev were writing their signatures on the INF treaty, my purse handle broke, sending chain links noisily cascading to the floor! Distracted and embarrassed and scrambling to pick up the pieces, I missed the full emotional impact of Ronald Reagan's finest hour.

During the day I had many opportunities to observe Mikhail Gorbachev in action—and I was impressed. He was charismatic and electric and I was fascinated by him, particularly by his aggressive body language. He was quick to laugh and even quicker to grasp ideas, his mind often racing ahead of the interpreter. I liked his bright brown eyes, which darted around like the cursor on a computer; he didn't miss anything. He and the President were comfortable with each other. The chemistry, as Nancy Reagan would later verify, was terrific.

Alas, as the world noted, the chemistry between the two wives was not quite so great. Mrs. Gorbachev was certainly not an easy person. Although very bright, she had a flinty feistiness and appeared overbearing, which seemed to me more a reflection of insecurity than arrogance.

The White House state dinner, attended by 120 guests, was a triumph, thanks to the minute attention Nancy Reagan had given to every detail. The receiving line took twice as long as usual, because the Gorbachevs had a personal word for each guest as they shook hands. Obviously they had been well briefed. Pianist Van Cliburn entertained—an inspired recommendation of Linda Faulkner, the White House social secretary. The performance ended with a sentimental rendition of "Moscow Nights," with the Gorbachevs and all of us singing along together. Afterward, bear hugs and kisses and a very emotional conclusion to an awesome day.

The next morning when I went to collect the Russians and escort them to the White House meetings, Gorbachev came bounding down the red-carpeted stairs of the embassy and greeted me with a cheerful "Good morning, Comrade Protocol."

Later, at the Secretary of State's luncheon everyone wanted a word with the Gorbachevs, who were remarkably gracious. It took two hours to move the guests through the receiving line. (My favorite vignette: tycoons Donald Trump, Ross Perot, and Malcolm Forbes in a huddle as they waited patiently in line.)

Gorbachev seemed amused as he watched me orchestrate the activities of my protocol staff. I must have looked agitated, because as Assistant Secretary Rozanne Ridgway came through the line she whispered, "Remember, Lucky, you're on *Candid Camera.*"

Shultz, however, was *not* amused. He was annoyed with me for changing the seating at his table without clearing it with him. I had, by now, observed that Raisa Gorbachev was a world-class talker. She was, of course, seated to the Secretary's right, but he would need reinforcements if anyone else was to get a word in. So I substituted Barbara Walters for Meg Greenfield—a brilliant editor and a favorite of the Secretary's—and moved Meg to Gorbachev's table. If anyone could hold her own with Raisa, it was Barbara. And Meg and Gorbachev would be a perfect combination.

Others at the table with Raisa were Senator Claiborne Pell, Congressman Tom Foley, Mrs. William Luers, wife of the Metropolitan Museum head, painter Andrew Wyeth, Mrs. John Heinz and Mrs. Alan Simpson, wives of the senators from Pennsylvania and Wyoming, and Arthur Mitchell, artistic director of the Dance Theater of Harlem.

At Mrs. Shultz's table, Gorbachev was on her right, followed by Chief of Staff Howard Baker, Meg Greenfield, Senator Sam Nunn, Mrs. Vincent Astor, PepsiCo's Donald Kendall, Susan Eisenhower, John Chrystal of Bankers Trust Company, and Senator Simpson.

Everything went splendidly at Mrs. Shultz's table, but it was a bit more contentious at the Secretary's. At his luncheons, Shultz always made it a practice to let each guest at his table put a question to the honoree. He introduced Teresa Heinz, using her background as an illustration that we are a nation of immigrants. (Mrs. Heinz is half Portuguese and half Swiss-German, Italian, and French, and was born in Mozambique.)

Teresa raised the subject of human rights in the Soviet Union, and Mrs. Gorbachev gave back the boilerplate answer, criticizing our treatment of the homeless and our unsafe streets.

Teresa responded that our problems might better be described as socioeconomic as opposed to human rights. "One involves humanitarian concerns; the other involves law." In an effort to be tactful, Teresa asked, "What do you think we can do together to find solutions to these problems?"

To which Mrs. Gorbachev replied, "What education do you have?"

"I have a B.A. and went to graduate school in Geneva," Teresa replied.

"I am a philosopher," said Mrs. G., "and I will give you a philosophical answer. At the moment of birth, every human being has a human rights problem."

Teresa felt they were in for a rambling discourse, so she interrupted. "Yes, but what can we do about our immediate problems—how can we work toward solutions?"

"These questions are obstructionist," Mrs. Gorbachev said.

Teresa refused to be put down. "I beg your pardon. That is not obstructionist. I care about the future, about my children and grandchildren."

It was time to change the subject.

Mrs. Gorbachev had just come from the National Gallery of Art and was upset to find so few Russian paintings in the collection. Mrs. Luers assured her that a large collection of Russian paintings hung at the Met. Barbara Walters spoke with Raisa about her favorite American writers—Joyce Carol Oates and Tennessee Williams. Raisa also talked art with Andrew Wyeth and ballet with Arthur Mitchell. It was a lively table, and George Shultz enjoyed more than anything playing the catalyst.

The highlight of the lunch was Gorbachev's gracious and sensitive toast. Noting that he was in the Benjamin Franklin Dining Room, named after one of America's greatest diplomats, the General Secretary said he wanted especially to praise the patient diplomacy of Shultz and Shevardnadze, whose work had made the INF treaty possible. Gorbachev insisted the two men stand. Shultz and Shevardnadze raised their champagne glasses to each other from across the room and the audience exploded in an ovation that lasted several minutes.

In the history of the State Department there had not been a luncheon like this: no one left until well after four o'clock. Gorbachev, whose energy never flagged, went back to his embassy and sparred with a group of invited editors for more than an hour and then hosted a return dinner in honor of President and Mrs. Reagan.

That evening at the Soviet Embassy party, I relaxed for the first time since the visit began. When I went through the receiving line, Gorbachev said to me, "This is the lady who gives all the orders," and turning to the President, he said with mock anguish, "Protocol rules our lives!"

The Soviet dinner began with caviar—passed twice—followed by a dozen courses ending with ice cream, then fruit, and finally blueberry tart. The evening concluded with a concert by Elena Obraztsova, a stunning blond mezzo-soprano, and star of the Bolshoi Opera.

Both at the White House and at the Soviet Embassy I noticed that these world figures were just like you and me. The Reagans and the Gorbachevs, the Shultzes and the Shevardnadzes autographed menu cards and programs for each other.

The heart-stopping moment in the Gorbachev visit came on the last day. As usual, I went to the embassy to escort Gorbachev to the White House for a meeting. He and his senior advisers had just given a breakfast in honor of Vice President Bush, and Bush decided to wait and accompany the Russians to the White House.

Bush was his usual cheerful and upbeat self as we sat together in a small waiting room near the front door of the embassy. He had enjoyed the exchange at breakfast, with Raisa and Barbara Bush present. Raisa had asked why Americans had such a negative view of the USSR. Did the schools teach properly? Was it the media's fault? Raisa and Gorbachev peppered the guests with questions, and sometimes contradicted and interrupted each other.

Our brief wait dragged on to a half hour, then an hour. My protocol people were upset that the Vice President was being kept waiting for so long. The White House people, at the other end of an open phone, were furious that President Reagan was kept waiting. The Soviets were in a big huddle, and constantly on the phone to their negotiating team, but we had no idea then what it was all about. (Later I learned that they were trying to reach agreement on how SDI—Star Wars—was to be treated in the joint declaration by Gorbachev and Reagan.)

Finally we departed in the usual sixty-car motorcade, Bush with Gorbachev, I just behind with Shevardnadze. Suddenly, the cars came to a precipitate halt at Connecticut Avenue and K Street, one of the busiest intersections in Washington.

This was unheard of in a police-escorted motorcade. Could there have been an assassination attempt? an accident? a heart attack? Shevardnadze's security people, guns drawn, hustled him out of the car. Armed Secret Service agents sprang from the cars toward the sidewalk. I headed for the crowd converging ahead. Vice President Bush stood back, looking somewhat bemused, but Gorbachev was in the midst of a group of Americans, pressing the flesh. The crowd went wild—and one young woman was captured on TV that night saying, "That guy is a PR genius!"

As we got back in the cars, my heart was still racing. Shevardnadze seemed extraordinarily calm, not the least bit shaken. A small suspicion crossed my mind. How did the TV cameras just happen to be at that intersection? Was that little adventure spontaneous or staged by the Soviets? I will never know, but I think the latter. In any case, it took a few years off my life.

I was waiting in the anteroom just outside the Oval Office while the final summit meetings were in session. The President's secretary asked me to pick up the phone—I had a call from Blair House, the President's guest house, where the multimillion-dollar restoration project was in full swing.

"Please, Mrs. Roosevelt," the project manager asked. "Can you come and see these paint samples on the walls?"

Dear Lord, I thought, here we are negotiating war and peace and I am doing paint colors! I dashed across the street, and returned just in time for Mrs. Gorbachev's arrival at the White House. She had had her coffee with Pamela Harriman and five other distinguished American women: Supreme Court Justice Sandra Day O'Connor, University of Chicago president Hannah

Gray, *Washington Post* publisher Katharine Graham, and Senators Nancy Kassebaum and Barbara Mikulski.

(Afterward, they reported that Raisa had talked nonstop, lecturing them about the Soviet Union. Barbara Mikulski remarked that that was the first time anyone had ever outtalked her. Nancy Kassebaum gave Raisa a letter from a prominent Kansas City doctor, complimenting Gorbachev for trying to curb alcoholism in the Soviet Union, and suggesting an exchange between the University of Kansas Medical Center and similar Russian institutions. Mrs. Gorbachev apparently followed through on this, and contacts were later initiated.)

The weather suddenly took a turn for the worse, and the White House staff debated whether to move the departure ceremony indoors. They gambled on outside, and it poured. I discovered to my amazement that the White House had only enough umbrellas for the Gorbachevs and the Reagans. Rex Scouten, the White House curator, took pity and gave me his own umbrella. But the mightiest men in the United States and Soviet governments lined up for the departure statements, stoically suffering the downpour, all prime candidates for pneumonia.

With the formal ceremony finished, we went home to dry off, so that we could get wet all over again. In the late afternoon Gorbachev had a press conference, scheduled to last for one hour, and then off to Andrews Air Force Base for an eight o'clock departure. We thought we had won that one, but never underestimate the determination of the Russians. Gorbachev outfoxed us by talking for two hours; he arrived at Andrews just before nine, as he had always intended.

I held my large umbrella over Gorbachev as he got out of the car. He looked embarrassed to have a woman holding his umbrella and ordered one of his aides to take it from me. I walked him down to the waiting Vice President and Mrs. Bush to say goodbye. Then, to my surprise, the Soviet leader, instead of going up the stairs, broke away and said goodbye to me.

I had worn a red wool coat, partly because it would make it easier for my staff to keep track of me during the nighttime departure made chaotic by the terrible downpour. Sure enough, the

Russian plane had no sooner headed down the runway than an irate caller telephoned the State Department to complain about my wearing red.

But nothing could dampen my spirits. I was on my way to a "wheels up" party with my heroic protocol staff. In the car I asked Gene to turn on the radio so we could listen to the President's report to the nation on the summit. Toward the end of the speech, I heard President Reagan say:

"A couple of years ago, Nancy and I were deeply moved by a story told by former *New York Times* reporter and Greek immigrant Nicholas Gage. It is the story of Eleni, his mother, a woman caught in one of the terrible struggles of the postwar era, the Greek Civil War, a mother who was tried and executed because she smuggled her children out to safety in America.

". . . Her final cry was not a curse on her killers but an invocation of what she died for, a declaration of love. These simple last words of Mr. Gage's mother were 'My children!'

"How that cry echoes down through the centuries, a cry for all the children of the world, a cry for peace, for a world of love and understanding."

Two years before, I had given the president a copy of Gage's book, *Eleni,* as a Christmas present, and thought no more about it. It was humbling indeed to realize that such a small gesture could have worldwide echoes as Ronald Reagan wound up the most triumphant week of his presidency.

TWENTY-EIGHT

China—the Drama Unfolds

*T*IANANMEN SQUARE! Like most Americans, I was glued to my television set during those weeks in the spring of 1989 when Chinese students fought and died for a more democratic China. But, as the Chinese army marched on the square and the bloody drama unfolded, I saw too the painstaking efforts by Reagan, Bush, and Shultz to build a solid Sino-American relationship come to an abrupt and tragic halt.

I had participated enthusiastically in building that relationship. Premier Zhao Ziyang, President Li Xiannian, Vice Premier Li Peng, General Yang Shangkun, Vice Premiers Yao Yilin and Tian Jiyun—for me, these were not just names in headlines. The men involved in the brutal power struggle I watched on TV had become my friends. We had crisscrossed the United States together on various official visits; I had spent more time with them on these trips than any other member of our government.

Before I became Chief of Protocol, the Far East had seemed strange and impenetrable to me, but much to my surprise, after so many Chinese visitors and after traveling to China myself, I found I had a special empathy for this nation of one billion people.

Nowhere in the world is protocol more important than in China. In ancient times the chief of protocol ranked near the top in the hierarchy of the imperial government. Because ceremony, outer appearances, and "face" are so deeply ingrained in Chinese culture, form always took precedence over substance, and this has continued under the Communist regime as well.*

Secretary of State Shultz understood this well. When we started planning the first exploratory visit, in October 1983, of his counterpart, Foreign Minister Wu Xueqian, the Secretary said in effect: "Lucky, I want to send the right signals with this visit. I want a program that will demonstrate the importance we attach to the China relationship."

The Chinese had been suspicious of the Reagan administration at the beginning—afraid that conservative Republicans, with their special ties to Taiwan, would make good relations impossible. Haig had worked hard to overcome this, and when Shultz took over, improving Sino-American relations was one of his foremost foreign policy objectives.

Shultz felt we could develop a productive relationship with China based on our mutual interests. He had recently returned from a successful trip to China and wanted to repay their hospitality in style. That was my job.

Normally, I did not meet foreign ministers at the airport (only chiefs of state or heads of government) but sent a lower-ranking emissary. But for Foreign Minister Wu I made an exception. The Chinese immediately "got the message" and the newspapers both here and in China gave special emphasis to the high-level greeting Wu was accorded. Wu was a cheerful and pleasant man, but also smart and perceptive. I liked his toothy grin, and we hit it off immediately.

That night Shultz made another "special" gesture—he had the Foreign Minister to an informal dinner at his house, and Mrs. Shultz did the cooking. (This so impressed Wu he later mentioned it in a toast in Chicago.) The next three days were filled with activity—a meeting with President Reagan, lunch with Vice Pres-

---

*Betty Bao Lord, the Chinese-born wife of Winston Lord, former ambassador to China, writes in her latest book, Legacies, that China has "a culture rooted in Confucianism, which accepts form, the more malleable, in lieu of content. To Confucius, the consummate realist, proper conduct, the more knowable, was the measure of man. To ask mere mortals to discipline their thoughts as well as their actions would be asking too much—form would suffice. And so Chinese embraced ritual, the ultimate form."

ident Bush, a large formal dinner in the State Department's Benjamin Franklin Room (the press duly noted that these were honors usually reserved for the top man), a luncheon hosted by the House Armed Services Committee, and a return dinner given by Wu at the Chinese Embassy.

I had my first run-in with Shultz during this visit. I casually suggested a gala evening at the Kennedy Center in honor of our visitor. The Houston Ballet was due to perform near that time. I checked with Roger Stevens, head of the Center, and he explained that the ballet company would have to come a day earlier and such an evening could be very expensive. Someone, either the State Department or a private donor, would have to guarantee most of the house and underwrite the cost of the many boxes needed.

Breathless with enthusiasm, I rushed to the Secretary's office to explain, seeking his agreement for the department to pay or permission from him to pursue the matter of private donors. I thought he would be impressed with my initiative.

Not at all. He was furious. "What ever gave you the idea that I wanted such an evening?" he asked. "And I do not want to be beholden to anyone."

In other words, cool it.

Later I asked Ray Seitz, Shultz's executive assistant, what I had done wrong, and he gave me the best piece of advice I ever got about dealing with George Shultz.

"You came on too strong, Lucky," Ray said. "The Secretary does not like to be crowded. He likes proposals to come to him in an orderly fashion and with the options clearly spelled out. And he wants time to think about them. But don't worry, he's probably already gotten over his anger."

In case he hadn't, however, the next day prior to an Oval Office meeting I slipped a note in his pocket saying, "O Venerable One! Please forgive worthless slave. Consider this at least a dozen kow-tows. Your humble servant, etc."

Even the best-planned visits can come unglued by some unforeseen incident. Had it not been for the alertness of Bunny Murdock, Foreign Minister Wu's visit would have come to a disastrous conclusion.

It happened in Chicago. Only twenty-four hours before Wu and his party were due to arrive there, Bunny learned that the Taiwanese community had asked the mayor to designate that day as "Republic of China Day." Bunny immediately recognized that official sponsorship of this Taiwan holiday would be taken as an insult by Wu and would spoil all that had been achieved by the visit. She quickly arranged for senior State Department officials to contact the mayor and alert him to the seriousness of the situation, and they negotiated well into the night. As a result, the Taiwanese celebrations took place without official sponsorship, and a threatening confrontation between the official People's Republic of China delegation and members of the Taiwanese community was averted.

Wu's visit was only a dress rehearsal. The real test came with the visit of Premier Zhao Ziyang, just three months later.

It was a brisk, cold January evening when Premier Zhao stepped off the plane at Langley Air Force Base, near Williamsburg, Virginia. He had already spent a pleasant twenty-four hours in Hawaii, his first rest stop, and we had decided to give him a second rest stop in Williamsburg before subjecting him to the full panoply of a state visit.

I liked Zhao immediately. He carried about him an air of authority and self-assurance, secure in the knowledge that he was Deng Xiaoping's protégé and anointed successor. (Who could have foreseen that five years later he would be stripped of his position, disgraced, and put under house arrest by that same benefactor?)

The next day in Williamsburg I rode beside Zhao in a horse-drawn carriage, accompanied only by attendants in Revolutionary dress and the ubiquitous Secret Service. I watched him go through his paces—smooth, quick-witted, an open mind absorbing every experience.

This was Zhao's first visit to the States and the first top-level visit since Deng's trip in 1979. Zhao impressed everyone from the President on down with his sophistication and intelligence and obvious good will. "He has the ability to be charming without giving up any of his positions," Mike Deaver observed. "Sort of like Reagan."

He sometimes sent important signals to his own countrymen. We were surprised that he wore well-tailored Western-style suits, explaining to reporters that not only were they "more comfortable" but also, "When the Prime Minister wears a Western suit, then nobody will fear to wear fashionable dress." He added that women should not be discouraged from wearing makeup or clothes which enhanced their looks.

Zhao was well-born, as Communist leaders go. His father was a wealthy landlord and he had been relatively well educated. A victim of the Red Guards during the Cultural Revolution, he was paraded through the streets of Canton wearing a dunce cap. He disappeared from sight for a number of years, but whatever he suffered then did not appear to have left him a bitter man.

Zhao was master of the graceful gesture. (When he learned it was my birthday during the visit he sent me beautiful red roses.) He never showed anger or annoyance and kept a good-natured smile on his face most of the time. He seemed to enjoy talking and joking with the likes of New York mayor Ed Koch or singer John Denver, and hammed it up for the cameras with little prompting from the photographers.

He was scheduled to visit the Sidwell Friends School in Washington, but it had to be canceled because of a snowstorm. When newspapers reported the terrible disappointment of the children, he insisted on scratching his formal departure ceremony the next day and substituting a visit to the school. I'll never forget the joy of those twenty students in the Chinese-language class when the Premier invited them all to come to China as his guests!

"I have five children and three grandchildren," he told me, "and we all live together, in the Chinese tradition." (Later I read that three of his children had been educated in the States, but he never mentioned it.)

He was fascinated by the Roosevelts—the "Luwasefu" in Chinese—and asked me many questions about the two presidents. But when we sailed around the Statue of Liberty, I told him about my own father, how he had come to America and prospered, and what Miss Liberty symbolized for me. "You can see, Mr. Premier, I am living proof that in America through study and hard work—and some luck—nothing is impossible," I said.

I watched his thoughtful face as the interpreter explained my words—and his eyes showed a keen appreciation for what I was saying. Five years later, when the demonstrators in Tiananmen Square raised up a Statue of Liberty, Chinese style, I thought of Zhao and wondered if that gesture by the exuberant and determined students had put another nail in his coffin.

Zhao had a superb interpreter the entire trip, but I almost blew it with her. As we moved in and out of our limousine, our feet sometimes got entangled and she seemed very huffy when I suggested we organize our feet a certain way. Apparently in China it is a faux pas to talk about feet, and she considered my comment an insult.

One other problem caused us momentary alarm. The Hotel and Restaurant Employees Union threatened to picket the Chinese for giving their return reception at a non-union hotel. By appealing to their patriotism we managed to persuade them not to carry out their threat and mar an otherwise flawless trip.

The Zhao visit ended in New York. As I saw him off—he then went to Canada for a state visit there—he told me, "I feel that Secretary Shultz is my friend, and I found President Reagan very open and honest. I like that."

This relationship remained a solid one throughout the Reagan years—and nothing gratified me more than the letter I found on my desk from Secretary Shultz on my return to Washington:

"I want to let you know how much I appreciated the outstanding job you and your staff did on the visit of Premier Zhao. Chinese comments . . . have been uniformly positive.

"The meticulous preparation and then follow-up . . . helped to set just the right atmosphere for us to pursue our objective: an improved U.S.-China relationship. From the initial arrangements and schedules to the day-to-day logistical support you helped make available throughout the visit, the final product was a great credit to the State Department and to this country.

"Thanks to all of you for your dedication to an important mission. I commend you on a job very well done."

The visit a year and a half later of China's President Li Xiannian and Vice Premier Li Peng was more of a cliff-hanger.

We had been working on the trip for months. The seventy-six-year-old Li was near retirement, so the real significance of the visit, scheduled to begin July 21, 1985, in Niagara Falls and ending ten days later in Hawaii, was to give Vice Premier Li Peng his first exposure to America and our China experts a chance to appraise him more closely. Li Peng was touted as the likely successor to Zhao, which indeed he was, albeit a bit premature.

However, on July 13, a robust and healthy-looking President Reagan went into surgery to have a cancerous growth removed from his colon. At this point, the Chinese party was already in Canada, making a state visit there before coming on to the United States. I received a letter of good wishes from President Li to be transmitted to President Reagan, but between the lines was the unspoken question, "Is the visit going to be canceled?"

All of us thought it would be. But to our amazement word came back that the state visit was on—and I was to proceed as usual. The Chinese could scarcely believe it. They kept checking with me, asking, "Are you sure? How could a man of seventy-three undergo major surgery and subject himself to the strain of a state visit ten days later?"

Well, Ronald Reagan showed them. As the world watched, he demonstrated not only physical courage, duty, and discipline, but also the force of the actor's maxim, "The show must go on." And the show did go on, reassuring the world and the financial markets that the affairs of the Republic were once again in strong hands. But we had a few glitches along the way.

My staff and I flew to Niagara Falls on Sunday, July 21. We had prepared a symbolic arrival ceremony in the middle of the Rainbow Bridge, which marks the Canadian-American border. A Canadian motorcade would bring the Chinese delegation halfway across the bridge and I would bring our motorcade to pick them up. Thus, the arrival of the Chinese on American soil made a great photo—the advance men and the media were happy, and the visit was off to an auspicious beginning.

Right away, President Li expressed his gratitude for our quick response after Reagan's illness was announced. "I am very impressed and appreciative that President Reagan honors me and the Chinese people by continuing this visit when his health is so precarious," he told me.

What the dear man didn't realize was that we were using his own delicate health as a way of slowing down Ronald Reagan, who was so gung-ho that Nancy was having a hell of a time persuading him to allow minor alterations to lighten his schedule.

President Li was frail—he had a bad back and was scheduled to have eye surgery as soon as he returned to China. Therefore we told the NSC that we needed chairs on the reviewing platform for the thirty-minute South Lawn arrival ceremony. (Normally the principals stood throughout.)

"Nothing doing" was the first reaction. The Reagans didn't want the world to think the President was an invalid. But, Mr. President, you don't want to embarrass your guest, do you? We don't think he can stand through the ceremony.

Much to everyone's relief, the President finally agreed to the chairs—and at the welcoming ceremony we were amused to see that, ten days after surgery, Reagan walked with his usual buoyancy and firmly gripped the hesitant Li by the elbow as he escorted him up the steps to the reviewing stand.

Then came another hitch, over the state dinner. Mrs. Reagan was adamant that the President retire immediately after the meal—before the East Room entertainment by opera stars Grace Bumbry and Gregg Baker.

Robert "Bud" McFarlane, head of the NSC, telephoned me in Niagara Falls and in his sepulchral voice said, "Lucky, we need your help. You must convince the Chinese to depart from the White House immediately after dinner, before the entertainment, otherwise the President won't leave."

"But, Bud, the Chinese are exquisitely polite. They would consider this terribly rude on their part. However, they will understand perfectly if the President goes upstairs early; they would feel they had to stay as a courtesy to Mrs. Reagan," I explained.

"If the President learns the Chinese are staying, he will insist on staying, and Mrs. Reagan won't hear of it. I don't care how you do it—but your assignment is to persuade the Chinese to leave early."

I discussed this at some length with my Chinese counterpart and got an insight into their curious mentality. "You see, Mrs. Roosevelt, before President Reagan's illness, our President did not want to stay for the entertainment—he is accustomed to early evenings. But now this special effort is such an honor by the Reagans, President Li feels he must show his appreciation by staying for the entire evening. He also said it would not be polite to leave early after so many presidents from America have visited China and he is the first Chinese president to come to America."

I was flummoxed. All this politesse—from both Reagan and Li—was going to kill them both and we could have a double funeral!

But we did hit on a solution. "What if both Presidents Li and Reagan depart immediately after dinner and Mrs. Li and Mrs. Reagan remain with all the other guests to enjoy the entertainment?"

That's one day I earned my salary. Both sides agreed to that simple solution. Mrs. Reagan also eliminated the receiving line and certain photo ops and the lengthy mix-and-mingle after dinner.

President Li was delighted with the evening, sitting next to Mrs. Reagan, who wore the handsome red brocade cheongsam (traditional Chinese dress) that had been his gift to her. She also had at her table Malcolm Forbes and Elizabeth Taylor, two Americans well known in China (and that was the beginning of their highly publicized friendship).

My favorite memories of Li's visit are those days on the road in Chicago, Los Angeles, and Hawaii. I had many conversations with the crusty old warrior, a veteran of the Long March, who began life in great poverty and worked his way up through the ranks of the Red Army. Later he became finance minister of the

Communist government and now President. Little as I knew about Chinese society, I could sense the gap between the peasant Li, the technocrat Li Peng, and the more polished Zhao Ziyang. Possible in those differences of background and education lies the explanation of the events which toppled Zhao and ruthlessly brought Li Peng to power.

I sensed in Li Peng a fundamental antagonism to America. And since he is now the Premier of China, his reactions at the time may help explain how he sees us.

Our prosperity had both a positive and negative effect on him, I wrote in my notes of the visit. "Li Peng sees the wonders of our country, but is reluctant at times to admit that they are the result of a free society. This would entail a wrenching ideological change because most of his orientation is toward Russia and the Eastern bloc. Nonetheless the seed is planted. Li Peng is reluctant to admit that his estimate of Communism's strengths may be wrong or that he may have been brainwashed (as a student in Russia), but this visit is the beginning of his re-education."

Of all the Chinese leaders I met, I found Li Peng the most difficult to read. It was hard to believe that his great patron and mentor had been Zhou Enlai, a man noted for his sophistication and charm. Li Peng was reserved, his reactions muted and complex, but he seemed quite candid in answering my questions.

What did he think of Gorbachev? (They had recently met in Moscow.)

"Gorbachev is his own man. I was very impressed that he had a briefing paper and never referred to it. He said he wants improved Sino-Soviet relations, but we must wait and see."

Li Peng said China and Russia had the same social systems, implying a natural affinity. I challenged that, noting that the Soviet system seemed much more inflexible. He agreed.

"America has never really suffered in a war," Li Peng stated. "Do you know who suffered most in World War Two? Russia, and then China."

We agreed that the future is in the Far East. "The world is not as the Americans would like to think it is—just Russia versus the

United States—but the new realities are China, Japan, and the land mass of Europe."

"On the contrary," I answered. "We not only acknowledge this, but everything in our postwar policy has made it happen— we forced postwar Japan to put aside militarism and develop economically, we built NATO, we encouraged the economic unification of Europe."

While Li Peng was a challenge to everyone on the trip, it was easy to talk to President Li, even though his advance billing described him as "stubborn, frank, and tough." Actually, we were somewhat bemused by him. We couldn't decide if he was bored, out to lunch, or simply inscrutable. However, I developed a real affection for him, and we even had a few laughs.

He was high on Richard Nixon. "The Chinese never forget a friend. We do not believe all those things about Watergate." Zbigniew Brzezinski, he said, was a "great strategist." He was not impressed by Carter or Ford and never mentioned Henry Kissinger.

One day, apropos of nothing, President Li started chuckling to himself, and said how smart we were to have bested the Russians in the purchase of Alaska. Another time, he observed it was much easier to run an army than manage an economy.

Li asked me about our tax structure. "Why does the President want to lower tax rates? What is your salary and what portion do you pay in taxes?" When I told him I paid 50 percent federal and 11 percent District income taxes he was shocked.

"We would not like to pay so much taxes either," he observed. "We don't have an income tax, but we have so little income there would be nothing left if we paid taxes."

But not all our encounters were weighty. In Chicago someone presented me with a large button flashing "Cubs" off and on in red lights like a neon sign. President Li was intrigued, so I pinned it on him just as he was about to attend a black-tie dinner in his honor hosted by Governor and Mrs. James R. Thompson and the Mid-America Committee.

Throughout the evening his flashing button proclaimed the Chinese leader a Chicago Cubs fan. However, I began to feel uneasy for fear that someone would think the gag had worn thin. I was, after all, responsible for the presidential dignity! But he turned aside all hints that I relieve him of it. When he went to the podium to thank his hosts, he got a huge round of applause as the sign blinked on and off! (And like all Chinese when applauded, he clapped back.)

In Hawaii, he caught me with my wet hair in a turban as I was rushing from the beach to my room, through the lobby. He was just going out for a stroll, and seeing me, he pointed and guffawed loudly—delighted to have caught me in a breach of protocol!

The chemistry between the Americans and the Chinese on the trip was terrific, and the only time I saw President Li and the rest of the delegation upset was over the matter of American condemnation of China's population policy—one child per family—and they were especially irked by the fact that we withheld funds for fear they would be used for abortion. The Chinese felt this was an internal matter and no business of ours to moralize or lecture them.

Li said his favorite stop was Chicago, and the city fathers certainly knocked themselves out for the delegation, laying on a visit to the Chicago Mercantile Exchange, another to the Braidwood nuclear station, and a boat excursion around Lake Michigan. And Chicago's merchants had filled their rooms with gifts.

The Chinese were also delighted with the warmth and hospitality in Los Angeles, where they visited Disneyland, and in Hawaii, where they were smothered with leis on their arrival. President Li was not very comfortable with so many garlands of flowers encircling his neck, so he took them and put them over my head, to the amusement of the photographers. Alas, this was the front-page photo in every Hawaiian paper.

Governor George Ariyoshi gave a memorable dinner for our visitors. The Chinese toured Pearl Harbor, and the nearby Polynesian village put on a colorful display of dancing and folklore.

On our way to the airport to say goodbye, I asked President

Li what had impressed him most about America. Without hesitating he answered, "The happy marriage between research in the universities and industrial development; and the prosperity of the Western United States due to the proper harnessing of water resources. Both of these are great lessons for China."

Not long after President Li's trip I was to learn for myself the accuracy of the saying "The Chinese never forget a favor."

When Wu visited in 1983, he invited me to come to China as his guest. I took that about as seriously as the Southern pleasantry "Y'all come and see us, hear."

Premier Zhao reiterated the invitation, as did President Li, but when Li said goodbye he warned, "Ambassador Roosevelt, you have looked after so many Chinese leaders on their visits to the States, you must now come to China. If you don't allow us to reciprocate, we will lose face. I will not permit any more Chinese officials to come to America until you visit China."

Again, I thought this his gracious way of saying thank you. It never occurred to me that he meant it—and that indeed this was the Chinese view of the situation. A few months later, Minister-Counselor Ji of the Chinese Embassy asked for a meeting with me.

"I come on instructions from Foreign Minister Wu," he said. "He extends once more his invitation to you and your husband to visit China and asks that you bring two others of your choosing as your entourage."

I loved the implication that I was so important I had to travel with an entourage! Clearly the time for decision had come, so after I checked with Secretary Shultz, the legal eagles, and the China experts, they all agreed that it was in the interests of the United States government that this trip go forward. I informed the Chinese that I wanted to bring Bunny Murdock, the assistant chief of protocol who had done so much to make every Chinese visit a triumph. She would choose her own companion. (It turned out to be the late Carroll de Erney, an inspired choice of Bunny's who added so much to the fun we had.)

I was scheduled to accompany President Reagan to the economic summit in Tokyo in early May 1986. The China trip would fit very nicely right after the summit. Archie could meet me in Tokyo and we would fly to Beijing together.

The PRC Foreign Office took charge of our lives the minute we four arrived. They had prepared our itinerary, which included Xian, Quilin, Shanghai, and of course the complete tourist tour of Beijing. They took care of our hotels and all our meals. An interpreter accompanied us at all times, and at least two "handlers" from either Protocol or the Foreign Office.

Foreign Minister Wu received me for tea, and the Vice Foreign Minister, Zhu Qizhen, and his wife gave a beautiful dinner for us at the Diaoyutai Guest House. (He subsequently was named ambassador to Washington.) Word had filtered back that I loved Peking duck, so the former ambassador to Washington, Zhang Wenjin, arranged a banquet for us at a noted Peking-duck restaurant.

But more was in store for us. Two days after our arrival one of our assigned sitters came to my room and in an awed voice told me President Li wished to invite the four of us to dinner. The aide informed me this was an unprecedented honor. President Li rarely entertained, and then only for heads of state or government. For a mere chief of protocol to be given a dinner in the same elegant guest house where Li had entertained President Reagan had stunned Chinese protocol.

There were seventeen at dinner, sitting at one round table set with a peach silk tablecloth, a centerpiece of bright flowers on a bed of green, and the finest Ming porcelain. And I tackled, with chopsticks, one of the most delicious meals I've ever eaten—eleven courses consisting of hors d'oeuvres, spicy squid's egg soup, braised delicacies, minced shrimp molded in the shape of a pomegranate, crown roast of lamb, fresh fish in cellophane, braised vegetables, eight-jewel rice pudding, pastries, fruits, and ice cream.

During the evening I said to my genial host, who looked ten years younger than when he had been in Washington, "Mr. President, this is an honor I will remember all my life. I do not deserve it."

"Yes, you do," he replied. "You were the first person to greet me when I arrived in Niagara Falls and you stayed with me until we said goodbye in Hawaii. This is the least I could do."

Later, in our exchange of toasts (the Chinese have endless toasts between courses and at the end of the meal—usually with a lethal rice wine known as mao-tai, guaranteed to produce a monstrous hangover), President Li made the predictable remarks about Sino-American friendship, but stressed the importance of friends such as ourselves handling our disagreements privately, as "gentlemen."

When my turn came I decided not to revert to the usual clichés. "Mr. President, dear Chinese friends. I come from a family who originated in Lebanon and who belong to a religious sect known as the Druze. The Druze believe that when you die your soul goes to China—which in their lexicon is the equivalent of heaven.

"What is so wonderful is that I did not have to die to get to heaven. But the Druze are correct. China is a form of heaven and all of us who have been the recipients of your hospitality must acknowledge that the Druze were indeed wise to have known this as far back as the eleventh century."

The strong Chinese wine enhanced my eloquence, and when I concluded, our hosts burst into applause. I had one more reason to bless my ancestors for helping me to rise to the occasion.

I came to love the Chinese, so for me Tiananmen Square was a personal heartbreak as well as an international tragedy. The careful efforts to improve Sino-American relations during the Reagan years were put on hold—one can hope only temporarily.

TWENTY-NINE

Asia—a Success Story

SECRETARY OF STATE Shultz always seemed happiest and most hopeful when dealing with the Asian nations. "The Pacific is where the action is," he would often remind us. "The Pacific is the future."

Perhaps it was because he attached such importance to the Japanese-American relationship. Perhaps the California orientation of the administration prompted him to look westward. Or perhaps it was the unmitigated economic success of so many Pacific nations that accounted for his great optimism. In any case, he made a believer out of me.

In the Far East, protocol was elevated to an art. Even the Koreans, whom my staff found to be the most rough-hewn, were punctilious about such matters. And at the end of his visit in April 1985, Korean president Chun Doo Hwan thanked Tim Towell for the "high degree of professionalism" of our protocol team, and added that in Asia "symbolism is an integral part of policy."

I have already described the ease with which my staff and I developed friendships and close working relationships with the Chinese. But the Japanese are another story. The differences between the two dominant nations of Asia are profound, and I am not sure that I ever understood the Japanese, much as I liked Prime Minister Yasuhiro Nakasone, who came to the United States at least once a year.

The language barrier is formidable, even with excellent interpreters. (I love the British diplomat's story of a Japanese translator who described "the Permanent Undersecretary" of the British Foreign Office as "the eternal young typist"!)

Japanese body language is just as mystifying. When they talk they stand farther apart than we do. Bows are very significant, and vary from a slight inclination of the head to a deep bend from the waist. The Japanese always seem to know exactly who bows to whom and how much. And in Japan a giggle or a laugh denotes embarrassment rather than amusement. In one set of instructions, we were told: "The Japanese equate emotion with insanity. Don't get excited."

The Japanese are so polite they hate to say no and will make every effort to prevent a direct confrontation of any sort. To avoid losing face—and because they are sensitive also to *your* losing face—"yes" does not necessarily mean agreement or acquiescence but simply "I understand what you mean."

And while this sort of dialogue gives the impression of compromise, the truth is the Japanese were the most inflexible and the most programmed group that we dealt with. Any variation on a schedule caused teeth-gnashing. When the Reagans at the last minute invited the Nakasones and their daughter to come and have an intimate breakfast with them at the White House just before departure, we thought everyone would be pleased—and, of course, the principals were. But the Japanese staff went into a tailspin. This was not on the program. How would they cope? We told them to relax; this was our territory and we could do it without the endless diagrams, motorcade pre-seating, and telephone monitoring that was their modus operandi.

The Japanese always brought the largest advance teams of any nation, excepting the Russians. I found the best way to have a visit come out the way we wanted it was to announce as holy writ our rules and procedures at the beginning. Then, instead of arguing with the Japanese over every detail, we found it made sense to let them do it their way, within our guidelines.

But sometimes our customs and theirs were in direct conflict. For example, on every visit Nakasone brought with him five members of the Japanese Diet. This apparently was etched in stone, and not bringing them would involve great political risk for the Prime Minister.

The Diet representatives insisted on meeting Reagan and having an individual photograph shaking hands with him. We never allowed outsiders to horn in on substantive discussions, and the President's schedulers objected strenuously. Nakasone insisted. Finally we gave up, and the Diet members, like a scene from Gilbert and Sullivan, filed in, bowed, shook hands with the President, and were escorted out of the Oval Office to their waiting cars. The entire performance took two minutes. But we must have spent two days hashing over the scenario.

Nakasone, who seemed to me restrained and dignified, was, by Japanese standards, a colorful extrovert. When he called the President "Ron" and the President called him "Yasu" it struck an incongruous note in my ear. I wondered if even Nakasone's wife called him that! There's no question, however, that the two got along famously.

Nakasone was also admitted to a very exclusive club, the other members being Margaret Thatcher and Mexico's former president José López Portillo. They were the only foreign VIPs received at Camp David during the Reagan presidency. The Reagans jealously guarded their privacy there, and did not want to start a competition among world leaders over who got invited to Camp David.

Whenever Nakasone came to Washington, Mike Mansfield, our octogenarian ambassador to Japan, also returned home with him. I found Mansfield one of the most admirable men I have ever met. Unflappable, with a wry sense of humor, and a face right out of a Norman Rockwell painting, Mansfield had presided over our Tokyo embassy for twelve years.

When we went to Japan for the economic summit in 1986, the advance men and White House staff took over, elbowing Ambassador Mansfield and everyone else out of the way. But Mansfield stood back and observed it all with great detachment and amusement, as the brash young types reinvented the wheel.

• •

Australia was of vital importance to us in the Pacific, and on my list of favorite VIPs Prime Minister Robert J. Hawke of Australia was near the top. This Labor Party leader, energetic and emotional, was a White House favorite as well, and although Hawke and Reagan wore different political labels, it was obvious they had a special affinity.

Hawke was full of surprises. He admitted quite frankly that he had once had a drinking problem and that he had been unfaithful to his wife Hazel. But everyone, including his wife and the vast Australian electorate, forgave him his transgressions and he kept being reelected. And we were delighted. A born politician, good-looking and with a very appealing personality, Hawke was widely recognized as a good friend of the United States.

We looked forward to his frequent visits, and after the first one Reagan and Hawke were on a first-name basis. No one was a greater fan of his than Ronald Reagan, and seeing their camaraderie simply reinforced my feeling that the President based his judgments on instinct and intuition far more than on ideology.

About once a year Lee Kuan Yew, the President of Singapore, came to town. At first I did not find him simpatico, but Reagan, Bush, and Shultz all held him in the highest esteem. I understood why only after I went to Singapore and saw what a remarkable transformation he had achieved in twenty-five years. From poverty and filth to prosperity and cleanliness—he changed not only the landscape but the habits of his people, and pulled them kicking and screaming into the twentieth century—sometimes by draconian measures. He also had the guts to punish drug traffickers with death, and force addicts off the streets and into rehabilitation centers. I ended up joining his chorus of admirers.

The Koreans were the toughest for my staff to deal with. "They are even more paranoid than the Japanese," one officer explained to me. "They always think they are being diddled, and they are so stubborn it is almost impossible to negotiate with them."

I always put a man in charge of the Korean visits, because

they were also given to strong-arm tactics. Once, when President Chun Doo Hwan was en route from the Washington Monument to his hotel, the motorcade passed by an orderly demonstration against the Korean president. The Korean security agents bailed out of a moving car and started beating up the protesters. Our own people had to plunge into the melee to break it up and remind the Koreans that in America we have freedom of speech and assembly!

The Koreans' negotiating tactics were exasperating; they would not take no for an answer. They went out of channels, and appealed to anyone they could think of to get their way. And if they were determined to win a point, they assigned dozens of people to work on that one issue. In the end, it was a war of attrition, and the Korean advance team frequently bested some of our most able protocol officers.

Only in October 1988, just as the Reagan administration was ending, did we come to know a more subtle Korean chief of state. The new President, Roh Tae Woo, brought a different type of entourage, and they made a very favorable impression.

Our relationship with the Philippines was unique in the Far East—a combination of paternalism, affection, and obligation to help this nation that had once been an American dependency. In retrospect, I should have realized that Ferdinand and Imelda Marcos' days were numbered. When they came on a state visit in September 1982—the first such visit in sixteen years—the signs were obvious. Security was unusually tight as dissident Filipinos gathered wherever they went to protest the Marcos regime. Stories of corruption and human rights abuses abounded in the press.

Both husband and wife seemed a bit louche to me, and I sensed they were on the defensive. They were surrounded by sycophants and security men—I even had to protest when the latter pushed me around. While Marcos seemed subdued and tended to tell war stories about his efforts against the Japanese, Imelda recounted her good works for the poor and downtrodden—anxious to impress us with her "devotion" to her people. This, of course, was before anyone knew about the money salted away in New York real estate, the collection of paintings, the 2,000 pairs of shoes, and all the other instances of extravagance and greed that subsequently came to light.

Undoubtedly, Imelda ran the show. Marcos was a more appealing character and easy to like. He was in very bad health, and Imelda made the decisions. She even tried to attend Marcos' meeting with President Reagan in the Oval Office, but she was turned down.

When Imelda talked about how much the Filipinos loved her, I couldn't decide whether she was a megalomaniac or a creature of limited intelligence. The first time I ever saw her—many years before—she had been a striking beauty, but now age and overindulgence had coarsened her features.

In 1982 it mattered enormously that Marcos was a staunch anti-Communist ally and welcomed our bases in the Philippines, which were the cornerstone of our defense posture in the Pacific. But the assassination of opposition leader Benigno Aquino in 1983 led irrevocably to Marcos' downfall. The transition to a precarious democracy under Aquino's widow, Corazon, chosen President in a free election, initiated a new era in Philippine history.

We all fell in love with Cory Aquino. That is, all except the Reagans—and at first I found it hard to understand, because the President, himself so warm and friendly, could not fail to appreciate Mrs. Aquino's human qualities.

Later it was explained to me by someone close to the Reagans. "The President felt very strongly about loyalty—when a friend got into trouble you did not abandon him. He saw what happened to the Shah and thought the way the Carter administration had treated him was a disgrace. It was not easy for Reagan to turn his back on the Marcoses in their last days."

Of course, explained this way, it is entirely consistent with the President's character. Happily, during Cory's visit she won over the President and their friendship blossomed, but not before the rumors flew that Nancy Reagan did not want to give a state dinner for Mrs. Aquino for the same reasons.

If the Reagans were struggling with their attitudes, there was no question about how Congress or the State Department—in a rare show of agreement—felt about Cory. She was the heroine of the hour, and her biggest champions were Senator Richard Lugar of Indiana, Congressman Stephen Solarz of New York, and Secretary of State Shultz.

When Shultz visited President Aquino in Manila she had given a dinner for him in Malacañan Palace, the official home of the Philippine president. But she apologized for the entertainment, pleading lack of funds after the Marcos excesses—whereupon Cory's daughter and her friends sang for the guests.

When President Aquino returned the visit in September 1986, the Secretary gave a brilliant dinner for her and also brought amateurs to entertain her—"The Goodtime Washboard Three," a trio that Shultz had gotten to know in San Francisco. Mrs. Aquino loved it.

Of all the dinners we gave at the State Department, I remember this as the most joyous. Nothing but cheers for this valiant woman—so feminine and soft-spoken but so determined to lead her country back to stability and prosperity after the years of Marcos' misrule.

Sitting next to me at the dinner was Congressman Jim Wright of Texas. Knowing that the yellow rose was the Texas state flower, I mentioned that Mrs. Aquino always wore yellow. "Why don't you get some yellow roses in honor of Mrs. Aquino when she delivers her speech tomorrow before the joint session of Congress?" I suggested.

Wright pulled out his memo pad and made a notation. And he did me one better. The next day, as members of the Senate and House filed into their seats, each wore a yellow tie and a yellow rose boutonniere flown in specially from Texas—a courtly tribute which Mrs. Aquino greatly appreciated.

Her speech was another triumph—one of the best ever delivered by a foreign guest, interrupted by applause eleven times, with a standing ovation at both the beginning and the end. Afterward, Senate Majority Leader Robert Dole congratulated her. "Cory, you hit a home run." And she, quick as lightning, replied, "I hope the bases were loaded."

They were. Some five hours later the House voted the Philippines $200 million in emergency funds.

From Washington, President Aquino journeyed to New York, Boston, and San Francisco. I never saw a visitor drive herself so. I pleaded with her to cut down on the number of events, but she felt compelled to reach out to as many groups as she could. She moved through it all with a serenity derived from the unshakeable conviction that God had entrusted her with this special mission for her people.

I cherish a letter she wrote me after her return to the Philippines, which said in part: "I appreciate in particular your concern over my extremely tight schedule. We are just glad we made it, and there was no question it was due a great deal to your personal attention. . . . If you may pardon a bit of female chauvinism, I think what you and I proved is that, what men can do, we can do better."

There have been six coup attempts against Mrs. Aquino since she took office. One day, one may succeed, but I doubt that we will see again soon a woman of power whose strength derives entirely from her moral authority.

In my office I had a huge, blown-up photograph of Indira Gandhi, the Prime Minister of India, arriving at Andrews Air Force Base, with Shultz walking along beside her—she was his first important visitor after he took office in July 1982. Next to that black-and-white photo hung a large color portrait of Pakistan's president, General Mohammad Zia-ul-Haq, which he gave me after his state visit five months later.

Within a few years both leaders died violent deaths—Mrs. Gandhi assassinated by her own Sikh bodyguards and General Zia killed by political enemies who planted a bomb on his plane. I kept their two pictures in my direct line of vision for the seven years I occupied that office. A salutary reminder, in the midst of my global activities, of the transitory nature of power.

Indira Gandhi and Mohammad Zia were natural enemies. They did not trust each other but wanted to reach an accommodation, and Reagan and Shultz did a great deal to help them along.

When Mrs. Gandhi came to Washington, it was the first time in ten years that an Indian prime minister had visited. The Indians were sure that our government tilted toward Pakistan—and maybe we did. But it was understandable. General Zia, warm, thoughtful, and very human, genuinely liked America and Americans. Later, he blotted his reputation irreparably by executing former president Ali Bhutto, father of Benazir Bhutto, who, in a neat irony, succeeded Zia.

Also responsible for burnishing Pakistan's image was one of the most brilliant diplomats of our time, Sahabzada Yaqub Khan, who cut a romantic, dashing figure in his impeccably tailored jodhpurs and jaunty cap. He represented Pakistan in Paris, Moscow, and Washington as ambassador and later became foreign minister, a post he still holds as of this writing.

Thus, at the beginning of the 1980s Pakistan was considered a staunch friend of America, while India proclaimed itself the leader of the "nonaligned" world.

We knew that the Pakistanis were monitoring every minute of the Indian visit and even asked to see a detailed schedule. We carefully considered their rivalry in every step of the planning and accorded them similar honors.

Both trips were major successes; both visitors went home with a better understanding of Ronald Reagan and his administration. Indeed, Mrs. Gandhi seemed quite beguiled by the President. She had met him at a conference the previous year in Cancún, Mexico, and took a fancy to him. It was then she decided the time had come to improve U.S.-Indian rapport, after a decade of chilly and querulous relations. The President seemed similarly inclined.

I had heard how difficult Indira Gandhi could be, a prima donna, willful and capricious. But not at all. She was on her best behavior. She never complained, not even when she and I were marooned in a car for an hour and a half in a torrential rainstorm, barely able to move in New York traffic.

Finally, we got to our destination and a protocol officer later asked me, "How on earth did you manage to keep a conversation going with her for such a long time?"

It was easy. I felt she must be very tired, so I said, "Prime Minister, why don't you take advantage of this bad weather to have a little nap. Just lean back and snooze, and I will wake you in time to pull yourself together before we arrive."

She nodded off immediately. And I have an odd memory of looking down at her feet—she was wearing white sandals—and noticing how beautifully her toenails were manicured and painted with bright red polish.

The only time she got testy was when Jerry Brown, who was running for the U.S. Senate from California, contrived to call on her so that he could get some publicity with the photo op. She did not like being exploited.

Armand Hammer, the head of Occidental Petroleum and noted philanthropist, also called on her, and she asked his advice about putting out an oil-rig fire in the Indian Ocean. Whereupon he picked up the phone, called Red Adair, the most famous oil-fire fighter in the world, and dispatched him immediately to India.

I did not remind Mrs. Gandhi that we had met before. I was that brash young reporter who twenty-five years earlier had followed her and her father, Jawaharlal Nehru, into Blair House, pretending to be a member of Nehru's official party. I was soon spotted by a Secret Service agent, who threw me out, saying, "Mrs. Roosevelt, it will cost me my job if you are caught here."

On the 1982 trip, Indira Gandhi brought her son Rajiv, and I remember what a good sport he was when trapped in a packed elevator for forty-five minutes at the National Press Club. In less than three years he would himself be Prime Minister. Thus, three generations of this family were to rule India, and I would participate in the state visits of all three.

After Rajiv Gandhi had succeeded his mother as Prime Minister, he came to America with his beautiful Italian wife Sonia in June 1985. Rajiv had star quality. How could any woman resist him, I thought to myself—devastatingly handsome, sensual, powerful, but at the same time tender, sweet, and soft-spoken? And there was a hint of tragedy about him, in itself tantalizing.

"Ambassador Roosevelt, you have not changed at all since I saw you three years ago" were his first words to me as I greeted him on the plane. And we both laughed as we recalled the elevator episode.

I traveled with Rajiv Gandhi throughout his visit, and he was tireless—never sleeping more than three or four hours a night. As we moved between appointments he, in his flawless English, gave me many insights into his thinking.

"I like President Reagan," he told me. "He is forthright, very human and easy to talk to. This sets the tone of our relationship. Our perspectives may differ, but we can cooperate to reduce the differences. I believe him and trust him."

Rajiv was pleased when crowds gathered to cheer him; he was surprised by their attention. He and his wife always held hands in the car, and one felt a genuine love between them. (I wondered how Sonia had managed to deal with such a strong woman as Indira Gandhi. In Indian culture the wife is almost a slave to her mother-in-law.)

"Our most important economic issue is our population policy," he said. He was against the rigid Chinese approach of limiting every couple to one child, but was most critical of the U.S. policy of cutting back on assistance for population control. I did not try to defend the Reagan administration's population policies, set by extreme right-wingers, both political and religious, who did not even believe in birth control.

He also talked about the importance of education for the poor. "We have an affirmative action problem similar to yours," he told me. "In India there is a great resentment from the middle class, who think that the Untouchables and the poor should not have any preference in jobs and college quotas."

At this time "Star Wars" was a big issue, and Rajiv could not understand why we insisted on pursuing SDI research.

I tried to explain. "We know the Soviets are involved in similar research. I can't believe you would prefer that the Soviets get ahead of us in all that technology. We are an open society and it is easy to monitor what we do."

I did not convince him, but I sensed that he was pro-West and as pro–United States as he could afford to be. He wanted genuinely to be nonaligned, but if he ever had to make a choice, I felt his heart would be with us. And so apparently did his country-men, because his suspected Western sympathies were cited as one reason for his defeat in the 1989 elections.

After his mother's assassination, Rajiv was a marked man as well. Our Secret Service took no chances; they had received a number of threats on his life. In all my years on the job, Rajiv Gandhi had the tightest security of any state visitor. It was for-midable. Tents were constructed to cover his comings and goings. We never entered a building by its proper entrance; I came to know the cellars and secret doors in every stop on our itinerary.

Everyone was issued a bulletproof vest except the protocol officers, and for the first time it occurred to me that in the event of an assassination attempt, I was the person closest to the target!

I chided the agent in charge. "Hey, how come I'm expend-able?" He was embarrassed. They were so busy worrying about the protectee that they gave little thought to anyone else. How-ever, in no time at all, they issued me a bulletproof vest—and to their dismay, I never wore it.

I am not the least bit brave, but I figured if a bullet had my name on it, then so be it. There are a lot worse ways to die than in the service of your country.

THIRTY

The Middle East

THE CHIEF OF PROTOCOL can have no favorites among nations or world leaders—at least not publicly—and certainly cannot let personal dislikes or political beliefs be apparent. Not only must he or she treat every country with the same dignity and consideration, but any variance from that is immediately interpreted in the international community as "sending a message."

Of course, protocol *is* often used to send a message—and no one reads the tea leaves of protocol more carefully than the Israelis and Egyptians, insisting that, in these matters at least, we have to be evenhanded.

I remember once when I was on vacation abroad and an Israeli VIP came to town. My deputy met him at the airport. These arrivals were always shown on TV, and someone telephoned my house and asked, "Why didn't Ambassador Roosevelt go to the airport to greet him? That is an affront to Israel." Fortunately, I had also been absent for an Egyptian arrival—but it showed me how carefully my actions were monitored.

These two important Middle East clients were constant visitors. The Israelis averaged three senior official visitors a year (and a dozen unofficial). Meir Rosenne, my favorite Israeli ambassador, called it the Tel Aviv–Washington shuttle, as he and I made our way to the airport to greet yet another of his countrymen. Rosenne was a superb diplomat and as funny as any TV comedian. No matter how hairy things got, he always had a good joke to tell me. His successor, Moshe Arad, a man of great elegance and class, was also a consummate professional.

The Egyptian ambassadors that I dealt with, first Ashraf Ghorbal and then Abdel Raouf El Reedy, were both remarkable men and made a real difference. The Egyptians were an anomaly, an Arab nation on the outs with the other Arabs because they had made peace with Israel. Egypt received almost as much foreign aid from us as Israel, and was a stabilizing presence in that volatile region.

Anwar Sadat was assassinated in the fall of 1981, and so Hosni Mubarak was the only Egyptian leader I dealt with during my seven years. President Mubarak visited Washington almost every year. His wife was a great beauty and, like Jihan Sadat, whom I had known and interviewed as a journalist, the product of an English mother and Egyptian father. Susan Mubarak was well educated and spoke perfect English, but she was more low-key than Mrs. Sadat and managed not to upset the Moslem fundamentalists.

The administration worked hard at keeping a symmetry between the Israeli and Egyptian visits. If Vice President Bush gave a dinner for the Israelis, then he had to give one, equal in size, for the Egyptians. If Mubarak was invited to lunch by the Senate Foreign Relations Committee, then they did the same for the next Israeli visitor. In only one area did they not compete. President Mubarak was a menace on the squash court, and the protocol office had a job finding players who could keep up with him.

Actually, the most difficult test for me was the visit of Amin Gemayel, the President of Lebanon.

It should have been easy—to greet and escort this handsome young man, a Maronite Christian and head of the Phalange party. In the fall of 1982, Gemayel had just become President. On this, his first visit, he had brought a Druze cousin of mine, Abbas Hamiye, as his chief of protocol, along with an entourage of high-level advisers representing every important religious sect in Lebanon. Gemayel was bringing a message of hope and the desire to heal Lebanon's sectarian wounds. It was U.S. policy to encourage this process—to support the Lebanese central government and to call for the withdrawal of Syrian and Israeli troops from Lebanese territory. (It does have a familiar ring to it!)

The night before Gemayel's arrival I felt restless and upset. Between intervals of disturbed sleep, I recalled the terrible letters we had received five years earlier about the devastation of Arsoun, my Druze family's village, by the Phalangists.

"It is fantastic . . . that we are still alive," my aunt had written us. "I am suffering a lot with the children and Najib [my uncle] to make them forget the horrible day we left Arsoun . . . the horror and destiny we faced and how all of us begged Sittu [my grandmother] to come with us, but she insisted with all her power to remain at home to keep it safe. She suffered a lot during her escape to a Christian friend. . . . After five days Showkat [the head of the Choucair clan then], with the Syrian soldiers, rescued her. She tells stories and stories of the barbarism she saw." (My grandmother died some six months later of a heart attack, attributed largely to the strain of her ordeal.)

"Poor Lebanon!" the letter continued. "Lebanon that used to be capped with the white snow and be washed with the blue of the Mediterranean is now capped with the black of mourning and watered with the blood of innocent people. . . . In Salima 140 houses out of 160 that belonged to Druze were razed to the ground after Phalangists killed the old, dragged the elderly in the village square, stripped old Druze women of their clothes, even crucified a Druze girl of nineteen after they exercised their male barbarism on her.

"As for Arsoun—like all other villages where Druzes have fed, sheltered and defended Christians to the very last moment, Druze houses were attacked, robbed and burnt. Not a single Druze house was spared and those of the Choucairs were burnt and demolished by these same Christians (could this be the teaching of Jesus Christ? We have learnt differently in the Protestant schools we have been to.) Arsoun today is a deserted village. Druzes who managed to escape . . . go there to witness the total destruction that has befallen them, while Christians, fearful of an act of retaliation, have locked their doors and left."

Apart from this vivid letter, we had learned of atrocities even more dreadful. After robbing an elderly cousin, Ismail Choucair, the Phalangists poured kerosene over him and burned him to death. In still another episode, the only son of Meliha Choucair—the sister of Showkat—was abducted and killed, his body later found in the trunk of a car, hacked to pieces.

As these stories raced through my mind, I wondered how I could be the gracious hostess, assist the President and Secretary of State in their important task, and keep my own honor and dignity intact. I did not share my misgivings with anyone—least of all my mother, who had the grace to make no comment at all.

The next day, I went aboard the aircraft that brought President Gemayel and welcomed him to the United States on behalf of President Reagan. My cousin, Abbas, made the introduction, and after the formalities were over I gave Abbas a cousinly kiss on both cheeks. I had not seen Abbas for more than twenty years.

Seeing this, Gemayel said, "How does Abbas rate a kiss, when he is only the Chief of Protocol—and the head of state gets just a handshake?"

"Because, Mr. President, you may be his president, but you are not my cousin," I said, and smiled despite myself.

The ice was broken, and the young President made a good impression on everyone. He brought Ronald Reagan a book on Lebanon, saying, "Lebanon is like California. Is it not a pity that such a beautiful country should be destroyed?"

His pleas were for naught. Gemayel was not the man, after all, to unite and save Lebanon, but we would not find that out until much later. By the time he left, I had kinder thoughts about him and I wished him well. Although his faction had been involved in numerous killings, he too had suffered. His brother had been assassinated and other members of his family had perished. In the Lebanese imbroglio, there were few clean hands.

As we said goodbye on the tarmac, he thanked me profusely and said how proud he felt to see a woman of Lebanese background fulfill such an important role. Then he kissed me three times—once on my right cheek, once on my left, and again on my right.

"That's the Lebanese style," he said. I knew this was being telecast to the Middle East and I wondered for a brief moment what my Druze relatives would think of that display of affection.

The subject of my background came up in only one other context—the Israeli visits. I was occasionally asked if I found it difficult, being of Arab origin, to play hostess to Israeli officials. The question offended me—as well it should have—but the short answer is no. Indeed, I felt it was a great opportunity to demonstrate that an Arab-American was just as American as anyone else. At the same time, to our Israeli visitors I wanted to show the best qualities of my ancestors—hospitality, sensitivity, warmth, and a sense of honor.

I saw myself as someone who could set an example. If I showed that affection and respect existed between myself and various Israelis, it would demonstrate that rapprochement between the Arab world and Israel was not impossible.

I have found that often I have more in common with my Jewish friends than my gentile ones, and probably, if I were to make a list of my closest friends since I left college, more than half of them would be Jews. This is no accident. I find we often are brought up with the special burdens and special awe of being first-generation Americans, we share many of the same insecurities, the same need to succeed, the same family structure. The Jewish mother and the Lebanese mother are not unalike.

This said, however, I confess that the first Israeli visit I supervised left something to be desired, for neither I nor my staff had mastered the daunting problems of giving a kosher dinner. And there were few caterers in Washington with the expertise needed. This dinner was a big one—given by the Vice President and Mrs. Bush in honor of Prime Minister and Mrs. Yitzhak Shamir in November 1983. More than two hundred guests were expected.

To prepare a kosher meal is quite a process. First, we had to rent a special glass dinner service. A rabbi assisted with the purchase of the food to be sure that it was truly kosher. Then he came to the State Department to inspect the kitchen. Everything was thoroughly scoured and aluminum foil put on all the work surfaces. The ovens were turned up very high to cleanse them of any residue. The caterers worked all day under the vigilant eye of the rabbi.

In preparing the first course—a kind of dumplings or quenelles that the caterer assured me was a favorite with his Jewish clients—the chef was ordered to throw out twenty-four dozen eggs because the rabbi had detected a trace of blood in one. That definitely did not put the chef in a good mood. At dinner, when the dumplings were served, they were as hard as walnuts and about the same color and size. I looked around the huge dining room of the State Department and saw that everyone was as baffled as I. The plates went back to the kitchen full. But I did notice that Shamir ate his with gusto—and I mentally gave him high marks for being a good guest.

But that was not all. There followed overcooked lamb with undercooked string beans, winding up with poached pears which were almost raw and slid all over the plate as we attempted to cut into them. Almost everything in the meal was a sickly brown color. I thought the evening would never end. My friend Kay Graham, chairman of the *Washington Post,* shook her head as she left saying, "Lucky, that meal was the worst—it really was the worst!"

But misfortunes never come singly. That same evening the Air Force Singing Sergeants, our favorite after-dinner entertainers, circled the head table and sang for the guest of honor, "Soon I'll Be Done with the Troubles of the World, I Want to Meet My Jesus."

In my happy relationship with Secretary Shultz, only one matter troubled me. As the years wore on, he seemed to become more and more disenchanted with the Arabs, particularly those on

Israel's border. Although he worked diligently on Middle East problems and met frequently with leaders of the Arab world, he had many moments of frustration.

In all candor, it is not difficult to get exasperated with the Arabs—they often shoot themselves in the foot. However, I felt that Shultz never quite understood their culture, nor their rhetoric. Being himself such a straight arrow, Shultz could not easily accept the Middle East approach of dealing indirectly with an issue. Arabs put a premium on not saying no. People might say one thing—for reasons of face and honor—and yet be willing, if not pressed publicly, to do the opposite. But preserving face is paramount.

Arab rhetoric tends to be sweeping, not intended to be taken at face value. I once tried to illustrate Arab hyperbole to Shultz by telling him about my gentle father's fury when I stayed out too late on a date.

"I'm going to cut your head off and throw it to the dogs!" he shouted at me in Arabic. I was cowering in my bedroom, door locked, not because I was afraid, but because I was laughing so hard. My father loved me more than life itself, but this was his way of venting his concern and his relief that I was safely home.

Shultz started out with high hopes. He, like President Reagan, pressured the Israelis to stop the bombing of Lebanon and eventually to withdraw. He was the architect of President Reagan's September 1982 initiative, which essentially provided for the return of the West Bank to the Palestinians, but affiliated with Jordan. The Israelis rejected it out of hand, and the Arabs were not clever enough to step up to the bargaining table and proclaim their readiness to negotiate.

Then followed so many heartbreaks—especially the May 17, 1983, agreement which Shultz negotiated with the Israelis and Lebanese, under the mistaken impression that the Syrians would acquiesce to a mutual withdrawal of Israeli and Syrian troops. Apparently, Shultz thought the Saudis and other Arabs would persuade the Syrians, but he was warned by some of his experts not to bank on it. And when the Saudis could not or would not deliver, Shultz felt betrayed.

There were other tragedies: the massacre of Palestinians in the refugee camps of Sabra and Shatila by the Phalangists while the Israelis, who might have prevented it, stood by; the bombing of the American Embassy in Beirut by Lebanese or Iranian Shiite fanatics, resulting in many deaths, among them Shultz's close friend and trusted CIA adviser, Robert Ames.

But the worst catastrophe in Lebanon was the bombing of the Marine barracks in the fall of 1983, leaving 241 Americans dead. I never saw George Shultz more devastated than when the Marines were killed. For him, it was a wound to the heart—not only because of his patriotism and deep love of the Marine Corps, but also because he felt responsible for the Marines being in Lebanon. He had fought bitterly with Secretary of Defense Caspar Weinberger to keep them there.

Also, he had pressed Weinberger to use the battleship *New Jersey* to fire on Syrian artillery positions in some of the villages overlooking Beirut. This shelling hit too many civilian targets and Weinberger ordered the firing stopped. (My own uncle was made deaf by a shell that landed in his apartment. Had he not fortuitously moved from his chair to the bathroom, he would have been killed.)

One day I showed the Secretary a photo album of my family—pictures taken in Lebanon in earlier, happier years. I wanted to put a human face to the innocent victims of these tragic events. One relative—a young woman who had recently visited in Washington—was killed, along with her unborn child and three other family members, when Israeli shells landed in their house in Abadieh, just above Beirut. Four other members of the same family were seriously wounded in that bombardment.

I wanted him to understand that most Lebanese, both Christian and Moslem, were not monsters but just ordinary people, helpless victims of the PLO, the Israelis, the Syrians, and their surrogates.

"We Americans are a good people—a decent people," he said, with more emotion in his voice than I can ever remember. He could not accept that in the Arab world we did not always appear so honorable, especially when we seemed to countenance the Israelis' invasion of Lebanon and their use of American-made cluster bombs, resulting in some 30,000 Lebanese civilian casualties.

Putting aside his disappointments, Shultz attempted once again in 1987 and 1988 to make a dent in the Middle East peace process by working with King Hussein of Jordan and later President Mubarak of Egypt. They tried, but the reality was overwhelmingly obvious: the Israelis and the PLO had the keys to peace in the Middle East and they did not choose to unlock the door.

Both Yitzhak Shamir and Shimon Peres were prime ministers of Israel during the eighties, and the contrast between the two was dramatic. I felt an enormous admiration and affection for Peres; he had soulful eyes full of compassion and understanding. Peres saw the Arabs as human beings, he was willing to gamble for peace, and he understood that any meaningful settlement would mean some concessions on Israel's part. I looked forward to his visits— and each time there was renewed hope that maybe, just maybe, he could pull the rabbit out of the hat.

But it was not to be. Shamir was the stronger and more ruthless of the two. He psyched Reagan and Shultz masterfully, appealing to their genuine sympathy for Jewish suffering in the Holocaust and their admiration for Israeli achievements. I watched Shamir's performance with some fascination. He reminded me of a pugnacious little troll. It was apparent that his only interest in peace was to thwart it. Sometimes I thought he was secretly laughing at Shultz—an opinion I never dared express until I read Thomas L. Friedman's brilliant book, *From Beirut to Jerusalem,* in which he gives voice to what I intuitively felt.

Friedman says that in dealing with the Israelis (and the Arabs too) one has to approach them like a good grocer; everything must have a price tag on it. There has to be a price for saying no and a windfall for saying yes.

Shultz never established with Shamir a price for saying no [writes Friedman]. . . . The effective American statesman [in the Middle East] must not only know how to establish a price

like a grocer but how to impose it as well. Shultz was wonderful at playing the good friend from America when dealing
with the Israelis in public. When he got behind closed doors,
however, when the television lights were turned off and it
was just he and Shamir sitting on the couch together, that was
the time for Shultz to switch from the Middle Western friend
to the Middle Eastern grocer, but he never did. Shultz, I am
told, was as avuncular with Shamir in private as he was in
public, and that simply won't work.

Nonetheless, George Shultz was probably the only person
who could have arm-wrestled Yassir Arafat, the head of the PLO,
to the ground and made him say the words recognizing Israel and
renouncing terrorism. When these conditions were met, Shultz
reversed the Kissinger rule of no dealings between the United
States and the PLO, and immediately opened up a dialogue with
the PLO. In the end, Shultz handed a real gift to the Bush administration, and gave Arab moderates a chance to try anew to find
peace in the Middle East.

In the Iran-Iraq war it was apparent that our national interest
lay in having Iraq (an Arab secular state) win the war with Iran (a
non-Arab, Persian-speaking, fundamentalist Moslem state). We
could not afford to have the Ayatollah's regime dominate the
area—it was bad enough that they had the leverage in Lebanon to
continue holding Americans hostage.

Thus, the administration, led by Secretary Shultz, reestab-
lished diplomatic relations with Iraq in November 1984. (Relations had been ruptured during the 1973 Arab-Israeli war.) I
watched with fascination the effective maneuvering on the part of
two brilliant Iraqi diplomats, Nizar Hamdoun in Washington and
Ismat Kittani at the United Nations, who worked hard trying to
overcome Iraq's negative image in America. Their efforts, coupled
with several visits from Prime Minister Tariq Aziz, helped change
the Middle East equation during the Reagan years.

The Iran-Contra debacle was a big domestic scandal, but in
retrospect and from my vantage point, it had no more than a

momentary effect on our relations with any other country. Of course, the Iraqis and other Arabs wrung their hands but the long-term damage was insignificant.

France's Prime Minister Jacques Chirac, when he visited Washington shortly after the scandal, told a group of congressmen, "We in Europe do not believe the United States has been weakened, nor has any harm been done to the President over the Iran affair."

I had no inkling of the events leading up to the scandal—none of the usual behind-the-scenes gossip. But when it did come, I was amazed at the naïveté and ham-handedness of National Security Advisers Robert McFarlane and Admiral John Poindexter. How did these American patriots—men I had worked with and thought I knew—get mixed up with a bunch of bazaar bandits, who stripped them to their undershorts before they caught on?

It certainly was not a noble page in American history, and the "arms for hostages" fiasco did demonstrate once and for all how dangerous it is to leave such things to amateurs instead of experts with solid knowledge of the mentality and language of the people they are bargaining with.

Our quarrels with Iran forced President Reagan to enunciate a firm policy in the Persian Gulf—and stick with it, sending the U.S. Navy to back up our determination to keep the sea lanes open and the oil flowing to the West. Our relations with the Gulf states—Bahrain, Saudi Arabia, Kuwait, Qatar, the United Arab Emirates, Oman, Yemen—were generally excellent.

I have already described the visits of many of the rulers from the Gulf. As I saw each of them depart, I always felt a slight tug at my heartstrings. Whether it was the Sheik of Kuwait, the Sultan of Oman, or the Amir of Bahrain, they invariably found their American hosts to be generous, gracious, and hospitable—qualities to which they attach inordinate importance. They went home with warm feelings toward America, with a sense that misconceptions had been dispelled and that they had won friends to their cause, subsequently and inevitably to be disillusioned.

The Gulf Arabs in particular place a great premium on honor; they follow the law of the tribe—their word is their bond. They did not understand that although Reagan, Bush, or Shultz might make certain commitments, they could easily be overruled or ignored by Congress, many of whose members were frightened of the pro-Israel lobby and beholden to Jewish supporters for their campaign funds.

A well-known Washington newspaperman once asked me at a Georgetown dinner party, "Lucky, how can you go on working for an administration which is so anti-Arab?"

That gave me pause. I thought the administration was pro-Israeli, but not concomitantly anti-Arab. The two did not have to go together. And personally, Reagan, Bush, and Shultz had all treated me with the greatest affection and respect. Never once had my Arab background been mentioned except with appreciation and approval.

I loved my job; I loved dealing with people from all over the world; I loved making them comfortable and happy and putting America's best foot forward. And finally, I cannot sustain negative emotions. They do not come easily to me.

I asked myself, when I disapprove of something in our Middle East policy, should I resign? My job was not a policy-making one. I wasn't really important enough to resign. What difference would it make if I did? A one-day splash in the newspapers and a long period of distrust before other Arab-Americans would be appointed to significant jobs.

I received letters from all over the country from Americans of Arab background saying how proud they were of me and how they wanted their daughters to identify with me. I felt I had a larger obligation to help instill in the Arab-American community a sense of pride in their origins. Their immigrant forebears started life in America as peddlers or small businessmen like my father. But their sons and daughters have become lawyers, doctors, politicians, journalists—you name it. They are usually conservative—fervent believers in free enterprise and the American dream—and they mostly vote Republican. They are fiercely loyal to America; most of them have little interest in the old world they left behind.

But there were moments when I suffered, especially over

attempts to "dehumanize" the Arabs—i.e., all Arabs are terrorists and therefore objects of loathing. When I look around the world at terrorist acts, I see that we do not hate the Irish, and yet the IRA has shown more sustained cruelty than almost any terrorist group. We manage to divorce the killers of Lord Mountbatten and the assassins who tried to murder Margaret Thatcher from the great Irish people. Likewise German, Italian, Japanese, Basque, Sikh, and Tamil terrorists—the list is endless. And, of course, terrorism was introduced into the Middle East as an instrument of national liberation by none other than the Israelis themselves, Shamir being a prominent practitioner in his early career.

But once "Arab" becomes synonymous with terrorist or other ugly stereotypes, then Arab lives are expendable, Arabs do not have names, Arab culture and the Arabic language can no longer be studied, because then you will be named an "Arabist." An Arabist, unlike, say, a Sinologist, is now a pejorative term, when once it simply described an honorable field of study. To be identified as an Arabist has become the kiss of death for a State Department career.

To deny the humanity of the Arabs makes them unworthy of compassion or understanding. Thus, in places like the West Bank or Gaza, southern Lebanon or the Golan Heights, they can be beaten and tortured, arrested at will, deported, their houses destroyed, their land confiscated, their trees uprooted and crops burned, their children locked out of their schools. And the world does not care.

Today Arabs are the new targets of bigots and haters. Arabs are just about the only ethnic group in America that one can still ridicule or caricature with impunity.

I would be less than honest if I said I had personally suffered much from these prejudices. I have had the protective mantle of the Roosevelt name, but my family and friends are not so fortunate. I speak for them all.

To deny their humanity is to deny my own.

THIRTY-ONE

Africa

At Arlington National Cemetery, the ceremony for laying a wreath on the Tomb of the Unknown Soldier never varies. Well, almost never. Crack ceremonial troops representing all the services are lined up on either side of the white marble memorial, all the way up the fifty steps to the actual tomb. There the VIP visitor, escorted by the commanding general of the Military District of Washington, pauses, places the wreath, and then stands at attention while a lone bugler plays taps.

I must have seen this hundreds of times, and it never failed to move me. But none of the protocol team will ever forget the day Kenneth Kaunda, President of Zambia, went to Arlington. Kaunda, one of Africa's senior statesmen, is the son of a preacher, and church music was an important element in his early life.

When Tim Towell went to the hotel to escort Kaunda to Arlington, he was not in his suite. Tim found the Zambian president alone in one of the banquet rooms, playing the piano and singing hymns to himself. "It soothes me," he explained to Tim.

That sunny October day Kaunda went through the usual paces, and after taps, instead of moving on, he simply stood there. From a distance no one could tell what was happening, but later we asked why he had paused for so long.

"I felt an urge to sing a hymn to the Unknown Soldier," he said. "And I sang 'Rock of Ages.'"

Kaunda cut an unforgettable figure on his visits to Washington—his hair gone white, his skin ebony—and he always wore a black or white safari suit and dangled a long white handkerchief in his hand.

The guitar was Kaunda's favorite instrument, so President Reagan presented him with a special made-to-order one. At dinner that night at the Vice President's house, Kaunda strummed and sang for the guests. That was one of the first dinners I attended at the Bushes' and I was impressed. They were superb hosts—it all seemed so effortless—and they made their African guests feel at home.

As a group, my protocol officers preferred the black African visitors above all others. With only a few exceptions the Africans were the kindest, the most gentle and compassionate. They were easy to work with and looked to my staff for guidance about everything.

Reagan and Shultz—and all of us—were particularly impressed with the President of Senegal, Abdou Diouf, and not just because he was a beanpole six feet, eleven inches tall. It was the only time I ever saw Reagan tilt his head upward to look his visitor in the eye, and it was the only time we had to request a special bed to accommodate a guest's almost-seven-foot frame.

Diouf was a Koranic scholar, very soft-spoken, with the eyes of a genuine sage. Without really being able to explain why, when I compared notes with Reagan and Shultz afterward, I found that we all had sensed a saintlike tranquillity about him.

Just the opposite was the Ivory Coast's Félix Houphouët-Boigny, a worldly Francophile and octogenarian who had ruled his country for forty years, making it one of the rare economic success stories in black Africa.

The Africans, of course, were genuinely exotic, with their dramatic costumes and unusual foods. A Soviet protocol officer told us about an African visitor to Moscow who arrived with twenty gazelles, ten monkeys, and dozens of birds.

"But we were not expecting any animals for our zoo," the Soviet official exclaimed as the creatures were led off the plane.

"These are not for the zoo," the African replied. "They are for our return banquet."

We never had live animals to deal with, but we certainly had technicolor arrivals. A great solidarity existed among the African diplomats. No matter which country's leader was visiting, all the North Africans and black Africans, many in national dress, would turn out to form a long receiving line. Adorable little children, with bouquets of flowers, were the first to greet the guest and his wife. And native drummers were permitted to herald their arrival and brighten things up at staid old Andrews Air Force Base.

Almost every important African head of state visited during the Reagan administration—all except the South African, who was never invited despite the accusations that the Reagan administration was too cozy with South Africa.

One of President Reagan's finest appointments, Chester Crocker, was Assistant Secretary of State for African Affairs for the entire eight years. Single-handedly, Chet Crocker directed our African relationships, with special attention to the resolution of the Namibian problem. And largely thanks to him, Namibia, Africa's last colony, was decoupled from South Africa, ending apartheid in that country. Namibian freedom was linked to the withdrawal of Cuban troops from Angola, and this too was achieved.

The 1980s, overall, were not a time for flashy successes but rather a steady, persistent improvement in our relations with most African nations. Sub-Saharan Africa went through a painful reassessment. A quarter of a century ago most of these nations—more than forty—had thrown off colonialism, thinking this was the cause of all their problems. Most were attracted to state socialism, which simply became state corruption on a grand scale—a far more efficient corruption than in any capitalist society. (In fact, the word "kleptocracy" has been coined to describe these countries.)

With the exception of Zimbabwe, Cameroon, Ivory Coast, Gabon, Botswana, Kenya and, of course, South Africa, they gradually became economic basket cases, even though many of the African nations are rich in natural resources.

They turned to us for assistance with their economic reappraisals. We were the source of honest economic advice, not ideological panaceas—economic "tough love," if you will. We broadened and diversified our African relationships, Ronald Reagan once again confounding his critics and understanding instinctively that African Marxism was definitely only skin deep.

One of my favorite memories is of the ebullient Samora Machel, Marxist president of Mozambique, bounding into the Oval Office and grasping our surprised President by the hand, "*Mi amigo,* Ronald!" he cried, pumping Reagan's arm and patting his back.

In my office we had to deal with the consequences of Africa's fiscal disarray almost every day. Certain nations could not pay the rent or upkeep on their embassies; they ran up bills, and merchants came to our office demanding we collect for them, since the embassies were protected by diplomatic immunity from regular prosecution.

I often wondered why each small African nation felt it had to maintain an embassy in Washington and another at the United Nations. This meant staffs, chauffeur-driven cars, and other costly perks for both ambassadors. Sometimes I would delicately suggest to an ambassador that perhaps he should find less expensive office space, or sell his embassy and move to a more modest one. My advice did not sit well.

In all our dealings with the Africans there was an undercurrent—an unspoken fear of racism. They were afraid of being the victims of white Americans' prejudices; they also feared being in a predominantly black city in which most of the crime was committed by blacks against blacks.

The Africans were the largest group in the diplomatic corps, and the only ones who asked for a special meeting with me as a group. They recounted their grievances to me, and I felt great sympathy and understanding for them. I remembered what it was like for me to grow up in the South with dark skin. I tried to be sensitive to their needs.

In our diplomatic relations with African countries we had to be alert to any possible slights or offense—and alas, these happened often enough to reinforce their complexes.

A glaring example was a request for a ten-minute photo op between Reagan and Denis Sassou-Nguesso, President of the Congo. The Congolese leader had been in New York for the opening session of the United Nations, and was also that year's chairman of the Organization of African Unity (OAU). Shultz had given a nice luncheon for Sassou-Nguesso and the OAU at the Morgan Library in New York. David Rockefeller had organized a high-level stag dinner at the Links Club. Governor Richard Thornburgh of Pennsylvania (later the U.S. Attorney General) had laid on a busy program in Philadelphia.

In Washington he was warmly welcomed, ensconced at the Willard Hotel, just across from the White House, and given both official and media attention. But what Sassou-Nguesso really wanted was some tangible evidence of a meeting with President Reagan—a quick photo. Both Protocol and the African bureau tried everything, and Vice President Bush interceded, yet for some reason it could not be arranged. Belatedly President Reagan, attempting to make up for the slight, managed to have a fifteen-minute phone conversation with him. The Congolese were not mollified. They felt this was a calculated insult to Sassou-Nguesso personally and to the OAU as an organization. I never found out why the President's schedulers were so insensitive—but all the hard work of Shultz and the department was shot for want of a ten-minute drop-by!

(Shortly after taking office, President Bush, possibly in an attempt to repair the damage, invited Sassou-Nguesso for a full-fledged state visit, which was a huge success.)

We found that successful African visits such as that of President Moussa Traore of Mali brought us more mileage than almost any other. In any African nation, every move of their head of state in America would consume the newspapers' front pages and be telecast in its entirety.

I remember also the enormous good will we generated for America when the Madagascar (Malagasy) ambassador to Washington died and we sent Associate Chief of Protocol Richard

Gookin to accompany the body home. This was the top news for days throughout Madagascar.

The United States also responded generously to the famine crises in Africa—and both private and government assistance went to Sudan, Ethiopia, and Mozambique, in particular.

The Reagan administration took a lot of heat over its South African policy, and in the end Congress overrode Reagan's veto of sanctions, and they were imposed. But in all the rhetoric I don't think anyone ever listened to what Reagan was saying. "Constructive engagement" was not a bad policy—it was an attempt to work with all parties in South Africa to shape alternatives to continued bloodshed.

Since Reagan left office, a more enlightened government has taken over in South Africa, and perhaps at last both blacks and whites have realized they must share their country or ruin it. A new generation is coming to power with the attitude that there is much to gain by negotiations, and everything to lose by violence.

While our activities in sub-Saharan Africa were relatively low-key, our relations with North Africa made great strides, and no one had more to do with this dramatically changed environment than Algerian president Chadli Bendjedid.

During the 1970s the United States and Algeria went through a rough patch—we viewed their Marxist orientation with the suspicion it deserved, but the change began when Bendjedid became President in 1979 and sent as ambassador to Washington Redha Malek, a brilliant negotiator and architect of the peace accord between France and Algeria.

Ambassador Malek had a key role in the Iran hostage crisis as mediator for the release of the American hostages in Teheran in January 1981. The success of the Algerian effort helped get the Reagan administration off to an optimistic and upbeat start.

When I joined the administration, Ambassador Malek was in the last months of his tour of duty in Washington. Because of all he had done for our country, I wrote Bill Clark and Mike Deaver recommending that President Reagan receive Malek to say goodbye (something normally not done) and once again thank him for his extraordinary efforts on America's behalf.

No one in the White House bothered to answer me—and the ambassador departed, an unsung hero. This disillusioned me but also made me determined that in these matters in the future I would deal only through the Secretary of State.

Since then one outstanding Algerian ambassador has followed another, and in the spring of 1985 Chadli Bendjedid became the first Algerian president to visit the United States officially.

His state visit was such a success that a few months later President Bendjedid sent his five children to tour the United States so that they might share with their parents what he termed a wonderful experience.

Since that date our relations with Algeria have improved dramatically. In addition, I am sure that what Bendjedid saw on his travels helped his determination to try a bit of *perestroika* of his own; the leaden hand of socialism is slowly being lifted.

Which brings me to a recent decision of the Bush administration. They no longer plan to offer state visitors a chance to tour the United States, but will invite them only to Washington. A big mistake and a terrible example of penny wise and pound foolish. In my experience, foreign visitors, especially those who have never seen America, learn much more about us as a people when they leave the stuffy confines of official Washington and see the "real America."

While our relations with Algeria were improving, the Reagan administration managed very deftly to preserve our traditionally excellent dialogue with King Hassan of Morocco, even though these two North African nations were frequently at odds with each other.

When pundits comment that ambassadors no longer make a difference, that they are mere messengers because of modern communications, I always think of Morocco's Ambassador Ali Bengelloun, who did such a good job that King Hassan had to send him back to Washington three different times.

Bengelloun first came in 1962 during the Kennedy administration, and in just three years this somewhat obscure embassy
was put on the Washington map. The capital's social life revolved
around their parties, cleverly orchestrated by the ambassador and
his wife Jackie. He invited leading White House, cabinet, and
congressional personalities and assiduously cultivated the press. In
short, he did what every ambassador in Washington should do to
be effective—but few manage to swing it.

Eventually the King recalled him, and after more than a decade of relatively inactive ambassadors, the Moroccan Embassy
declined in prestige and importance. The King finally decided to
send the Bengellouns back in 1977 and they remained through the
Carter and first Reagan administrations, once more making the
Moroccan Embassy an important catalyst in Washington's political and international society. But again the King recalled
Bengelloun, and in no time at all, Morocco seemed off the radar
screen. It only took the King five years this time to send
Bengelloun back to Washington at the beginning of the Bush
administration.

Ali Bengelloun had that rare natural instinct—he knew how
to bring people together in a way that served both Moroccan and
American interests. I felt that almost all the ambassadors in Washington could profit from watching his smooth operation, and learn
how to improve their countries' image here.

Not much could be done about Libya as long as the bizarre
Muamar Qaddafi ruled the country. Often I thought how lucky I
had been to visit Libya in 1968, before this quirky character took
over. Although a well-kept secret, Libya has the most exciting
Roman ruins in the world—Leptis Magna, a complete Roman
city, until this century buried under the sand. Leptis was uncov-
ered by an Italian archaeologist, whose nephew, Italian diplomat
Marcello Guidi, and his wife Gioia spent a day showing us through
the ruins. Imagine having a picnic lunch, complete with champagne, in that deserted ancient city.

Fifteen years later Marcello Guidi would be Italy's chief of protocol and my mentor when I attended my first chiefs of protocol conference just before the Paris summit. His advice: "Trust your instincts. Never say no directly. Never take no for an answer."

Our relationship with Tunisia, which has always been good, continued on a smooth path despite the big bump when the Israelis bombed the PLO headquarters in Tunis, resulting in more than one hundred Tunisians killed.

Archie and I always had a sentimental feeling about Tunisia because of Habib Bourguiba, the man who led the country with a benevolent but firm hand from independence until he was replaced in November 1987. During World War II, as an intelligence officer, Archie had come to know and admire him.

I first met Bourguiba in 1952 in Istanbul, and he became a great hero of mine. He was returning to Tunisia after being imprisoned by the French, and garnering world sympathy for Tunisian independence. His sharp, laserlike blue eyes and his eloquence made an indelible impression on me, a girl just out of college. "Bourguiba is absolutely wonderful—a moderate—not a hothead at all," I wrote home. "I cannot imagine the French could be so stupid as not to follow the course he advocates."

A few years later Tunisia was free, and Bourguiba sent his son, also named Habib, to help open an embassy in Washington. I was then a reporter for the *Washington Star* and did the first interview with him in the United States. Thus began a long friendship with Habib and his wife Naila, which lasts to this day.

Before relinquishing power, Bourguiba's fondest wish was to make a final official visit to Washington. His son and daughter-in-law accompanied him, and I thought once again of the way this job of mine completed so many circles.

The elderly statesman suffered from failing sight and was not entirely with it. His blue eyes were hidden behind dark glasses, and he carried a cane. He leaned on President Reagan, who piloted him tenderly into the Oval Office and later into lunch. But flashes of his old spirit surfaced from time to time.

As he and Reagan sat down to lunch in the White House,

Bourguiba noticed his interpreter, Sophia Porson, a woman of a certain age, but transformed into a veritable goddess through the old man's eyes.

"The interpreter has beautiful eyes," he said, and leaning forward, added in an emphatic voice, "If I were forty years younger, I would propose to you." Sophia blushed. Nothing like this had ever happened to her, a professional to her fingertips.

"Translate what I said," President Bourguiba insisted, until she did so, which left the President and both official delegations in stitches.

Everyone in our government was disposed to indulge the grand old man, and we did everything we could to make this— undoubtedly his last trip—a happy and memorable one.

THIRTY-TWO

South of the Border

*I*T IS VERY UNCOMFORTABLE to sleep in the same bed with an elephant," said Mexico's President Miguel de la Madrid in a meeting with our legislative leaders during his 1984 state visit to Washington. He was trying to explain the way Mexicans feel when grappling with the United States over bilateral issues.

"The United States sees us as primitive, touristic, and folkloric," he continued, lamenting the lack of empathy between our cultures and our disregard for Latin sensibilities. And as if determined to prove him right, one of the senators told the Mexican finance minister, Jesús Silva Herzog, that he should run for office because his first name had immediate recognition. Of course, in the Spanish-speaking world, Jesús is as common a first name as Joe is in the United States.

The Latin-American portfolio was a difficult one for the Reagan administration, what with an intractable Cuba, Marxist Nicaragua, guerrilla warfare in El Salvador, and a festering Panama. But the President and Secretary of State preferred seeing the Latin-American glass as half full instead of half empty.

The contrast between the political map of Latin America at the beginning and at the end of the 1980s was cause for optimism. Only a decade ago, most Latin Americans lived under totalitarian or authoritarian regimes; now they had peacefully evolved to democratic republics, with duly elected leaders—Brazil, Argentina,

Uruguay, Ecuador, Bolivia, Guatemala, El Salvador, Peru, Honduras, had all made the transition.

My job was receiving these new leaders, many of whom turned to the United States for assistance and guidance in moving their countries toward freer economies as well. Almost all were in dire economic straits.

Over the decade every elected leader visited us, with the exception of Peru's Alan García. Aside from the fact that he was no friend of the United States, García blotted his copybook with Shultz when, in a speech to the United Nations, he attacked us for being the main market for drugs. Shultz took great offense at his speech, as did U.N. Ambassador Vernon Walters, but as I read it today, I still cannot understand why it caused Shultz to explode. What García said about American consumption of drugs was extremely tactless, but true.

Chile's Pinochet and Paraguay's Stroessner were never invited; they were kept at arm's length, as they were the only right-wing dictatorships still surviving. As of this writing even that has changed, as well as the new look in Nicaragua; now the map is all one color with the exception of Cuba.

I felt very comfortable with our Latin visitors. Having lived in Spain for four years and speaking fluent, though grammatically dubious, Spanish, I had the benefit of instant communication. Surprisingly, few South American leaders spoke English—almost as if to thumb their noses at us. They did not come to North America to be educated; they preferred going to Europe and studying French as their second language. Even the Portuguese-speaking Brazilian leaders communicated with us in French or Spanish, rather than in English. This cultural defiance of the "Colossus of the North" reveals much about our past failures with our Latin neighbors.

It has been observed that Spaniards are Arabs who speak Spanish and practice Catholicism. And as a generalization this applies to the Latins as well, even taking into account the strong Indian influence in much of the region.

In my dealings with the Latin Americans, I saw so much that

I instinctively understood: the way they respond to charismatic leaders rather than ideas; the way they personalize every action or pronouncement; their strong sense of *amor propio* derived from the Arab *sharaf,* or honor; their contradictions of machismo and tenderness, of cruelty and kindness. Fate is something they accept, combined with a deep religious faith—the Moslem *Inshallah* long ago became the Catholic *Si Dios quiere* (God willing).

Because personal relationships are so important in Latin cultures, our visitors were particularly anxious to have an ongoing dialogue with Ronald Reagan. And for his part, the President was a master at conveying affection, appreciation, and a certain machismo—the big *abrazo,* the gracious homilies. Latins are intuitive; they immediately recognized a good and honorable man in Ronald Reagan—even when they did not always agree with him, as in the case of Nicaragua.

No one had a greater personal affection for President Reagan than the late José Napoleón Duarte, President of El Salvador. Duarte was a noble character, with a Latin sense of theater. In the midst of reviewing the troops on a state visit, he departed from the script, walked down the South Lawn to the American flag, and as a gesture of respect, brought the flag to his lips.

I thought to myself, "Oh, Lord, the Latin-American press will crucify him for toadying to the gringos." Later, he told me he didn't care. "My country is still free because of America's help. I want the world to know that we appreciate it."

Years before, Duarte had lost several fingers on his left hand from being tortured by the military government; more recently his daughter Inés, a mother of three children, had been kidnapped and held captive by Marxist guerrillas for forty-four days. Shortly after her rescue, Duarte brought Inés to Washington to help her recover from the trauma. Her only wish was to meet President Reagan.

Normally, Oval Office visits did not include wives and children, but we made an exception. As I walked her into the Oval Office, Inés ran to President Reagan and threw her arms around him, hugging and kissing him, crying all the while.

By Duarte's next visit, we had learned he had cancer, and as he came back for periodic treatments, it soon became apparent that the disease was terminal. He was gallant to the end—a rare human being whose capacity for love and reconciliation should have been a beacon for his countrymen.

Secretary Shultz also did well with Latins, although he was less demonstrative than the President. They respected Shultz; he was someone they could trust. But the foreign policy establishment who dealt with South and Central America had their problems.

The Assistant Secretaries of State for Inter-American Affairs during my tenure were Thomas Enders, Langhorne A. (Tony) Motley, and Elliott Abrams—men I liked and respected. Enders, a brilliant career Foreign Service officer, was pure Anglo-Saxon, six foot eight, with patrician blond good looks designed to destroy the *cojones* of every diminutive Latin American worried about his virility. In fairness, once they got to know Tom, they joked about his looks and one South American leader said to him, *"Nos mandan un gringo y media"* (They have sent us a gringo and a half).

Tom Enders was viewed suspiciously by the White House— he had run afoul of both Mike Deaver and Mrs. Reagan—and by conservative elements in Congress, who thought he wasn't sufficiently doctrinaire. The liberals found him too conservative, however, so he couldn't win on the Hill.

Tony Motley was quite the opposite. An Alaskan businessman, and an ardent Republican with great political instincts, he was born and raised in Brazil and spoke fluent Portuguese. He had been ambassador to Brazil; he understood his constituency, and more important, he knew how to keep the White House happy by constantly touching base with Deaver and Jim Baker. But he had no stomach for the bureaucratic and congressional infighting. He was not a hard-liner, and after two years on the job he left to return to the private sector.

The last and longest-lived in the job was Elliott Abrams, who combined youth and brilliance and who certainly did not suffer fools gladly. The Congress did not cotton to his conservative views or his manner. The son-in-law of Norman Podhoretz, one of the leaders of the neo-conservative movement, Abrams had a keen intellectual grasp of the area, but I wondered if he lacked the emotional empathy. And because of the administration's priorities, during his tenure he was consumed with the issue of Nicaragua—the Contras *vs.* the Sandinistas, and the Iran-Contra scandal.

In the State Department, I worked with all the regional bureaus, and it was no secret that the Far Eastern and African were considered the best. They were staffed with first-rate professionals and headed by men of extraordinary competence and knowledge of their areas. The European and Middle Eastern bureaus came next, but by universal agreement, the Inter-American bureau was always at the bottom of the list.

My protocol staff, both career and political appointees, shared this assessment, and nothing I experienced proved to the contrary. It baffles me. Spanish is the easiest language to learn; we have a huge Spanish-speaking population in our country; there is every good political reason for attracting superior minds to the Latin-American area. And yet, motivation seems to be lacking. Why don't we have a coherent, long-range, and effective Inter-American policy?

I made an effort to bring home to Secretary Shultz and any others who would listen the need to focus on Latin America in other than geopolitical or economic terms—the need for us to understand and appreciate Latin-American culture.

For example, South American writers, especially novelists, provide a rich, exciting intellectual experience. Literary figures have a special status in Latin America and are considered the keepers of the national conscience. I felt they were the key to winning the struggle for Latin minds and hearts.

I saw no sign among our officials of any awareness of this important ingredient, totally missing from our South American equation. So I asked Secretary Shultz if he would allow me, from time to time, to arrange private lunches for him with Mexico's Octavio Paz or Carlos Fuentes, Peru's Mario Vargas Llosa, and any others I could persuade to come to Washington for this purpose.

Shultz thought it a great idea, and we started off with a winner. I telephoned Vargas Llosa, the great Peruvian writer recently turned politician, and he flew over from London for a lunch, with only the three of us present. As a result of that meeting Vargas Llosa and Shultz became friends, and still exchange letters. Also, the President and Mrs. Reagan agreed to include Vargas Llosa in a state dinner scheduled that week. But when I called Vice President Bush's office, his staff showed no interest—a big disappointment because I felt that one day Bush and Vargas Llosa might be running their respective countries and they should get to know each other.

Mario returned to Washington in 1989, a declared candidate for the Peruvian presidency. I had left government by then, but I telephoned friends at the National Security Council and the White House to urge Bush to see him. To my surprise Vargas Llosa was unknown to them, even though he is one of the most important political and literary figures in the Americas, the author of more than ten novels translated into every major language, and is on any short list of candidates for the Nobel Prize for literature.*

President Bush's staff did not reflect his own oft-stated interest in South America, but when Bush himself speaks or acts, he makes a strong and favorable impression on Latins. After his visit in 1985, Belisario Betancur, then President of Colombia, wrote me: "For my part, each time I gain a greater admiration for Vice President Bush, for his understanding, his intuition, his communication. He will very soon be President of the United States."

Betancur brought in his party a number of luminaries from Colombia's artistic community—among them the famous painter Botero—but he could not persuade Colombia's world-renowned author Gabriel García Márquez (*One Hundred Years of Solitude, Love in the Time of Cholera*) to come, mostly because of the McCarran-Walter Act of 1952, which was so offensive to South American intellectuals. (The law would not allow former members of the Communist Party to enter the United States, and many Latin writers had joined the party in their youth to protest con-

* Vargas Llosa, a favorite for the Peruvian presidency, lost the election in a surprise upset in June, 1990.

ditions in their own society. The law has recently been revised.)

Betancur also wrote me, "I know of your friendship for writers, as you are yourself; and for journalists, as you are also. I wanted to be a journalist and writer, but politics prevented me. I have mentioned to my friend García Márquez your admiration for his work." How pleased I was that the President of Colombia remembered our discussions about writing and writers—not protocol or politics.

When Venezuela's President Jaime Lusinchi came on a state visit in 1984, he brought Pedro Berroeta, a leading Venezuelan writer, in his official party. "Even though I must concentrate on economic matters on this visit," Lusinchi told me, "I want Americans to have a broader understanding of Venezuela, so I have included representatives of the intellectual life of our country."

I thought to myself, will the day ever come when our President has the guts to take a leading American intellectual as part of his official party instead of the usual White House operatives?

The meeting that meant the most to me personally was between the Cuban poet and writer Armando Valladares and Shultz. I had read Valladares' book, *Against All Hope,* a devastating account of his twenty-two years of suffering and torture as a prisoner of Fidel Castro. It was as painful to read as Jan Valtin's *Out of the Night.*

I tracked down Valladares through his American publisher. He lived in Madrid but happened to be in the States when I called, and agreed to come to Washington. His beautiful wife Marta, who had waited for him during all those years of his imprisonment, accompanied him. Valladares spoke no English, and as Shultz wanted to limit the luncheon to the couple and myself, he asked me to interpret. Luckily, Marta spoke enough English to rescue me.

Valladares used this opportunity to make an impassioned plea for Shultz's help in liberating the remainder of the political prisoners abandoned in Castro's jails—some for more than twenty-five years. He spoke rapidly, in an unfamiliar Cuban accent difficult to follow. But the thought of helping to free these prisoners focused my mind. When I couldn't translate literally, I grasped the sense of his remarks and made my rendition as eloquent as I could.

"Mr. Secretary, the men I shared those years in prison with are my brothers, more so than my own flesh and blood. It is my mission now to secure their release," Valladares concluded.

Shultz was deeply affected by Valladares and shortly thereafter took steps both to cut through our own red tape and to persuade Castro to liberate those long held in his jails. That September 15, 1986, when I saw on TV those sixty-nine former political prisoners land in Florida into the welcoming arms of their families, I wept with them. Nothing in my seven years as Chief of Protocol meant so much to me.

The following Christmas, I received a box of red roses. Enclosed was a Christmas card with the photo of two adorable little boys. I turned the card over and read: "Fernando and Carlos Alberto Valladares." It was Armando's way of saying thank you, not just for himself, but for his sons.

There is a sequel. Valladares was anxious to focus world opinion on Castro's cruelty and inhumanity. He felt a lot of missionary work needed to be done to alert European and South American intellectuals to the nature of Cuban totalitarianism. He mentioned that Cuban political prisoners testifying before Congress were bewildered by so many apologists for Castro in both the Congress and the press.

I suggested to Elliott Abrams that a man so sincere, so courageous and so attractive, might be very valuable in the battle for freedom and democracy in South America. I have no idea if my recommendation planted the seed, or if others thought of it independently, but in 1987 Armando Valladares was granted U.S. citizenship and joined the United Nations Committee on Human Rights. President Reagan appointed him head of our U.N. delegation to that committee in 1988, and as of today Valladares continues in that position.

Generally speaking, the Latins were the most fun-loving of our foreign visitors. Knowing Spanish made it possible for me to enjoy their sense of humor and share in their jokes. I also was able to pick up bits of gossip not contained in my briefing papers.

For example, one head of state—hardly looking like a sexual athlete—arrived with his wife, his mistress, and his former mistress, and our biggest problem was to avoid putting the current mistress and the past one in the same car. Another unlikely Lothario had a different glamorous creature with him on each visit. Sometimes the accompanying officials discreetly brought their mistresses instead of their wives, but we pretended not to notice.

The Latins loved to dance, and several complained about being hustled out of the White House after a state dinner, and not being given an opportunity to dance like the rest of the guests. The Reagans had the custom of walking their guest of honor out the front door to his or her waiting limousine immediately after the entertainment concluded. In most cases, this was just fine with the guest of honor—who was usually tired after a long day of meetings and ceremonies. But from the younger heads of state, especially Latins, we frequently heard complaints. They found this discourteous, and the wives were terribly disappointed not to have a twirl around the dance floor with President Reagan.

We reported this to the White House and suggested that they consider tailoring the departure to suit the wishes of the guest of honor. Nothing doing. Mrs. Reagan wanted them to go at a certain hour, then she returned with the President to start the dancing, and soon afterward quietly slipped upstairs to bed while the rest of the guests continued dancing.

The Latin Americans were also vocal about their treatment at the United Nations. Each year, when the Secretary went to New York for the opening two weeks of the General Assembly, he and Mrs. Shultz entertained extensively, grouping delegates geographically.

Because they constituted such a large group, the Inter-American delegates and their wives were usually invited to a reception at the U.S. mission. The first year, I observed that very few attended, or they only came for a few minutes. They did not like being kissed off with a mere reception while the Africans or the Arabs got a meal. I suggested the Shultzes try a luncheon instead, using an attractive setting such as the Morgan Library. This resulted in almost 100 percent attendance, and Secretary Shultz became a believer.

Each year, Mrs. Shultz gave a luncheon for the chief delegates' wives on Malcolm Forbes's yacht, and the husbands were very envious. Finally one complained, "Ambassador Roosevelt, I do not understand why you discriminate against men. Why are the husbands not invited to see Mr. Forbes's yacht?" So the following year we did a dinner for them aboard the yacht—the biggest success of all.

The Costa Ricans have been special favorites of mine since my days as a journalist. They always seemed so sensible in a world given to pointless posturing and high drama. I suppose the fact that Costa Rica has never had an army stuck in my mind.

President Luis Alberto Monge, literally Mr. Five-by-Five, endeared himself to me when, after several visits, I heard him observe to an aide, "There really is much to be said in favor of a woman chief of protocol"—whereupon, I am told, he appointed one.

His successor, Oscar Arias Sánchez, was impressive even before he won the Nobel Prize for his peace proposals for Central America. He was serious almost to the point of lugubriousness, and I sensed the White House had lost patience with his attempts to bring Nicaragua's Daniel Ortega into line by quiet persuasion as opposed to keeping up the pressure through the contras.

This earnestness of purpose would manifest itself throughout his presidency and he used the Nobel award to set up The Arias Foundation for Peace and Human Progress. Among its first projects was the integration of women into the Central American economy and I am sure the inspiration for this project came from his beautiful, articulate wife Margarita, a Vassar graduate whose liveliness made up for his quiet, low-key manner.

Even while negotiating war and peace in Central America however, we had a Marx Brothers–type incident when the Ariases came for cocktails with the Vice President and Mrs. Bush.

The waiter asked President Arias what he would like to drink.

Arias turned to his wife and said, "Margarita, what do you want to drink?" But the waiter only heard "Margarita" and rushed off to fetch one. A margarita is almost pure tequila, with just a touch of lemon or lime juice, and when the waiter returned with the drink, the other Costa Ricans opted for margaritas as well. I'm not sure the Bushes ever knew why their party was so lively!

Temperamentally and philosophically the opposite of Arias was Ecuador's President León Febres-Cordero. He was aptly named, a tall, vigorous, attractive man with masses of white hair and a bushy mustache, giving him a leonine appearance and a passing resemblance to Theodore Roosevelt.

Febres-Cordero was first proposed for a working visit, but I prodded Shultz to persuade the White House to make it a state visit. A millionaire businessman, León Febres-Cordero was a vocal advocate of a free market economy; he had rescheduled Ecuador's foreign debt, and was trying to put the country on a sound economic footing. What's more, he supported Reagan's position on the Nicaraguan contras, one of the few Latin Americans to do so.

Febres-Cordero also shared Reagan's and Shultz's position on terrorism, and had recently paid a heavy price for it. In a speech at a National Press Club luncheon, Febres-Cordero said, "I'll tell you what I would do with terrorists. I would shoot them."

That was not braggadocio. Three months earlier, a group of terrorists had held hostage a wealthy banker and relative of Febres-Cordero. Government forces located their hideout and asked the kidnappers to surrender; they refused, so Febres-Cordero ordered an assault and everyone was killed, including the hostages. He felt terrible about the outcome, but still believed he had done the right thing. Later, in a philosophical moment he said to me, "We leaders today, we seek these positions, but only when we are in them do we realize how our decisions have so many ramifications."

On this trip Mrs. Febres-Cordero took a shine to Barbara Bush and announced that as soon as her husband finished his term as President (he was prohibited from succeeding himself) she was going to Florida to campaign for George Bush and get all the Latin voters behind him.

•   •

Of the South American leaders that I met, few were as nice as Argentina's President Raúl Ricardo Alfonsín, an appealing man with the doleful brown eyes of a basset hound. To him fell the job of reestablishing democracy in Argentina after four decades of military and Peronist governments. He started off with high hopes, and when he came to Washington he was riding a crest of popularity both at home and on the international scene. But a seating gaffe at the White House dinner almost ruined the trip for him.

President Alfonsín, of course, was on Mrs. Reagan's right. But without checking it out, Mrs. Reagan decided to seat a fellow Argentinian, blond, beautiful Amalia Fortabat, on Alfonsín's other side. Mrs. Fortabat is the most famous woman in South America—an outstanding industrialist and philanthropist. But she had supported the opponents of Alfonsín. The photos of that evening, with Alfonsín and Amalia side by side, appeared in all the Argentine newspapers, to his acute political discomfort.

The next day Alfonsín seemed upset. His ambassador asked me why the seating had been thus. I told him the truth—that the White House social office was not attuned to the politics of Argentina and did not check the seating with the State Department. I did not add that Mrs. Reagan had forbidden her staff to show the seating to anyone until immediately before the dinner.

As I reviewed the seating at Mrs. Reagan's table—the guests chosen for Alfonsín to meet—I could understand his puzzlement even more. Among other guests at the table were Argentine tennis star Guillermo Vilas, golf pro Lee Trevino, jazz musician Peter Fountain. Alfonsín was a serious man, a human rights activist, and a student of literature, law, and social studies. He did not speak English, but there were dozens of distinguished Americans who spoke fluent Spanish and could have been placed at his table, showing greater sensitivity to his interests and pride.

Alas, Argentina's problems proved to be far more intractable than anyone thought in March 1985. When Alfonsín left office in 1989, the economy was in shambles. He was judged a failure, and my heart went out to this well-motivated and honorable man. I wondered how many more failures Argentina's fragile democracy could survive.

On these visits, I spent a lot of time smoothing ruffled feathers—especially the upsets caused by sometimes irresponsible reporting in our press. One of the worst episodes was with the leader of our most sensitive neighbor of all, Mexico's President Miguel de la Madrid.

Columnist Jack Anderson chose the very week of de la Madrid's state visit to publish a story attacking him as corrupt and in the same mold as previous Mexican presidents who had regarded their office as a six-year license to steal. In fact, we believed de la Madrid was honest and doing everything he could to change this image of the presidency. And so he proved to be, having left office with his reputation intact.

President de la Madrid was so aggrieved by these allegations he demanded that the State Department issue some sort of statement denying them. I warned Shultz of how upset our visitor was, but there was little he could do.

Few bilateral relationships are more important to the United States than that with Mexico, sharing as we do a 2,000-mile border. But no relationship is more prickly either. The Mexicans simply do not trust us; they cannot put aside bygone hurts.

The Mexican foreign minister, Bernardo Sepúlveda Amor, was not a favorite of Secretary Shultz because he frequently took third-world, anti-American positions; the two of them had clashed on a number of issues—a reflection of the difficulties of our relations with Mexico.

But I found Sepúlveda brilliant and delightful to work with, having known him in his previous incarnation as Mexican ambassador to Washington. Slim, elegant, and very handsome, with bedroomy dark eyes, he enchanted the women on my staff, and they all thought up excuses to work on the Mexican visits.

The wariness between the two foreign ministers was in part substantive, but I have a feeling it was also the result of those cultural differences which so often impeded our ability to understand one another. When I visited Mexico years before as a journalist, it had come as a shock to learn how unpopular we are south of the border. Since most of us do not return the hostility, it is depressing to see our motives constantly questioned and old wounds never allowed to heal.

The Brazilians are a totally different breed. Originally a colony of Portugal, they are the only country in South America speaking Portuguese. Like us, they had a large slave population, making them the most racially mixed population to our south. They are not full of angst about us; they regard themselves as our equals. They too have a huge land mass, an immigrant society, and a wild west.

I have traveled in Brazil and found it an intriguing, bewitching country, but I was always disappointed by the leaders who came from Brazil. They did not seem worthy of that glorious people, and reflected, with remarkable accuracy, the recent history of a troubled nation.

In May 1982, President João Figueiredo, a former general, made a state visit to Washington. Military men had governed Brazil for almost twenty years. Figueiredo was unhappy with our pro-British stance in the Falklands War, so the visit was on again, off again. Finally he decided on a truncated visit, coming to Washington for only two days. With a nation full of simpatico, outgoing people, it was extraordinary that the Brazilians had a president so austere and withdrawn.

The Figueiredo visit is etched in my mind forever, because of a White House goof. I constantly lectured my protocol staff, "Never give foreign visitors their own food or their own entertainment; they do it better than we ever can." Thus my heart sank when I learned that a samba troupe had been chosen as the entertainment at the Brazilian state dinner. Surely, our vast entertainment industry could have produced something representative of the United States! I also knew the Brazilians hated the patronizing "folkloric" image Americans had of Brazil (carnival in Rio, black magic in Bahia, etc.).

The entertainment was a disaster—not only a samba troupe, but an inferior samba troupe. Usually, Brazilian samba dancers are

gorgeous and sexy mulattoes—redeeming features in any entertainment—but the White House managed to find the only ugly
mulattoes in Brazil. And they made up in vulgarity what they
lacked in beauty or ability.

The Brazilian political picture had changed completely by
January 1985, when Tancredo Neves was elected President in a
vote by the Brazilian electoral college, an interim process en route
to free national elections. The President-elect preferred not to wait
for the full state visit, and came to see Reagan two weeks after the
election. The trip probably contributed to his tragic death shortly
thereafter.

I was alarmed as he got off the plane that freezing January day.
He wore a wool muffler around his face, and his only response to
my greeting was a prolonged, hacking cough. He looked pale and
fragile as he was bundled into the waiting car. As it turned out,
Tancredo Neves would never fulfill his electoral mandate. He died
in April 1985. Vice President José Sarney took office and eventually
made a state visit to Washington, in September 1986.

José Sarney, a poet and intellectual, started with high hopes,
just like Alfonsín. And again, the Reagan administration was responsive. They pulled out all the stops, including an invitation to
address a joint session of Congress.

When I was told that Sarney's favorite poet was Walt Whitman, this seemed like a good omen to me, and we arranged for
President Reagan to present Sarney with a handsome leather-
bound set of Whitman's complete works. No state gift was a
greater success. President Reagan was particularly pleased when
Sarney closed his address to Congress with a quote from Whitman's poem to the Brazilian people heralding the birth of the
Brazilian republic in 1889, "Welcome, Brazilian Brother—thy ample place is ready. . . ."

For the Sarney visit, the White House entertainment was the
American crooner Paul Anka—at least an improvement on the
samba dancers—but I would have been prouder of something a
little more classical for a man of Sarney's poetic sensibilities.

There was no visit by a South American leader where some
problem of sensitivity did not arise. And as far back as 1984, with

the visit of the President of the Dominican Republic, Salvador Jorge Blanco, I began writing memos to Shultz about the forth-coming 500th anniversary of Columbus' discovery of America in 1492. The Dominicans have a special claim on this celebration, maintaining that their islands were the site of Columbus' first New World settlement, Isabella.

Since planning was beginning years ahead of the event, I wrote Shultz, "The 500th anniversary . . . is a wonderful oppor-tunity for us to affirm our sense of community with the Caribbean nations and Central America in particular. Let's not let it slip out of our hands." Alas, 1992 is just around the corner, and we have done precious little about it.

Thinking back over the Reagan administration's Inter-American policies, I feel more than anything else a sense of lost opportunities. I agreed with our efforts to help the Nicaraguan freedom fighters and our support to the moderate forces in El Salvador. I also applauded the Caribbean Basin Initiative, an effort to stimulate economic development in the region. But at the same time, with Ronald Reagan's power as a communicator and ability to convey a noble vision or cause, I believe we could have forged a new era of North-South relations.

I wanted the President to say: "The American dream is not just for North Americans. We share a common vision that all things are possible, that no man need be limited by ancestry or class, that our societies are essentially meritocracies, and that wealth should not be despised, but likewise should never be the only measure of our values."

I felt it was time to show that we really are partners; to put behind us the "gringo" stereotype; to show that we have grown in understanding and sensitivity, just as they need to mature in their reactions to us. Only if we deal as equals can we have a true meeting of minds.

And finally, I could hear the President urging our Southern neighbors to put aside the negative, leftist shibboleths, and accen-tuate the positive—our common dreams, our common respect for liberty and law.

Where, oh where, was Peggy Noonan?

THIRTY-THREE

Europe

T HE RIGHT HONORABLE Margaret Thatcher, Prime Minister of the United Kingdom of Great Britain and Northern Ireland: a formidable title and a formidable woman. But the Margaret Thatcher that I saw bore very little resemblance to that demon the British press loved to criticize and caricature. Oh, she was an iron lady all right. I saw the "iron" from time to time, but I saw a lot more of the "lady."

She was Reagan's first and last official visitor, and during his presidency she came to Washington at least once a year, sometimes more. I would guess that she was Ronald Reagan's favorite visitor. She certainly was one of mine. What a woman! Indefatigable, courageous, forthright, and sharp, but also courteous, thoughtful, and very feminine.

It was said that Ronald Reagan and Margaret Thatcher were so attuned politically and economically, they were natural friends. But I think there were other dimensions to their relationship. One of the reasons Mrs. Thatcher liked Reagan so much was his lack of pretension, intellectual or otherwise. He set for his administration certain simple and clear goals and stuck to them. He was as honest and steadfast as she. He also appealed to the womanly side of her—and she could be surprisingly gentle and kind.

My first encounter with Mrs. Thatcher was in June 1982, when Alexander Haig was still Secretary of State. Together we met her at Andrews Air Force Base in Maryland and then heli-coptered in. She wasted no time with small talk. The Israelis had invaded Lebanon and she was outraged by events in the Middle East. Haig shrugged and tried to change the subject. He did not want to hear about it, but offered the argument that the PLO arms cache the Israelis had found was ten times what they expected and was Soviet-made. That did not impress her. Haig seemed an-noyed; his face turned strawberry red. I wrote, "She is one bright and tough lady. I really like her and she gave me several knowing nods as she lectured Haig and I nodded back!"

Apparently, Haig did not really take offense, for he praised the Prime Minister mightily in his memoirs. One of my favorite Thatcher stories comes from Woody Goldberg, Haig's special as-sistant.

Haig had to stop off for an important, and possibly confron-tational, meeting with Mrs. Thatcher on his way back to the States from the Middle East. As they sat down with her, Woody whipped out his notebook.

"Now, Woody," she said. "This is still nice time. I'll tell you when to take notes."

On Mrs. Thatcher's next trip I had occasion to appreciate her still more when she downplayed an unintentional snub. Secretary Shultz was at the United Nations in New York and Kenneth Dam was acting Secretary of State. Somehow, Dam's staff erred on Mrs. Thatcher's arrival time, and he did not show up to greet her. Of course, I was there, and made the appropriate apologies— having no idea what had happened to Dam.

"My dear Ambassador Roosevelt, think nothing of it. We have handled this rather well, all by ourselves," she said, smiling to the waiting press and photographers. Nothing fazed her; she never lost her good manners or her cool.

Unlike most male heads of state, Mrs. Thatcher traveled light. Her entourage was the smallest we ever dealt with. She was so secure, both emotionally and intellectually, she did not need hordes of tom-tom beaters to impress people with her importance. She never brought a maid or hairdresser but relied on local talent.

She managed nicely on only four hours sleep—to the despair of her staff, who were normal folk and tended to look green around the gills after a Thatcher visit! On almost every trip she began her days at 5:45 A.M. She could do four morning TV shows—ABC, NBC, CBS, and CNN—in an embassy drawing room, moving from one corner to another so the backgrounds would be different for each show.

My favorite story of Mrs. Thatcher's stamina was her December 1984 arrival in Washington after a nineteen-hour flight from Hong Kong. The welcoming committee had assembled at Andrews Air Force Base, when a heavy fog suddenly enshrouded the field. We heard her plane approach and then zoom back up into the sky. The pilot radioed, "No visibility, impossible to land. We're heading for Dulles Airport."

That was an hour away by car. I felt the welcomers were expendable, but what to do about the cars—including the armored limousine for Mrs. Thatcher—and her Secret Service detail, waiting to pick her up? With no assurance that her plane would be able to land at Dulles, we decided to gamble.

"Tell control at Dulles to find some way to prevent Mrs. Thatcher from deplaning until we get there" were my instructions as we scrambled into the cars. With police escort and sirens blaring we made it to Dulles Airport in forty minutes—what with the fog and slippery roads, the wildest motorcade I've ever been in. Mrs. Thatcher had landed, and as we pulled up on the tarmac she tore out of the plane and down the steps. That thoroughly sensible woman wanted to get right in the car and head for the embassy.

I started to apologize, but she beat me to it. "My dear Ambassador, I am so sorry for all the trouble and inconvenience we have caused you."

"Prime Minister, you must be exhausted. I hope you were able to get some sleep on the long flight."

"Oh, no. I never sleep on planes," she replied.

Apparently so. When her plane refueled in Hawaii, as a courtesy the commanding general of Hickam Air Force Base had gone out to greet her, even though it was the middle of the night. But instead of polite chitchat while the mechanics did their work, Mrs. Thatcher said, "General, I have always wanted to see Pearl Harbor. Would it be too much of a bother?" And off they went.

By my calculations Mrs. Thatcher had been awake some twenty-seven hours when we arrived at the British Embassy two hours behind schedule. It was midnight, and I could see that her traveling companions were exhausted. As I was saying goodnight at the door, however, the butler and footmen took everyone else's coats and I saw her look at her watch and say to the ambassador, "Now then, could we meet in the library in fifteen minutes for a briefing?" Then she turned to an assistant and said, "Please have the hairdresser come at six forty-five in the morning. I would like to be called at six." I watched transfixed as she disappeared up the grand staircase of the British Embassy, talking in her calm and measured voice but not wasting a precious minute.

Because her time was so valuable, Mrs. Thatcher respected other people's timetables as well. She was always punctual, or even early. "Better I wait than keep the President waiting," she said to me.

The Prime Minister was particularly courteous to the people who served her. I will never forget the delight of the Blair House staff when on her departure she asked to have them all assemble in the drawing room. Whereupon she made a gracious speech, then circled the room shaking hands and thanking each person individually. She was equally thoughtful of the police and Secret Service who guarded her. Once, after saying her goodbyes, she walked up the steps to her plane and then noticed an officer she had failed to thank. Back down the steps she came to shake the surprised policeman's hand.

Each year at the Economic Summit of Industrialized Nations I had an opportunity to observe President Reagan and Mrs. Thatcher, along with President Mitterrand of France and the Prime Ministers of Japan, Italy, and Canada, the Chancellor of Germany, and the head of the European Community. A different country hosts each year, and when it came our turn in 1983 we staged the summit in Colonial Williamsburg.

I greeted each arriving leader at the helicopter landing and then escorted him in an open carriage, complete with coachmen and outriders in period costumes, to President Reagan, waiting at the entrance to the Governor's Mansion. Crowds gathered along the route, waving and cheering each VIP as he went by. Mitterrand, Kohl, Nakasone, and Fanfani barely noticed them; Canada's Pierre Trudeau doffed his hat to the occasional pretty young thing, but Prime Minister Thatcher responded not only with queenly waves of the hand, but by leaning over and speaking to them as we passed. "How very kind of you to come," she would say, or "How good of you," or "Thank you for your warm greeting."

That night the President hosted a dinner at Carter's Grove Plantation. Each leader arrived in his own motorcade, in reverse protocol order. The President greeted at the door, and then I took the guest into the drawing room, making small talk until I had to return to the President and take the next guest in.

President Gaston Thorn of the European Commission came first, followed by Fanfani of Italy, Nakasone of Japan, and Kohl of Germany. But when I returned with Trudeau, Kohl had disappeared.

"Where is Chancellor Kohl?" I asked.

"He stepped outside on the terrace to talk with the press," said Fanfani.

"Please, Signor Fanfani, won't you go outside and make him come in? The press has been told that coverage is limited to a group photo. This will throw everything off."

Fanfani must have been all of five foot four, and Chancellor Kohl was a foot taller—a big bear of a man. I don't know how I thought Fanfani was going to drag Kohl back inside.

I disappeared to fetch Prime Minister Thatcher and told her what was happening. The minute she walked into the drawing room, the fractious boys stopped misbehaving. Trudeau greeted "Maggie" with a kiss, and the other men came in quickly from outside. Soon they formed a circle around her; she dominated the conversation and they hung on to her every word, attentive pupils listening to their teacher. Finally President Reagan, escorting Mitterrand, joined us, and they too formed part of the circle around her. It is one of my favorite vignettes of Margaret Thatcher.

In our travels together, Mrs. Thatcher had a disarming way of asking my opinions about economic or political questions as though they mattered. This was a part of her charm, of course, and one couldn't help but feel flattered.

We also talked about the problems of dressing for the public eye—whether to wear a hat and look smart in the day and then have our hair all mussed for a later appointment. Both of us found that so much standing for public ceremonies had caused our feet to increase by a half size, and we moaned over the difficulty of finding shoes both comfortable and chic. We carried almost identical handbags—short straps, square shaped, with side pockets for quick access. Her suits were conservative, well cut and of the finest English woolens. As time went on, she seemed to become more clothes-conscious, and on her last visit actually changed costumes five times in one busy day.

In my job I saw a lot of pompous people—it went with the territory. Margaret Thatcher not only eschewed the pompous, but she could shrink self-important types with a steely glance. She also knew when and how to stroke their egos. In Washington, she refused to let high-ranking officials call on her, as protocol would dictate. Instead, she called on them—a nice gesture, but also she preferred to see officials in their own environment, the better to assess them. When someone such as Shultz did call on her, she herself greeted him at the embassy porte-cochere and, when he left, escorted him to his waiting car.

I enjoyed observing Mrs. Thatcher in almost any role, but nothing was more fun than to sit through one of her press conferences. The punches Mrs. Thatcher landed often left smug reporters reeling. Our pundits and TV anchors, accustomed to American-style politicians who think a press conference is just a photo op with sound, learned quickly that this woman took no prisoners. Ask a foolish question and you got lanced with an intellectual rapier that left you skewered to the floor.

I grew very fond of her husband Denis, who seemed to relish his role as the amiable British businessman totally supportive of his famous wife but with no desire to share the limelight. (I don't know if he realized there is a Denis Thatcher Society in Washing-

ton, made up of husbands whose wives are more famous than
they.)

The Thatchers' last visit to Reagan's Washington was in November 1988. Denis arrived at Blair House ahead of his wife and
was shown to the spouse's bedroom of the master suite. The room
is decorated in the most extravagant flowered silk moire, covering
the walls and windows, the bed and its canopy—as feminine as a
room could be. He was offered his choice of that bedroom or the
adjoining chief of state's bedroom, which was more masculine.

"Oh, no," he said. "I love this room. It makes me feel happy.
And anyway, Margaret must be in the proper room."

During this farewell sentimental journey Mrs. Thatcher paid
an emotional and glowing tribute to Ronald Reagan, terming his
presidency one of the greatest in American history.

She also looked to the future. Of Bush she said, "We know
him as a friend, we admire him as a man of unrivaled experience,
and we respect him because he stands for all that is best in America."

And she concluded, "President Reagan has a unique style
which the world has come to know and love. George Bush too
will have his own style. But I think we're very fortunate in the
Western world that for the first time we shall have continuity of
policies stretching over a second presidency . . . that gives enormous confidence and stability to the feeling of the world."

Canada, although our hemispheric neighbor, was always
placed administratively in the European section of the State Department, and from a protocol standpoint, I found it a curious
anomaly that the Queen of England was still their queen and the
Canadian prime minister was outranked by the Queen's representative, the governor general of Canada.

Like most Americans, I made the mistake of thinking the
Canadians are really just like us, but their large French-speaking
population does give them a European orientation and makes for
a unique three-way cultural amalgam of English, French, and
American.

When Reagan first came to office, he put a high priority on

our Canadian relationship, but everything that was wrong with it seemed to get in the way; by the time he left office, everything that was right about it had triumphed. This was largely due to the polar differences between Liberal Prime Minister Pierre Trudeau and his successor, Conservative Brian Mulroney.

Trudeau had become an anachronism by the time Ronald Reagan became President. He was a bit flaky—a man of the sixties and the anti-Vietnam syndrome. He seemed to enjoy being at odds with the United States, the big bogeyman, and cast Canadian foreign policy more in a third-world mold. Naturally, this did not endear him to Reagan.

But all that changed when Brian Mulroney became Prime Minister. Here at last, in this handsome son of Ireland, Ronald Reagan found his political soulmate. And there was great personal affinity as well. Both men had more than their fair share of Irish charm, both were eternally cheerful, and both had beautiful and adoring wives.

Mila Mulroney, a native of Yugoslavia, spoke five languages and was a warm and radiant woman. She had an all-inclusive manner which embraced everyone she met. As Reagan said to Mulroney on observing their two wives together, "You know, Brian, for a couple of Irishmen, we certainly married up."

The Mulroneys had a great marriage. She fussed over him and was delightfully uninhibited in showing her affection, even occasionally chucking the Prime Minister on the cheek. When I went to the hotel to escort Mulroney to address a joint session of Congress, Mila sent him off with an encouraging kiss, and then called down the hall to us, "Check and be sure that I didn't leave any lipstick on his cheek."

Although Americans responded positively to this dynamic couple, the Prime Minister did have some political fallout in Canada from his affection for the United States. "America-bashers are a minority in Canada; however, they are the trendy sophisticates," he said, adding that his opponents point the finger: "There goes Mulroney down to Washington to hold hands with his pal Reagan."

Talking with a group of American congressmen, I heard Mulroney make a remarkably generous comment: "There is no question that everyone now recognizes America's leadership. For example, at a NATO meeting or at a summit meeting when the President of the United States arrives, something happens. I sense it. He represents power and generosity. I have felt the resurgence and booming of United States self-confidence under this administration. The American psyche is a great thing to behold, even though it affects us [Canadians] negatively."

To me, Mulroney's words were a sign of the maturing of the Canadian-American relationship. And this made possible some impressive accomplishments, capped by the treaty which created a Canadian-American free trade zone.

Mulroney's final visit to Washington during the Reagan presidency was in April 1988, and he went to have drinks with Bush. We had been on the go all day, and in the car Mulroney ran a razor over his five o'clock shadow, finishing just as we pulled up to the Vice President's residence.

The two men talked mostly about the campaign, and Mulroney told Bush: "About the time of the conventions, the Democrats will be ahead. Don't let that discourage you. Don't let the Republicans start fighting among themselves. Your most important task will be to keep the right wing in line."

Mulroney said in politics it was best not to hold grudges, and Bush replied that Barbara had a long memory and found it hard to forgive people who attacked her husband.

"Mila feels the same way," said Mulroney. "Do you think it's because women are less forgiving than men?"

Just as Margaret Thatcher seemed quintessentially English in character and looks, François Mitterrand, the President of France, conformed to the popular image of a Frenchman—high cheekbones, aquiline nose, thin lips, and an air of bored cynicism.

For me, Mrs. Thatcher was instantly understandable; Mitterrand was not. I found this austere, aloof intellectual almost impossible to read, and undoubtedly my poor French added to that impenetrable wall.

I thought of my mother, who had taught French to so many

students in Tennessee and yet had been unable to persuade her own daughter of its joys. "You'll be sorry," she often said, sadly predicting I would never be truly cultivated without benefit of the French language.

Of course, mothers are usually right. And I did feel stupid that first Mitterrand visit when I went aboard the Air France Concorde and stammered like a six-year-old, *"Bienvenue à Washington, Monsieur le Président."* I daresay my accent was so bad it offended his ears—I had been told that he spoke the most elegant, the most literary French imaginable.

In any case, I gave up and from then on Christopher Thiery, the brilliant interpreter who always accompanied Mitterrand, was our link. Such was Thiery's genius that whatever Mitterrand's tone, Thiery would mimic it perfectly, even to the Gallic shrugs and gestures. When Mitterrand paused, pouted, or misspoke, Thiery would do so. And when Mitterrand ventured a laugh, Thiery would laugh in exactly the same place.

I first met François Mitterrand when I accompanied President Reagan to the Versailles summit in May 1982. I would not say it was love at first sight for either of us. But I did come to have a deep respect, and in the end, a grudging affection for President Mitterrand.

His week-long state visit in 1984 was an unforgettable endurance test—I recall that in one day we flew from San Francisco to Peoria, Illinois; drove from the airport some forty miles to Galesburg to see a working pig farm; flew to Pittsburgh where he met with some university professors; from there to New York's Kennedy Airport and the long drive into the city. The March weather was terrible, and as we sloshed around the pig farm someone thrust a piglet into Mitterrand's arms. The photographers went crazy, but the imperturbable French president never unbent.

For me, the turning point came on the Fourth of July, 1986, when we were driving from Kennedy Airport into New York City. He and Ambassador Emmanuel de Margerie were discussing his speech, to be delivered that evening commemorating the

Statue of Liberty's 100th birthday. (I understood French a bit better than I spoke it.)

Suddenly Mitterrand turned to me. "Madame Roosevelt, I would like to conclude my speech with an English phrase. What would you suggest?"

I thought a minute. "Well, Mr. President, how about 'Happy Birthday, Miss Liberty'?"

His eyes lit up and he said with a strong French accent, " 'Appy Birrrrthday, Mees Lee-berrrr-tee."

"Perfect, Mr. President. Now let's practice it a few more times."

And sure enough, that night he concluded an eloquent French speech with this English phrase, and throughout the United States it was the television bite on the evening news!

No two men could have been more different, intellectually and temperamentally, than Ronald Reagan and François Mitterrand. I sensed a certain disdain in Mitterrand's attitude toward Reagan, and certainly Reagan could not have been enchanted with Mitterrand's socialism—although in only a few years it would prove to be more pragmatic than doctrinaire.

But Reagan always thought big—and he saw that in matters of foreign policy he and Mitterrand were much closer. Both he and Shultz felt that Mitterrand played a very constructive role in world affairs. Early on, Mitterrand supported the deployment of U.S. missiles in Europe; he participated with us in America's ill-fated venture in Beirut; he sent troops to Chad when Libya tried to take over.

Mitterrand was always critical of our Central America policy, but from the beginning he saw the urgent need for dialogue between Reagan and Gorbachev and did all he could to push East-West talks. It is to both leaders' credit that they came to work so harmoniously, but according to Rozanne Ridgway, then Assistant Secretary of State, it was Ambassador Joe Rodgers, a political appointee who had Reagan's ear, who finally convinced Reagan that he could do business with Mitterrand.

The French visits were among our most difficult ones—and

not just because of the language barrier. Bunny Murdock, who spoke excellent French, time and again saved the day. The French advance men were as demanding as our own. And French security tried hard to rough up Bunny, but she always managed to stand her ground.

Most interesting to me was the rivalry between the French Foreign Ministry and Mitterrand's own staff, very similar to the turf battles between the White House and the State Department. Jacques Attali, his senior adviser, and Jean-Louis Bianco, who administered Mitterrand's staff, seemed to control access to the great man, and one or the other always accompanied him.

I disagreed with the White House staff mentality vis-à-vis the French. When I came aboard, the advance teams for the Versailles summit, both French and American, had already established an adversarial relationship. I listened to their negotiations and couldn't believe my ears. For example, this discussion about a luncheon Mitterrand proposed to give for Reagan:

"President Reagan will arrive for lunch at two o'clock," said the American advance man.

"Well, that is a bit late. President Mitterrand would prefer to invite President Reagan for one o'clock, which is the time he usually has his lunch."

Since I knew that President Reagan normally lunched around twelve, I thought our team would be delighted at the earlier hour. Not at all. For reasons unknown to me we insisted that President Reagan did not wish to lunch before two. After more haggling, they agreed to have the luncheon at one thirty.

As it happened, President Reagan did not arrive until two o'clock, but it was no fault of his. The widow of a military atta-ché, Colonel Charles Ray, who had been assassinated in the streets of Paris, was scheduled to see the President just before lunch. Reagan, touched by her sacrifice, gave more time to the meeting than had been planned, and was late for lunch.

This got Mitterrand's dander up, so he was exactly twenty minutes late for President Reagan's subsequent dinner in his honor at the American Embassy in Paris.

Again, at the Tokyo economic summit, the punctilious Japanese had orchestrated every move. Reagan, being the ranking chief of state, was scheduled to arrive last to the opening session. But Mitterrand was late, so the Reagan motorcade circled downtown Tokyo, waiting for the French president to go in turn. Finally, Reagan, who hated playing games, told his driver to ignore protocol and proceed. Let Mitterrand come when he felt like it!

I'm afraid such one-upmanship went on for years—and came to a head during Mitterrand's attendance at the Statue of Liberty celebrations. President Reagan, naturally, was Mitterrand's host. It was meant to be a happy and carefree occasion, but the staffers working on the scenario treated every move as a battle maneuver.

For example, Mitterrand was particularly sensitive to the awkward protocol of his arriving first on Governors Island (where the festivities were to take place) and being kept waiting while Reagan's helicopter flew in twenty minutes later. The visit was almost canceled three times over this argument—exacerbated by advance-man mentality.

Likewise, I thought it bad manners during the television spectacular for the Reagans to enter after the Mitterrands. They should have come in together and sat in the same box instead of separate boxes.

Small matters in themselves, but I often wondered why all the macho types—on both the French and American sides—broke so many bones over details which in the final analysis were simply questions of good manners and good taste.

After this trip, I wrote Shultz: "Bunny and I both have the feeling that it's time to wipe the slate clean. Enough is enough."

Helmut Kohl was Chancellor of Germany during most of Reagan's two terms, and he and the President formed a strong personal and political bond. The Chancellor came to Washington at least once a year, usually bringing with him Vice Chancellor and Foreign Minister Hans-Dietrich Genscher, an important political figure in his own right.

The strong, effective bilateral relationship they developed—it soon became "Ron" and "Helmut"—was vital to both countries and to world peace. I think what Reagan liked most about Kohl was his unambiguous voice. Kohl believed that partners should be dependable and predictable. "We are not wanderers between two worlds. Our position is clear; we stand by our friends. We have learned that lesson from history," he said.

An informal survey among my staff revealed that they found the Germans the most demanding and exacting of the countries we dealt with (followed by the Israelis and the Japanese). The Germans knew exactly what they wanted and were ill disposed to compromise. This came as a surprise to me, because on the ambassadorial level I found them very easy.

Kohl was a creature of habit. He refused to arrive at Andrews Air Force Base, which was easiest for us and where we could control security. Instead, he arrived at Dulles Airport, where Lufthansa, the German airline, had a huge terminus. This was his way of showing the flag.

He insisted on the same suite at the Watergate Hotel because he liked the view of the Potomac River. He made no official plans the first night and always took friends to dinner at Filomena's, a folksy Italian restaurant in Georgetown.

Kohl took up lots of space. He was not only very tall, but broad as well. When we were rehearsing the horse-and-carriage arrival at Williamsburg, we got the biggest man we could find to test the carriage—worried that it might collapse under Kohl's weight.

He always seemed in a hurry, and with his large strides I had to run to catch up. At times, he would notice that I wasn't beside him, turn around and, with a look of embarrassment mingled with exasperation, pause and wait for me. I often wondered if underneath that brusque exterior was a teddy bear; but I'll never know, since he spoke little English and personal communication was minimal.

I accompanied Chancellor Kohl on his rounds to the Senate, the House of Representatives, and the National Press Club, and I recall particularly one of his observations. On the East-West question, as far back as 1984 he noted that Germany and the Berlin Wall were at the center of Europe, and the overall world situation was reflected at the German border. "But changes are under way," he said prophetically. "The East-West division will not last forever. We Germans insist on the right to unity. It is a fundamental right."

While the British, French, and Germans became constants, it was left to the Italians to provide variety. I came to know a half-dozen Italian prime ministers—the average term was less than two years—and they each, upon assuming office, felt they had to come to Washington.

The Italians, knowing that their politicians lead ephemeral lives, have cleverly maintained one of the finest career diplomatic services in the world. And they usually send their top diplomat to Washington. In my years, Reinaldo Petrignani was ambassador—and he was a master. Every few months he would be in my office, working on yet another visit by a new Italian prime minister (technically, president of the Council of Ministers). It was not enough that we arrange a visit, sometimes at very short notice, but each new prime minister had to be accorded the same hospitality and honors as his predecessors. Otherwise the Italian press would interpret this as a message—either that the Italian-American relationship was floundering or that we had a preference in prime ministers.

In all candor, I could hardly see any changes in our relationship with Italy, no matter who was prime minister. The Italian government—thanks to the permanent bureaucracy—seemed to operate on automatic pilot.

We had only one real problem with our delightful Italians. They were addicted to long, flowery toasts after dinner, in Italian, which then had to be translated into English. The visitor usually began his speech with Christopher Columbus and omitted nothing after that date which touched on Italian-American friendship. I remember one evening sitting through a forty-minute discourse, after which Vice President Bush rose to make the return toast.

"Ladies and gentlemen, you have just heard a brilliant dissertation on the state of Italian-American relations. I really feel there is little I can add to that, so won't you all join me in a toast to our guest of honor and to Italian-American friendship." We clinked glasses, silently toasting Bush as well for sparing us further torture!

(Everyone could learn from the Chinese about speeches and translations. When the Chinese visitor rises to make a toast, he reads only the first paragraph in Chinese, then the interpreter reads the rest of the speech in English. To mark the end of the toast, the visitor then says the last sentence in Chinese and lifts his glass.)

During the decade of the eighties, democracy was firmly established in both Portugal and Spain. The Portuguese repulsed Communist attempts to take over, and the moderates finally wrested control. The Spaniards consolidated the return of the monarchy and the stability of their governmental institutions by twice electing Socialist Felipe González Márquez as Prime Minister.

In the beginning, González was regarded with some suspicion by Reagan and Shultz, and the feeling was mutual. In a 1989 interview in *Time* magazine, González revealed his earlier trepidations: "I used to have little faith in the U.S. and this was still true when I came into office. . . .But I changed as I came to know the U.S. a little more. Americans want so much to be liked. But they also have enormous power, and that is not easily compatible with the affection of other people. This gives me a feeling of tenderness toward them."

Soon after taking office, Shultz made a trip to Spain, and he and Felipe González took each other's measure. They both liked what they saw, and this resulted in an invitation to González to come to Washington.

I looked forward to meeting him, and I was not disappointed. It was easy to see why he was such a popular politician, and catnip to the ladies—charismatic, impish, his dancing eyes sparkling with good humor and joie de vivre. So Andalusian and so Spanish.

Reagan also liked González, and over the years of his presidency our relations with Spain had their ups and downs, but in the end they seemed rather solid. My disappointment was our inability to exploit Felipe González as an interlocutor in both South America and the Middle East.

Prime Minister González believed there should be a triangular relationship between Europe, the United States, and Latin America, and he wanted to play a larger role vis-à-vis South America. As a prominent Venezuelan official told me, "Look, Felipe is young, and is going to be around for a long time. You Americans do not appreciate the role he can play in South America."

I think this is because our leaders are so European oriented they do not think in Hispanic terms; they have not made the mental jump which comes with a knowledge of Hispanidad—the world of Spanish-speaking peoples who look to Spain as the mother country the way we look to England.

Likewise, our government has never understood the Arabs' affinity for Spain. To both North Africans and Middle Easterners, Moorish Spain represented the pinnacle of Arab civilization and culture, when Cordova was the intellectual capital of Europe. Spaniards appreciate and understand Arabs in a way that few Europeans can, and could be an important bridge for us in dealing with intractable Middle East problems.

The Irish came once a year—on St. Patrick's Day, of course—bringing shamrocks in a Waterford bowl as a gift to the Irishman in the White House.

The Yugoslavs also came annually—each time a different president of the Federal Executive Council, which rotated yearly. It is perhaps a comment on the drabness of Communism that I remember nothing distinctive about any of them!

The Greeks, as long as Andreas Papandreou was in power, were not invited to Washington. Despite his virulent attacks on the United States, no foreign leader worked harder to get an invitation to the White House. He tried working through Greek-American Republicans, but their pressure did not succeed. No matter how much we wanted warmer relations with the Greeks, Papandreou made it impossible, even though a liberal faction in the State Department kept advancing reasons for inviting him. Happily, they did not succeed. We conditioned his invitation on an agreement over our military bases there.

The State Department was also opposed to receiving Constantine, the former king of Greece, even for an informal off-the-record call. I urged the Secretary to see Constantine—if only to tweak Papandreou's beak—but he refused. Nancy Reagan was a bit bolder. She invited the ex-king to tea, and President Reagan just "happened" to be strolling by on his way back from the Oval Office and joined them.

The Greeks' nemesis of course was Turkey, and we had excellent relations with the Turks. But there isn't a more hypersensitive country in the world! The Turks resented the power of the Greek lobby but recognized that with such a large ethnic Greek community in the United States, Congress would tilt toward Greece in matters of foreign aid. The Turks constantly pointed out how steadfast they were and what ingrates the Greeks were. What really stuck in their craw, however, were the Armenians who were determined to have Congress pass a resolution condemning Turkey for the genocide of Armenians some seventy years ago.

We planned a state visit for Turkey's President Kenan Evren in the spring of 1988 and were able to arrange all the trappings the Turks asked for, plus a trip up the Hudson in Malcolm Forbes's yacht, stopping for lunch at David Rockefeller's estate. Nonetheless, at the last minute the Turks canceled the visit. Why? They feared the Armenian resolution would pass Congress just as the visit was beginning. To the Turkish president, this would be a gratuitous insult. It was beyond their comprehension that the President could not prevent such a slap by the Congress. Actually, the resolution never did pass, and the Armenians are still trying.

In July, we got the Turkish visit back on track, but it almost came apart again because of another perceived slight—this time by Vice President Bush. He was in the midst of the 1988 presidential campaign. The Turks thought the Vice President had promised to fulfill his traditional role as guest of honor at a return dinner to be given in Washington by the Turkish president. However, Bush's staff had long before committed him to an important fund-raiser in California. (It was not lost on the Turks that the governor of California was an Armenian-American.) The Turks appealed to Secretary Shultz, tactlessly indicating that he was not high ranking enough to be a substitute! Nothing worked, and they canceled the dinner. Bush sent a handwritten letter of apology, but they were not mollified.

The visit continued as scheduled, but the Turks were also unhappy that the Forbes yacht was no longer available—it had been moved north for the summer. Then when we went to call on Speaker of the House Jim Wright and Chairman Dante Fascell of the House Foreign Affairs Committee, the Turks were kept waiting for twenty minutes due to an unexpected roll call.

The next day, Senator Robert Byrd—whom I often found to be arrogant and rude—kept the Turkish president waiting thirty minutes, and Evren was fuming. When the Senate meeting did get under way, Byrd delivered an impassioned pro-Turkish speech, but it was lost on Evren because his interpreter keeled over, fainting from exhaustion in the middle of the translation. Finally, I was sure that a hex had been put on the visit when a protocol officer found Reagan's gift to President Evren—a beautiful Steuben piece—broken and left behind in the hotel room. We never knew what happened, but Steuben helpfully replaced it.

Every European country was important to us, and basically our relationships were productive and successful—with the Benelux countries (Belgium, the Netherlands, and Luxembourg); the Northern tier (Sweden, Denmark, Norway, and Finland); and Austria, positioned as it was on the edge of the Iron Curtain, then about to disintegrate.

One of the most significant events of the Reagan presidency occurred almost unnoticed by the press and pundits in July 1988 when Karoly Grosz, the new Hungarian Communist Party chief, paid an official visit to Washington—the first by a Hungarian leader in forty-three years.

I had by then seen so much of the Russians that I took their "new look" for granted. But the surge toward democracy and freedom in Eastern Europe arrived almost unannounced. It was Grosz's visit that woke me to the possibility of the miracle we would all be witnessing in 1989—the destruction of the Berlin Wall and the liberation of Eastern Europe.

THIRTY-FOUR

Moscow—
Lilacs and a Full Moon

As THE WIFE of a former senior CIA official, I accepted as holy writ that the Soviet Union would always be off limits to me. I never expected to see Moscow—and certainly not as a guest of the Russian government.

But then, never in my most bizarre fantasies could I have imagined watching Ronald Reagan deliver a speech at Moscow State University under a bust of Lenin, or going with him to the Danilov Monastery, recently restored as the headquarters for the Patriarch of the Russian Orthodox Church.

When people ask me what were the highlights of my years as Chief of Protocol, certainly the trip to the Moscow summit in May 1988 as a member of the President's official party has to be near the top of the list.

Jockeying for a place in the presidential entourage on major trips abroad was one of the great indoor sports at the White House. The truth is that presidential travel, the courtiers and outriders, had gotten completely out of hand. Everyone argued they were indispensable; everyone wanted to be where the action was. Sometimes I traveled with the President, but often I did not, as I was too busy preparing for the President's visitors coming to Washington. However, I wanted to go to Moscow more than anything, so I was thrilled when Howard Baker, Chief of Staff at the White

House, told me I could be a member of the official delegation. But until I actually got on the plane I was afraid someone might pull rank and bump me.

So that the Reagans would be well rested for the Moscow summit, they traveled ahead for a three-day stopover in Helsinki, but many of us preferred to leave a little later and go straight to Moscow.

It is also more fun *not* to be on Air Force One. (This is heresy, I know.) On the presidential plane I would be lucky to get one of the better guest seats and, of course, I would have to sleep sitting up. But on a backup plane, someone of my rank usually ended up in the presidential suite—complete with a sofa bed and private bathroom. It was bliss.

On the trip to Moscow I shared the presidential suite with Charles Wick, the head of United States Information Agency. We joked about our "sleeping together" and Charlie, something of a wit, kept insisting, "I want everyone to understand that our relationship is *not* platonic." The plane had been Air Force One in an earlier incarnation, and the stewards pointed out the rack installed for Lyndon Johnson's Stetson, and another for John F. Kennedy's pipe.

I slept all the way to Moscow, and woke to find we were landing. It was a clear sunny day, temperature in the 70s. A Soviet protocol official greeted me with an armful of salmon-pink roses and escorted me to a waiting car and an assigned interpreter.

The Reagans were due the next day, and the airport had already taken on a festive air. Huge red banners said "Welcome, Mr. President" in both English and Russian, and the otherwise drab decor was brightened with pots of red geraniums everywhere.

The official party was housed at the Mezhdunarodnaya, or the Mezh, as we dubbed it, a cavernous tourist hotel. I was given a clean and comfortable suite, with a television set in each room and a fine view of the river. However, the decor was Communist Party drab—in every shade of brown—and left much to be desired. The windows were filthy and streaked, a condition which seemed to be endemic in Communist countries. (This was also true of every hotel we stayed at in China.)

Before leaving Washington, Bunny had given me a list of necessities to take—towels, washcloth, toilet paper, Kleenex, soap, air freshener, sink stopper, and lots of snack foods, just in case I missed meals.

At a security briefing, we were told to assume that all our conversations were bugged and that we were being observed by hidden cameras. No hanky-panky, no loose conversation; in other words, don't do anything you wouldn't want seen on TV or recorded by a listening device.

All this was second nature to a CIA wife, but I was amused by some of the younger female staffers who brought dark shower curtains with them, hoping to hide their nudity from the curious eyes of the KGB. I decided to hell with that. If they got their jollies looking at a naked middle-aged woman, then who was I to deny them their fun!

Soviet Chief of Protocol Vladimir Chernyshev had arranged for me to have a tour of the Kremlin Museums, sightseeing around the city, and finally, a trip to the Bolshoi Theater to see a stunning production of Rimsky-Korsakov's *Le Coq d'Or*.

The next day, Sunday, the Reagans were due in the afternoon. I gave two of our top interpreters a lift to the airport welcoming ceremony, and thought what a wonderful window on history they had—they would be the only outsiders who were witnesses to the substantive discussions. And how discreet they had to be!

The top brass of the Soviet Union filled the VIP lounge, and after passing through a security cordon, I greeted first the Shevardnadzes, giving them both affectionate kisses; Dobrynin, who complained that I didn't kiss him; and then the Gromykos, he far more genial than I had ever seen him. (From a protocol point of view, he outranked Gorbachev, for he was President of the Soviet Union, a largely ceremonial office. This was later changed, with actual power and protocol rank coinciding. Gorbachev was made

President—chief of state as well as head of government, just like our own President.)

When someone explained to Mrs. Gromyko who I was, she said, rather gravely, "That is a very important job."

Maybe. But it was all I could do to keep my composure and act important. Instead, I wanted to shout and wave when I saw Air Force One taxi to a halt. The Russian welcoming delegation, led by the Gromykos, walked toward the plane and greeted the Reagans and the Shultzes rather informally, without a receiving line. Then the Russians escorted their guests to a reviewing area marked by a handsome red Bokhara carpet. Troops marched in front of them in staccato goose steps, very precise—a good show. Afterward the Reagans shook hands with a long line of both Russians and Americans.

I rode in the motorcade with O'Bie Shultz. Friendly crowds lined the roads all the way into town. The Shultzes had been in Helsinki with the presidential party, but O'Bie said she never set eyes on the Reagans during the entire three days there.

The next day I spent some time walking around Red Square, which was not at all what I had expected. Having only seen it on TV, usually in winter, the square had seemed sinister to me—either all gray or covered with snow as some huge military parade marched before the cameras. Now, in summer, I saw the cheerful red brick and the fabulous Cathedral of St. Basil with its multicolored onion domes, as fanciful as a Walt Disney movie.

I will never see lilacs again without thinking of Moscow. The white and lavender blossoms were in bloom everywhere in the city, their perfume sweet and seductive. The Soviets had even managed to produce a full moon shimmering over the river. Everything was exciting—even the special restaurant in the hotel for the official party, where we gorged on smoked sturgeon and all the caviar we could hold.

The people seemed well dressed and healthy, and I was struck by their homogeneity—obviously their minorities did not live in Moscow. But what startled me was the total absence of commercial life. So few stores for such a big city; no advertising (maybe a blessing!), few restaurants. Still, Moscow was far more beautiful than I had expected, though most of the Communist architecture was drab and monstrous. The Soviets, like Texans, think big is beautiful.

They were beginning to restore the colorful Czarist buildings and churches, and we saw a wonderful example of this on the Reagans' afternoon outing to the Danilov Monastery. The priests greeted us on arrival, an impressive sight with their black beards and black headdresses and cassocks, relieved only by massive gold chains and crosses. They chanted liturgical music in the resonant basso profundo voices I always associate with Russian singing.

The Reagans were given a tour of the newly painted pink stucco church and bell tower and shown the restored icons. The priests wore a light aromatic scent, and the gleaming floors gave off an odor of beeswax. The rooms were handsomely furnished, complete with crystal chandeliers.

"All the renovations have been paid for by the labor or money of the faithful," a priest told us. At the time, I wondered if this was another Potemkin village, but in the years since, so much has happened to bring back religious freedom to Russia, now I am convinced it was genuine.

The official gifts the Reagans gave the Gorbachevs and others in Russia were of consuming interest to the press. It was difficult to keep them a surprise until the gifts were actually presented.

While visiting in the mountains of North Carolina earlier in the year, I had seen a stunning quilt made by some local women. I thought it might be perfect for Mrs. Reagan to take to Raisa. My friend Martha Hanes Womble had commissioned it for the Dolls House, a project started by the Hanes family to encourage mountain crafts. When I got Mrs. Reagan's approval, I asked Martha Womble to arrange for Mrs. Julia Spidell to make another one. Martha volunteered to underwrite the cost of it.

"Martha, whatever you do, be sure to swear your ladies to secrecy. If word leaks out ahead, I might even have to cancel the order," I warned. (In this case, an idle threat.)

Fat chance. Mrs. Spidell, whose more than 700,000 stitches

produced a work of art, just couldn't resist spilling the beans to the North Carolina papers, and later she was written up in *People* magazine.

We made several suggestions for the President's gift to Gorbachev, and he chose a replica of his favorite Remington bronze of a cowboy.

Probably nothing on the Moscow trip thrilled me more than going with the President to the House of Soviet Writers, a club of writers, artists, and filmmakers. In the wood-paneled dining room we were given a superb lunch of blini with black and red caviar, hazel-hen with bilberry sauce, and ice cream and pastry, plus white wine, red wine, and champagne—struggling artists they were not! Every person in the room was a Russian celebrity, and of course, I immediately recognized the poet Yevtushenko, a real heartthrob, dressed all in white, à la Tom Wolfe.

The President's speech was more literary than usual and was well received. Some of the Russian speakers were frank to criticize their own country as well as ours. One speaker told the President, "If you succeed in eliminating war, you will be entitled to become an icon—Jesus Christ in the middle with you and Gorbachev on either side."

Someone asked the rhetorical question, "What does acting have to do with politics?" And I heard Sam Donaldson in his usual booming voice say, "Good question."

I will take to my grave the picture of Ronald Reagan addressing a large auditorium of attentive Russian students with an enormous bust of Lenin on a ten-foot pedestal behind him. I had heard that the White House advance people tried to persuade the Soviets to remove the bust, but I'm glad they didn't succeed—there's so little whimsy on a trip like this. The students seemed prosperous and well dressed, and I assumed they were the sons and daughters of the top Soviet bureaucracy. I wondered what went on in their minds as President Reagan delivered a speech inveighing against bureaucracy in any country, saying it restrained economic growth.

The President was in good form and got a huge ovation, but

I later learned that the speech was not carried on Soviet TV, as the Soviets had promised.

"It's exciting to be part of history, but I am getting jaded," I wrote in my notebook in Moscow. "Every day is part of history and when it comes in daily increments it becomes normal. Whatever is on the front pages is what I am a part of."

Even so, I still found mind-boggling the dinner given by President and Mrs. Reagan in honor of the Gorbachevs. It was held at Spaso House, the ambassador's residence, and I was shocked to see this former Russian palace now furnished with government-issue broadloom carpeting and inappropriate works of abstract art—the result of our parsimonious attitude toward our embassies. These majestic rooms should have been enhanced by Oriental carpets, handsome curtains, and fine oil paintings in keeping with the period of the house.

But never mind the decor. There, collected under one roof, was the most extraordinary group of Soviet citizens ever assembled—everyone from dissidents Elena Bonner and her husband, physicist Andrey Sakharov, to the ranking Soviet political figures—Gromyko, Shevardnadze, Nikolay Ryzhkov, Yegor Ligachev, Aleksandr Yakovlev, Marshal Akhromeyev, to name a few. Liberally mixed with them were the leading musicians, ballerinas, writers, and scientists of the Soviet Union.

Every table (there were twelve round tables in all) was celebrity filled and challenging. At my own, presided over by Chief of Staff Howard Baker, the ranking guest was Ligachev, who had emerged as the sharpest thorn in Gorbachev's side. Conversation was a bit awkward at first. I heard Baker making small talk with Ligachev and then, as if wanting a little relief, he threw the conversational ball to me, across the table.

Not expecting this, I reverted to Southern belle in my confusion. "Oh, Mr. Ligachev. It's very exciting to meet you, after reading so much about you in the American newspapers."

He seemed surprised and replied that what I read probably wasn't very complimentary, and I, not a very good liar, resorted once again to some blarney. "But you are *very* famous."

He chuckled and after that the table became more animated,

with Pushkin Museum director Irina Antonova, writer Victor Yerofeyev, noted hockey coach and goalie Vladislav Tret'yak, Fyodor Burlatskiy of the Soviet Human Rights Commission, Ambassador Dubinin, Mrs. Dave Brubeck (wife of the jazz musician, who entertained after dinner), orchestra conductor Gennady Rozhdestvensky, and Mrs. Dmitriy Yazov, wife of the Minister of Defense. The spouses of almost all the government dignitaries attended the party—a departure from past practice. And we were surprised to see how slim and well dressed they were. I had expected hefty ladies in dowdy clothes.

The choice of Dave Brubeck for the after-dinner entertainment was enthusiastically received. Gorbachev was asked, "Do you like jazz?" and he replied, "I like good jazz, and this is good jazz."

We were gathered in the once beautiful ballroom of Spaso House, temporarily ruined by the demands of security. The Secret Service had insisted on covering the lovely French doors and windows with white curtains that must have come straight from Sears Roebuck. But not even ugly curtains could dampen the warm and bubbly atmosphere. The party was a smash, and certainly the most memorable dinner I have ever attended.

On the feminine front, the Nancy-Raisa exchanges were reported ad nauseam by our press. Certainly Mrs. Gorbachev's manner could be grating, but I kept wishing Nancy would not let it get to her. I wanted her to rise above the provocation, smile sweetly and look ingenuous with her beautiful brown eyes wide open. I was surprised that a woman as controlled as Nancy Reagan would let herself get rattled, in full color on international TV. I wanted to shout to her, "Smile, Nancy! Smile!"

Part of the problem was that no one dared tell the First Lady such things. And Mrs. Reagan also was a victim of the advance-man mentality—the idea that all those foreigners are out to make "our guy" look bad and "their guy" look good. I suspect they greatly exacerbated the Raisa problem. "They turn everything into a contest of wills," I wrote. "It all seems so childish. We should be more relaxed, as befits a great country. It is a great mistake to play games with these people."

I always felt that the Russians had a monumental inferiority complex as a nation, hypersensitive to any possible snub. I remember a comment by Librarian of Congress James Billington, a brilliant Russian scholar, who said that being on the Moscow trip gave him real insights into the importance of the symbolic in our dealings with the Russians.

The Moscow summit did not yield any great new initiatives, but a number of smaller arms-control accords were initialed by Shultz and Shevardnadze. As this was taking place Ambassador Matlock observed, "This is the first time in some forty years that the United States and Soviet foreign ministers have gotten along." And commenting on Shultz's success, Dr. William Graham, the President's science adviser, said, "Shultz is a logician. A very strong and tough negotiator, but always patient and courteous."

I was one of the few Americans privileged to witness the formal ratification in Moscow of the INF treaty signed at the White House the previous December. This final formality took place in one of the Kremlin's ornate halls, and as we waited almost an hour for the principals to appear, I had a chance to reflect on the grandeur of the moment.

Senate Majority and Minority leaders Robert Byrd and Robert Dole had flown from Washington for the occasion, having shepherded the treaty through the Senate. All the important Soviet players were in place, and in the back of the room, waiting to record it for posterity, was the press pool, let by the dean of White House reporters, UPI's Helen Thomas, in a bright red dress. Hiding on the stairs leading into the gold-and-white and brilliantly chandeliered room were some of my faithful protocol staff—Pam Gardner, Shelby Scarbrough, and Leslie Laudenslager, all of whom had been in Moscow for the previous three weeks helping with summit preparations. I was so pleased that they too could be witnesses. Too often, those who did the grunt work never got to see the final production.

I thought how sweet it must be for Shultz, Ridgway, Powell, Baker, and all those who had worked so long for this moment. But most of all, what a glorious hour for the President!

Then I did something rather tacky. I stood up and snapped photos of Gorbachev and Reagan as they signed—the only time I ever allowed myself the indulgence of taking a photo while on duty (a real no-no for a chief of protocol). I couldn't resist, but I got my comeuppance. The photos all turned out to have a strange blue cast, so my version of the great INF finale might better be entitled "Rhapsody in Blue."

The real celebration came in the evening—a gala at the Bolshoi Theater, in which the premier Russian dancers performed sensational solos and pas de deux from the great ballets. Such an evening would have had audiences in America hysterically shouting "Bravo!" and clapping for encores. But the Moscow audience was strangely muted, perhaps inhibited by so much Soviet brass in attendance.

We had been assigned a large box to the right of the presidential box, or Czar's box as it was known. When we arrived we found the entire front row of our box taken up by former ambassador Anatoliy Dobrynin and his family and other members of the Politburo. With me were Colin Powell and most of the senior members of the President's official party. I thought it strange from a protocol point of view—if not plain bad manners—that none of the Soviets acknowledged us, or made any attempt to offer us the front seats—as would have been automatic in a similar situation in America.

Dobrynin had been dean of the diplomatic corps during my first four years as Chief of Protocol, and he and I were thrown together on many occasions. I found him amusing and quick-witted, but underneath that glibness and charm was a tough man, agile enough to survive in Washington through all the Soviet rulers from Khrushchev to Gorbachev.

After the performance, the Reagans and Gorbachevs, Shultzes and Shevardnadzes had an intimate celebration at the Gorbachevs' dacha, while the rest of us went on to other parties—winding up the evening at Armand Hammer's Moscow apartment—a somewhat shabby place brightened only by some nice paintings. But what really took me aback was the dirty stairs we climbed to his sixth-floor apartment. The bannisters were covered with dust—as if no one had touched them in months. Why didn't he order them cleaned, I wondered. Where was the janitor or the caretaker? Suddenly, on that staircase, I had an odd flash of insight as to why *perestroika* was going to have such tough going. Pride in work and service had long ago been corrupted by the low expectations of an egalitarian society.

The next day, the President gave a moving farewell to the embassy staff at Spaso House and we set off for the airport, Charlie Wick and I once again traveling together. We were supposed to go directly to the airport, but our driver mistakenly followed the President's motorcade, headed for the departure ceremony at St. Catherine's Hall in the Kremlin. We ended up watching the farewells in the huge gold-and-red hall lighted by six mammoth gilt chandeliers.

The only rain on the entire trip fell during the airport departure, but it was an insignificant damper on a week of exhilarating events. I thought this would be my last meeting with the Soviets before I hung up my shingle as Chief of Protocol but one more dramatic encounter was still to come.

Six months later, Gorbachev decided to come to New York to make a major speech at the United Nations. It was also a chance for him to say goodbye to Reagan and to touch base with President-elect Bush.

Since he was coming to the U.N., the White House gang decided there was no need to have my protocol team involved. The President would not go into New York City, but instead would give a lunch for Gorbachev on Governors Island. That would be arranged by the White House advance team. They wanted to keep the numbers on the island to a minimum.

It had been announced that the Gorbachevs wanted to see something of New York—and to my horror I heard they planned to visit Trump Tower. Of all the sights that might discourage the Soviet leader about our society, I would put that monument to conspicuous consumption at the top of the list!

It seemed to me that things were getting a little out of hand, so I brought this to Shultz's attention.

"I don't think it's right for no one to represent the President in New York," I told him. "You cannot leave Gorbachev—the most important man in the world today—to run around New York with no one from the State Department or White House accompanying him. What if something should go wrong? And certainly someone representing the President has to greet him at the airport. Even if the White House doesn't understand protocol, the Russians do!"

By this time, I was pretty worked up. "And furthermore, can you imagine President Reagan arriving, say in Leningrad, and not having some biggies from the Soviet government there to greet him?"

Shultz knew what he was going to say long before I had finished. "Lucky, I want you to do exactly what you think is right. Go to New York, see that he is properly greeted and seen off, and keep an eye on everything else."

That's what I did. And by the time I got to Kennedy Airport on the day of Gorbachev's arrival, a real free-for-all was developing between U.N. officials and the U.S. Customs Service. We in Protocol had a happy relationship with customs officials all over the country; they trusted my staff and never gave them a hard time. But sometimes the United Nations people forgot that they were permitted access on sufferance, and they could be arrogant. Customs threatened to throw several U.N. bigwigs off the tarmac; they would not permit any U.N. protocol officials to approach the Soviet aircraft.

I waded into this and managed to cut a deal with customs before the Russian plane touched down. I would personally be responsible for my U.N. colleagues, and they would go only where customs allowed. Crisis averted.

It was exciting to welcome once more the Gorbachevs to America, and after a few words of greeting my United Nations colleague Ambassador Ali Teymour delivered an eloquent and lengthy welcome. I was so impressed and wished I had Ali's gift for words, when I noticed Gorbachev's busy bright eyes darting impatiently about. Perhaps brevity wasn't a bad thing after all!

Gorbachev's speech the next morning at the United Nations

was dramatic—announcing the Soviets' intention to sharply cut their military forces—but more important, giving his bold vision of a new world order where force would no longer be an instrument of foreign policy. Normally at the U.N. no one pays much attention to the speeches and the delegates rarely applaud, but the atmosphere was electric and the Soviet leader got a warm ovation. I thought to myself, "This man is thinking conceptually and running circles around us. What a showman!"

Later, he lunched with President Reagan and President-elect Bush, did a quick turn around Times Square, and was guest of honor at a reception given by Javier Pérez de Cuellar, the Secretary General of the United Nations.

Malcolm Forbes was among the hundreds of guests, and he and I ended up conversing with Foreign Minister Shevardnadze. We congratulated him on Gorbachev's speech. He told us that Gorbachev had been working on that speech for over a year, which put to rest the rumors here that he had hastily put the speech together to divert attention from his country's internal problems.

Shevardnadze had greeted me with a warm embrace; it was a joy to see him again. Even through the language barrier I felt a rapport and understanding with him. But he seemed very subdued.

"How did the day go?" I asked.

"Here, everything has gone very well, but not in my own country. The earthquake in Armenia has been very bad and there are many deaths."

That was my first realization of the seriousness of the earthquake which killed tens of thousands in Soviet Armenia. I was not surprised to be called around midnight and informed that the Russians had decided to move their departure up a day.

A very somber group assembled at the airport the next morning. As Gorbachev went to the podium to thank the American people for their generous outpouring of sympathy for the earthquake victims, all of us formed a semicircle about ten feet behind him. I was wearing a Russian sable hat to protect me on that cold December day.

But the camera plays strange tricks. I was nowhere near him, yet for weeks afterward I heard from friends around the world who said they had seen me standing *beside* Gorbachev as he made his farewell remarks—and everyone complimented me on the fur hat. I thought once again how difficult it was for a woman protocol chief to fade into the background!

I also thought how terrible it would have been not to have a personal representative of the President on this occasion, not only for a routine protocol farewell, but also to express the President's condolences on a day of national mourning in Russia.

THIRTY-FIVE

On Being a Woman

As I CIRCLED the globe on this extraordinary carousel, interviewers often asked me, "What has been your most exciting experience?" And I would predictably respond, "Working for the President, the Vice President, and the Secretary of State," or "Meeting Gorbachev and watching the Soviet-American relationship gradually thaw."

And yet, as I conclude this book I ask myself what, in the final analysis, has given me the greatest challenge, and perhaps the greatest joy, in my life? I must admit that the most sweeping adventure of all is being a woman.

I often read about women who wish they had been born men. I find it difficult to empathize with them. Perhaps it's because I come from a long line of strong women and have never felt any road should be closed to me just because I am a woman. Contrary to popular belief, strong women have existed in the Middle East since the Queen of Sheba and Zenobia of Palmyra. The first wife of the Prophet Mohammed was a prominent merchant of Mecca and financed him in the early days of his mission. A later wife fought for power on the battlefield a few years after his death.

At the same time, Middle Eastern women have another tradition in their history—that of the odalisque. And I must confess, I find them rather fascinating as well. These women of the harems developed certain instincts for survival and used whatever weapons were at hand, so to speak.

A friend of mine, the beautiful Druze poet Nadia Tueni, once wrote about her role as a woman: "There is a road to truth which the Middle East knows. It is the shortcut to knowledge, by instinct. And I am not a rational or logical person. I believe in magic and superstition and I have no complexes about it. I am not ashamed of it."

And while Nadia's attitudes are also part of my heritage, I would not minimize the effect of being raised in Tennessee, where the Southern belle and the steel magnolia were one and the same woman.

This probably explains why I am not a militant feminist. It would be impossible for me to consider men the enemy. And while I cherish my women friends, I have to say that, in the professional arena, I have found women at times more mean-spirited than men and envious of other successful women. The only journalist who ever trashed me or trivialized me was a woman; the few bosses who were capricious and petty were women.

As a boss, I tried very hard to learn from my own experiences, and I certainly pushed the women on my staff to aim for the stars. To me, their success was also my success.

On balance, my experiences with men, both personally and professionally, have been positive. As friends they were loyal and generous; as bosses and colleagues they were generally easier to work with.

All of this is by way of preface. I feel I owe my readers an explanation of why I, then the only female chief of protocol in the world, would recommend that President Bush select a man as my successor.

It wasn't because of those innumerable mornings when I arrived at my office exhausted from trying to balance my protocol duties and my home life and exclaimed to my secretary, "What I need is a wife!"

It wasn't because I had to waste so much valuable time going to the hairdresser, changing clothes as many as three or four times a day, and generally worrying about my appearance.

And it certainly wasn't because of any lack of appreciation for my performance in the job. On the contrary, Reagan, Bush, and Shultz were more than generous in their praise of me.

So why would I want to turn over this plum position to a man?

During ten of the previous twelve years, the Protocol slot had been held by a woman and it was rapidly coming to be regarded as a "woman's job." That was said in pejorative tones, implying that it was sissy stuff—tablecloths and flowers—something no red-blooded American male would aspire to.

In truth, my concerns *were* feminist. The position was being downgraded *because* it was perceived as a woman's job. When this view began to permeate liberal and feminist attitudes, I felt it was time to restore some balance and redefine the duties.

I'll never forget my annoyance on reading a newspaper article about Pamela Harriman's future, should the Democrats capture the White House in 1988. Stuart Eizenstat, domestic policy chief for President Carter, commented, "Harriman should be given a substantive position . . . in the next Democratic administration. She shouldn't be the *protocol* person."

It is true that a chief of protocol does not make policy; however, he or she has to know what the administration is trying to achieve. Protocol's input can make a big difference.

Actually, Pamela Harriman, because of her intelligence and substantive knowledge, would have brought so much to the job. To make the correct decisions about protocol, one has to understand substance; one's effectiveness is limited only by one's ignorance of foreign affairs.

When I took the job, I discovered that before each important visit the Secretary of State was given a "pre-brief" by everyone concerned with the visit, but the chief of protocol was not included. I asked why and the answer came back, "I guess no one ever thought of it." From then on I was included, and to my surprise, at my first pre-brief, much of the discussion was about my areas of responsibility.

Thanks to George Shultz and others in the State Department

hierarchy, I was allowed to run my shop with almost a free hand. They wanted a strong administrator and understood that the job required, more than anything, *diplomatic* skills.

But at the White House I was always walking on eggs. The staff never understood my duties. They saw me either as a glorified advance man or as the hostess with the mostess. The first was a threat to them, and the second was a threat to the First Lady.

Of course, the chief of protocol is often in attendance with the President and his wife at public events. For a woman, it's a delicate balance. If she is a sad sack, not well dressed or well groomed, that would reflect badly on the White House; if she is noticeably attractive or too much in evidence, that could become an annoyance to the First Lady.

A man has none of these problems. His suits are dark and nondescript. At galas, he is in black tie, the perfect uniform. In photographs, he is barely noticed; he does not detract from the picture. After the first few weeks, I became adroit at stepping out of photos, but it was tiresome dancing around trying to disappear when I also had duties to perform.

Often outsiders assume that a female chief of protocol works for the First Lady and that she is in charge of the wives of visiting heads of state. In reality, I rarely accompanied Nancy Reagan, and almost never escorted the wives of our visitors. Nonetheless, I would often be invited to the events for spouses rather than to the stag event for principals. These mistakes were easily corrected, but they do reflect the public perception of what a female chief of protocol does.

A member of the administration—presumably to compliment me—said that a woman made a much better chief of protocol because men wanted to sit at the table, and women were willing to take a back seat.

Actually, as the President's personal representative, the protocol chief needs the status that goes with "sitting at the table." If he is shunted off to the kitchen, it means he is not very important—and means that the President does not regard his guest as worthy of high-level attention.

A woman chief can never be "one of the boys." For me, that

is not a complaint—I am more comfortable in the traditional feminine roles. And I could never have pictured Ronald Reagan sitting around with his feet up, relaxing with his female Chief of Protocol.

Not being "one of the boys" was no impediment in Washington, but it became a major problem when traveling with the President and his male entourage. Not only were there occasional limitations to a woman's movements depending on the customs of the country we were visiting, but there were also problems with physical arrangements such as bedrooms and bathrooms.

But don't misunderstand me. I think a woman brings very special and desirable talents to the role of chief of protocol. Many visiting heads of state, after observing our heavily female operation, complimented me by saying they were determined to place more women on their protocol staffs. Indeed, the Canadians just recently appointed their first female chief of protocol.

While we are way ahead of the rest of the world on women protocol chiefs—four out of twenty-one chiefs in our history have been women—we are still far behind when it comes to women in the highest reaches of government. It always struck me as odd, especially when a female chief of state was visiting.

Historically, some of Europe's strongest monarchs have been women—Elizabeth I of England, Catherine the Great of Russia, Isabella of Spain. And yet America, the home of the emancipated woman, still has fewer women at the highest levels of government than, say, Pakistan or Costa Rica!

The women heads of state that I came to know were all—with no exceptions—outstanding. They had to be. The burden of proof was on them; and they have proved convincingly that women can run the affairs of men—and do it as well or better.

Margaret Thatcher, Indira Gandhi, and Corazon Aquino I have already described—and equally impressive were Prime Minister Gro Brundtland of Norway, President Benazir Bhutto of Pakistan, and Prime Minister Eugenia Charles of Dominica. I remember Reagan and Shultz were particularly taken with Vigdis

Finnbogadottir, the bright and beauteous blond president of Iceland.

If there was one characteristic these women shared, it was, to put it crudely, the ability to cut through the "baloney." (Once Prime Minister Charles arrived on an earlier shuttle from New York than she had originally advised us. Not wanting to cause us any trouble, she sat patiently in the airport, perched on her suitcase, until the visits officer showed up to escort her into town.) They traveled with much smaller entourages and they cared much less about matters of face than the men—a sign of their own self-assurance. But I did notice that not one of them failed to use her femininity as an extremely effective weapon. They did not try to rule like men. Their wisdom had a universal quality about it—the certainty that being a woman had distinct advantages.

I was often reminded of Henry Kissinger's famous remark when asked why he had such success with women though not exactly a Rudolph Valentino. His answer: "Power is the ultimate aphrodisiac."

Well, it should come as no surprise to discover that women with power also turn men on. Successful, self-assured women have a heightened sexual awareness, a knowledge of their own worth, which projects confidence. Men are often tantalized by them, and find such women a great challenge.

The aura of power and success rarely attaches to very young women; this magnetism and attraction tends to come as a woman is entering middle age. It is a special dividend—perhaps nature's compensation for no longer being in the first blush of youth.

When I read Carolyn G. Heilbrun's book *Writing a Woman's Life,* I was intrigued by her opinion that women after fifty require new attitudes and new courage. "Women with security of some sort—tenure, an assured place, financial means—are in danger at this stage of choosing to stay where they are . . . I do not believe that death should be allowed to find us seated comfortably in our tenured positions. . . . Instead, we should make use of our security, our seniority, to take risks, to make noise, to be courageous, to become unpopular."

Those words got to me. They came at just the right moment. My friends kept asking, "Now what? After that glamorous life, after living for seven years with presidents and kings, after being at the center of power, won't everything seem an anticlimax?"

Actually, no. A certain amount of government service is a great experience. My husband loved his thirty years in intelligence; I loved my seven years in diplomacy. But it is time for a change. All my life I have been constricted by my husband's job or my own. For security or policy reasons, I could not always write what I wanted; I could not take jobs I would have liked.

And now I am free. It took forty years to arrive at this point, and I want to savor every minute of it. The possibilities are endless, but I will heed Carolyn Heilbrun and look for the riskier paths.

No matter what is next on my agenda, however, I can never forget that being born in America made it possible for me to break away from the shibboleths of the past. The advantages and opportunities that have come to me, as a first-generation American, would have been beyond the wildest imaginings of my ancestors.

I can never do enough to express my gratitude to this country or the pride I take in being an exponent of the American dream. Our message of political, religious, and economic freedom still illuminates the world, and if sometimes we fall short of our own highest ideals, then all the more reason why people like myself must cherish that dream—nurture it, respect it—and never, *never* take it for granted.

Epilogue

AT THE BEGINNING of this book I expressed my belief that how we deal with adversity defines us. I had no idea that I would soon be put to the ultimate test.

Archie, who since the moment we met had made every day of my life a joyous one, died on May 31, 1990. During the winter he had suffered from endocarditis, a bacterial infection of the heart valve, and after gallantly recovering, he then had to contend with congestive heart failure. But he was not a grandson of Teddy Roosevelt in name only. He kept his zest for work and insisted on following a normal routine, so we thought he was making a remarkable recovery.

Sweetly and gently Archie lived his life, and sweetly and gently he left it. He went to sleep one evening and simply did not wake up. I believe God loved him very much to have taken him so tenderly.

Although he was only seventy-two when he died, he made up for that in excitement and fulfillment by achieving success in three different careers—government, banking, and writing. He took as the theme of his life these lines from a work of James Elroy Flecker:

We travel not for trafficking alone;
By hotter winds our fiery hearts are fanned:
For lust of knowing what should not be known,
We take the Golden Road to Samarkand.

And so he traveled the road of life in passionate pursuit of knowledge—the more exotic and esoteric, the more ardent was his search. This mature, cultivated mind belonged to another century perhaps, but with his brilliance he combined the innocence and playfulness of a six-year-old boy.

When he made me his companion on this golden road, neither of us could have foreseen what a fantastic journey it would be. None of my own achievements, modest by comparison, could have been as rewarding without his encouragement, his generosity of spirit, and his enormous capacity for both giving and receiving love.

Even now, in my profound sadness, I can only think how incredibly lucky I have been, how favored by God and by fate.

Index